Winner of the Jules and Frances Landry Award for 2024

SOUTHERN BIOGRAPHY SERIES

WILLIAM JOHNSON, CA. 1845

THE

Barber

OF

Natchez

Reconsidered

WILLIAM JOHNSON *and* BLACK MASCULINITY
in the ANTEBELLUM SOUTH

Timothy R. Buckner

LOUISIANA STATE
UNIVERSITY PRESS
BATON ROUGE

Published by Louisiana State University Press
lsupress.org

Manufactured in the United States of America

DESIGNER: Andrew Shurtz
TYPEFACE: Garamond ATF

COVER ILLUSTRATION: *Natchez under the Hill, Mississippi,*
ca. 1850, by Frederick Hawkins Piercy. Courtesy the
New York Public Library, Digital Collections.

LIBRARY OF CONGRESS CATALOGING-IN-PUBLICATION DATA
Names: Buckner, Timothy R., 1974– author.
Title: The barber of Natchez reconsidered : William Johnson
    and black masculinity in the antebellum South /
    Timothy R. Buckner.
Description: Baton Rouge : Louisiana State University
    Press, [2023] | Series: Southern biography series |
    Includes bibliographical references and index.
Identifiers: LCCN 2023004052 (print) | LCCN 2023004053
    (ebook) | ISBN 978-0-8071-7994-9 (cloth) | ISBN 978-0-
    8071-8054-9 (pdf) | ISBN 978-0-8071-8053-2 (epub)
Subjects: LCSH: Natchez (Miss.)—Social life and customs. |
    Johnson, William, 1809-1851—Diaries. | African American
    barbers—Natchez—Diaries. | Masculinity—Mississippi—
    Natchez—History—19th century. | African Americans—
    Mississippi—Natchez—History—19th century.
Classification: LCC F349.N2 B775 2023 (print) | LCC F349.N2
    (ebook) | DDC 305.38/896076226—dc23/eng/20230419
LC record available at https://lccn.loc.gov/2023004052
LC ebook record available at https://lccn.loc.gov/2023004053

for Nathan and Norah

Contents

Acknowledgments

I FIRST READ about William Johnson more than twenty years ago, and while I have worked on various projects over those years, I always wanted to return to write a book like this one. Though some of the research on this book began in the early 2000s, I wrote the first draft during the COVID-19 lockdown while my family and I were sequestered from work and school, mostly wearing earbuds so as not to hear my children during their Zoom classes. Luckily, my kids are cool enough that I'd want to hang out with them even if we weren't related, and my wife is mostly tolerant of my brand of weirdness, which allowed us to get through this without going completely stir-crazy. Video conferencing technology allowed me to keep in touch with many friends when we could not meet in person and offered a critical break from the stresses of writing. That very strange period will undoubtedly receive a lot of attention from future historians. Thankfully, the staff at Troy University helped me to transition my courses to an online format that kept my students from falling behind and allowed me the time to make progress on this book, but I am most grateful that my family and most of my friends made it through with only mild inconveniences; many were not so lucky.

Troy University has supported this book in many ways. The Faculty Development Council awarded me a summer research grant to make a trip to Natchez, which proved invaluable to this book. A sabbatical I took in 2013 for a different project indirectly led me back to this one. I am fortunate to have a group of colleagues in the Department of History and Philosophy who are excellent scholars and teachers. Their support and friendship have made my time in academia much brighter. David Carlson was kind enough to read a skeletal draft of this book and made important suggestions. Two of my closest friends at Troy, Nathan Alexander and Rob Kruckeberg, passed away well before their time, but I greatly appreciate all I learned from them. Countless students have contributed to this book without their knowledge as I tried out ideas in classes and sharpened my focus by reading their work.

Academic lives, like all of them, I suppose, move in bizarre ways. Not too long ago, I was prepared to walk away from writing history entirely during what I think of as my academic-midlife crisis. I was drawn back by the excellent work produced by scholars writing in the fields of slavery and Black masculinity in the American South; much of that appears in the notes and bibliography of this book. I am deeply thankful for LSU Press and the reviewers of this manuscript who offered me the chance to make my own contributions.

The Barber of Natchez Reconsidered

Introduction

BEFORE THE CIVIL WAR, William Johnson was Natchez, Mississippi's, wealthiest and most well-respected Black resident. Johnson was born to an enslaved mother and a white father and released from bondage by the Mississippi legislature in 1820. He trained as a barber and became a prominent business owner and member of the community in Natchez. Despite the restrictions placed upon him by Mississippi's racist laws, Johnson achieved a high degree of financial and social success—he owned several properties in town and eventually a farm nearby. His diary is the single richest surviving source on free communities of color in the antebellum South, yet interpretations of his life have mainly focused on his psychological relationship with the white planter class. Edwin Adams Davis and William Ransom Hogan first published Johnson's edited diary in 1951 and a companion biography in 1954. The two works are meticulous, explaining Johnson's references to people and events within Natchez in detail beyond the diarist's sometimes very brief entries. Their work has provided several generations a better understanding of Natchez in this era and a sense of how race and class functioned within a small but important southern town.

At the same time, though, the biography is as much an artifact of its era as the diary itself. The 1973 edition of *The Barber of Natchez* includes a quote from the *Alabama Review* in which a reviewer contended that the biography "provides a commentary on the question as to whether the Negro can be assimilated into American Society."[1] Two other quotes from James Dickey and James Baldwin provided in this edition clarify that at least partly what the authors wanted to do with this biography is to argue whether or not the goal of assimilation was possible." Davis and Hogan found that Johnson maintained an "isolated position at the top of his class."[2] Essentially the flaw in their interpretation was their assumption that Johnson separated himself from other African Americans because he had the racial sensibilities of a slaveholder but could not mix with whites because he was Black. This simple binary did not apply to the lived experiences of the people of Natchez. Johnson was an enslaver, but he also was deeply connected to the Black community as a craftsman who offered a path to freedom and respectability to the boys he took on as apprentices. Being Black kept him from legal equality with whites, but he did interact daily with other men via the various activities reserved for men in the antebellum South. While his race certainly kept him from full acceptance, his gender allowed him to create a multitude of complex relationships in and around town.

As problematic as Hogan and Davis's concerns about integration are for modern readers, several other interpretive issues with their analysis are grounded in the historiography of race, slavery, and the South in the era in which they edited the diary and wrote their biography. For example, it is difficult to see how these authors could have concluded that Johnson was isolated. In many ways, Johnson was the nexus of Natchez: his barbershop—operated by himself, his apprentices, and the men he enslaved—trafficked not only in hairstyles but in news and gossip about issues personal, local, and national. Johnson was an avid reader of politics, a frequent gambler, and an observer of day-to-day life. He was a family man with a network of business associates and friends throughout the region with whom he intermingled daily. Davis and Hogan's assumption that Johnson was isolated resulted from his inability to be what they call a "gentleman," which is to say because he was not white, Johnson was unable to engage with the upper-class whites with whom, they argue, he had much more in common with than with other free people of color or certainly with the enslaved or poor whites. Yet, the supposition that Johnson wanted to be white or belong with the planter class socially is not supported anywhere in Johnson's two-thousand-page diary or the letters and record books he left behind.

Unfortunately, most scholars who have used William Johnson's life in their work since the publication of *The Barber of Natchez* have conflated Davis and Hogan's analysis of Johnson with the diary itself.[3] Focusing on the diary, what comes through is that the life Johnson detailed was a masculine one very connected to and protective of a community of free people of color. Work, competition, trades, fights, women, race, and politics were discussed in a world of men, sometimes bound by race but often not. Over the last decade, there has been a growth in Black masculinity studies in the nineteenth century, which has refined and complicated how Black men established themselves as men in this era.[4] Part of this scholarship rests on a rejection of eighteenth- and nineteenth-century American definitions of manhood as exclusively reserved for whites. American and particularly southern notions of masculinity required independence, boldness, public displays of bravery through physical confrontations with other men, and an ability to provide for and control their dependents: women, children, and enslaved people.

Generations of scholars have established that gender is not a static category but rather, as Gail Bederman has argued, "a historical, ideological process" in which individuals are positioned or position themselves as men or women. Gender roles, she argues, are a "dynamic process," and "at any time in history, many contradictory ideas about manhood are available to explain what men are, how they ought to behave, and what sorts of powers and authorities they may claim, as men." Taken together, scholars who study white and Black men in the antebellum era agree that the status of "manhood" could be reached only through tests and conduct, visible to the broader public, that set them apart from women. Scholars of white masculinity in the South have recognized that expressions of manliness and claims of belonging in a community of men required public performance. Bertram Wyatt-Brown's *Southern Honor* established that white men, especially elite white men, claimed manliness via establishing a public reputation, usually of bravery or a willingness to fight, but sometimes through grand expressions of hospitality. Other scholars have questioned how much nonelite men subscribed to the culture of honor, but public performance, especially of a competitive nature with other men, was the key. That competition could include violence, success in business, gambling, military titles, adherence to evangelical Christianity, and mastery over families and enslaved workforces.[5] The institution of slavery restricted most Blacks from this definition of manliness; thus, lacking manly qualities could define one as a "slave." These notions of separating masculinity and slavery have a long history but were most forcefully expressed in the rhetoric of colonial resistance leading to the American Revolution, as powerful white men complained that Parliament's actions were "enslaving" them, leading to expressions of patriarchal rage.[6]

In nineteenth-century America, the definition of masculinity could not be separated from discussions of race and slavery. Most of the markers of masculinity relied on independence, the ability to provide for and protect a family, and exercising a public role in society. This was the era in which states dropped the property requirement for voting, meaning that all white men could vote, creating a sense that, at least in terms of participation in government, all white men were equal. Of course, creating that sense of equality meant keeping nonwhites or nonmales from accessing full citizenship. The institution of slavery further solidified a distinction between whites and Blacks: enslaved Black men lacked independence by definition. They could not provide for or protect families in the ways that free men could. Moreover, enslavers usurped the roles of husband and father in multiple ways by not recognizing marriages of the enslaved, splitting families through sale, or sexually assaulting enslaved women. Slaveholders' ideas about paternalism further reduced the opportunities for enslaved men to engage in masculine behaviors that white men took for granted. As one enslaver wrote in 1860, "The African negro is physically a man, mentally a child—treat him as such." Placing themselves at the head of the "family," enslavers negated traditional masculine behaviors for enslaved men.[7] Lacking manly qualities like boldness and independence, especially treasured in "frontier" places like Natchez, Mississippi, could define one as a slave or a child.[8]

Whites' narrow definition of manliness found an analogue in how African American abolitionists described themselves: one could either be a slave or a man, but not both. Some of the most famous African American abolitionists of the nineteenth century shared the notion that violent resistance to slavery was the only way for Black men to claim masculinity. Frederick Douglass used his fight with Edward Covey to show how "a slave was made a man."[9] David Walker's *Appeal* insisted that men must protect their families via armed revolt to overthrow slavery and to claim America as their own. Both championed an idea of heroic masculinity that required Black men to fight back against slavery and its debasement of Black men. As Walker wrote: "Throw away your fears and prejudices then, and enlighten us and treat us like men, and we will like you more than we do now hate you ... for America is as much our country, as it is yours—Treat us like men, and there is no danger but we will all live in peace and happiness together. For we are not like you, hard hearted, unmerciful, and unforgiving. What a happy country this will be, if the whites will listen."[10] Johnson no doubt agreed with Walker that whites should treat free Black men such as themselves as men and agreed that colonization of Liberia was an insult; however, Johnson did not share the antislavery sentiment. Though most African Americans in the South shared similar experiences of oppression under slavery, some lived in ways that diverged from the majority, and as one author has written, their lives "contradict our expectations of a unitary 'black' subject and racially 'representative' texts."[11] Instead of finding solidarity with the enslaved, Johnson supported the rights of his fellow free people of color. When those rights were in danger during the summer of 1841 in Natchez, he wrote despairingly in his diary, "oh what a country we live in," which, though not in the same spirit as Walker's "what a happy country this will be, if the whites will listen," contained a similar disdain for the treatment of African Americans.

Such ideas that only violence or resistance to slavery could make a Black man a man have shaped how generations of scholars have viewed Black masculinity. That notion created the argument that enslaved men fell into either the "Sambo" stereotype, the childlike dependent who needed enslavers to survive; the rebellious "Nat," who either fought or ran away from enslavers; or "Jack," who accepted the dominance of whites but rebelled or disengaged from work when mistreated.[12] Studies focusing on the enslaved community rejected these ideas and contended that enslaved men found ways to demonstrate their manliness, if not to whites, at least to the communities to which they belonged.[13] Some of the most recent scholarship modifies but agrees that communities of enslaved African Americans collectively resisted aspects of slavery and asserted masculinity.[14] Of course, these stereotypes are just that and negate the genuine differences in the actual lived experiences of enslaved men. The life stories of Black men, enslaved and free, in the Slave South, belie these simplistic dichotomies.

More recent research has made it clear that there were multiple Black masculinities and, thus, various ways of being a man within enslaved communities. David Stefan Doddington has argued that there were many different ways that enslaved men could assert manliness but that the performative nature of masculinity was not always in comparison to, or for the benefit of, whites. Black men could show they were men through resistance to slavery, being hard workers, demonstrating authority over others, and even violence between enslaved men. In *Contesting Slave Masculinity,* Doddington makes the crucial point that agency does not have to stem from resistance to slavery, and Black men could assert their manliness beyond rebellion. Men established themselves not only by revolting against enslavers but by becoming drivers and overseers. Enslaved men competed with one another to prove their manliness; in those contests, some won, and others lost, and both had to deal with those repercussions.[15]

Just as agency does not mean resistance, Black men did not only assert masculinity by fighting for freedom. Historians have traced the lives of famous and lesser-known enslaved men through their narratives or how children have remembered their fathers in postemancipation interviews. These individuals offer a vital view of Black masculinity. However, because often we still see these men narrowly—the man who was good at fighting was able to assert his masculinity in this way, the man who bragged about sexual exploits in another—this only offers a small sample of how Black men publicly displayed manliness.[16] These limited demonstrations were probably not the only way Black men conceived or expressed their masculinity. The child of a plantation driver might have remembered her father as an authority figure, but perhaps he was also a kind and caring father despite how he might have behaved within his job. Exhibitions of masculinity shifted depending upon circumstances; Black men expressed themselves differently depending on relationships, contexts, and types of interactions. Representing individuals as articulating only one kind of masculinity is not a flaw of historical analysis; it is a flaw of sources. Unfortunately, because of the lack of available sources, we rarely get the complete picture of how enslaved or free Black men lived.

Unlike for most enslaved men or even other free men of color, we have a large amount of material on William Johnson. Though he was free, that certainly does not mean that Johnson did not have to deal with racist repression, and it would be wrong to argue that he lived the same kind of unfettered life as his white contemporaries. Still, Johnson's freedom, material wealth, and education provided him with a wide range of experiences and opportunities to perform masculinity in various ways. Via these voluminous sources, we can trace Johnson's multiple masculinities and those of the men he enslaved, his apprentices, fellow free men of color, his sons, and others. His diary offers the chance to track how he changed over time: as his family grew, his business expanded and became more complicated, how he handled the dispute that led to his murder, and how his influence lasted long after his death. In other words, Johnson's life offers the most comprehensive view of Black masculinity of any single subject in nineteenth-century America. Unlike Frederick Douglass's autobiography, Johnson did not craft his narrative for public consumption or offer a retrospective construction of moving from slavery to freedom to further the cause of abolition. Johnson's diary was private and rarely self-reflective; instead, it served as a place to record daily events he viewed as essential and meaningful. Unlike Douglass, who revised his life story in several editions and offered a direct view of heroic resistance to slavery as the only significant expression of masculinity, Johnson engaged in many different modes of manliness. His roles included a master craftsman trying to impart not just skills to his apprentices but also an example of how to be free and Black in the antebellum South, a father and husband attempting to raise and protect a family, and a man willing to risk his reputation and fortune on gambling and sporting events. Johnson embodied these masculinity types and expressed triumph and frustration in these ventures. Throughout Johnson's life, he viewed masculinity as an expression of respectability and valued competition, assertiveness, participation, and protection of one's family and community.

Johnson's relationship with his white father is difficult to determine. He learned much about being a man from James Miller, a free man of color from Philadelphia, who married William's sister, Adelia, and set up a barbershop in Natchez. Miller took Johnson on as an apprentice shortly after arriving in town. After adulthood, Johnson eventually purchased Miller's shop, which allowed him to create a business and lay claim to the kind of "self-made manhood" valued by nineteenth-century Americans. In taking on apprentices, Johnson used their labor, taught them his trade, and imparted his ideas about respectable behavior through punishments and rewards. These hard-learned lessons enabled his apprentices to live as free people of color within a slave society. Miller taught Johnson the trade that helped him establish respectability based on economic independence and a reputation for honest dealings with his all-white clientele. By serving whites and enslaving people, Johnson demonstrated that he was no threat to the racial order of the South.[17] While some free people of color purchased slaves and held them in only nominal bondage, Johnson did not. His interest in enslaving people was financial, and he could be as cruel as any white enslaver in dealing with punishments. Still, he also took some interest in helping the enslaved men better their positions and occasionally offered them significant autonomy.[18]

Everyone who worked in the barbershop was a Black man or boy, but the entire clientele was white and mainly, but not exclusively, white men. Johnson created a reputation for respectability and a shared sense of manliness with his clients within the shop. Johnson wrote a lot about the men who were his customers; sometimes, he wrote about them as "gentlemen," which seemed to be the highest compliment he had, but other times referred to them as "rascals," his biggest insult. Of course, only white men were referred to as gentlemen, though rascals could be white or Black. These terms usually were expressions of how Johnson viewed their reputations. Sometimes he referred to young people who he did not think would amount to much as "small potatoes." Most of his other insults were reserved for young Black women he viewed as possessing questionable sexual mores: "strumpet" and "buster." When the mixed-race apprentices in his shop pursued young women he thought of as strumpets or busters, he often referred to the boys in racial terms, most famously calling Bill Nix a "pure, pure negro at heart."[19]

At times his customers related stories to him about fights or duels between other men who lived in town or nearby. In other instances, Johnson and his workers saw these confrontations firsthand from their position in the heart of downtown Natchez. In describing these fights, Johnson often judged these men's performances, their bravery or cowardice, and their skills or lack of them. Johnson's opinions of the men he encountered came from their behaviors rather than racial distinctions. Stories exchanged in his shop offered the chance to discuss local and national politics to supplement what he read in the newspapers. He frequently expressed opinions about white politicians. However, Johnson never writes of wishing to be a white man or lamenting that he could not participate socially or politically with them. The barber vied with many men at the racetrack and in other competitions. Though he could not vote, he participated in politics by attending events, engaging in civic service, helping with fire prevention, and placing bets on the outcome of elections.

Johnson raised a family in Natchez. He married a free woman of color, who, like himself, had been born into slavery, and the couple had ten children. His mother, also freed by his white father, lived nearby, and he helped her manage her household, including those she enslaved, though he was also frequently exasperated by her. Unlike her son, Amy Johnson openly lost her temper in public, and Johnson spent considerable space in his diary worrying about what she might do next. Being free and Black in antebellum Mississippi was, by no means, a comfortable existence, as the government and several of its leading citizens made it clear that they should not be allowed in the state. Of course, this was the case everywhere in the

Slave South as free people of color found themselves under suspicion of being dangerous to the peculiar institution. Johnson and others in Natchez carved out lives for themselves, sometimes by slipping underneath the view of whites, but at other times through boldness and working within law and custom to establish niches and reputations that could protect them when movements against free Blacks threatened their lives and livelihoods.

Johnson had an extensive network of friends, neighbors, and business associates he socialized with virtually every day when not working. As a younger man, Johnson frequently spent his nonworking hours competing with other men in various contests: betting on horses, shooting matches, cards, dice, hunting, and fishing, to name a few. Johnson recorded his wins and losses, rarely seeming to take either very seriously, even though sometimes he lost more than his barbershop earned in a day or a week. He attended auctions to buy products cheaply for his household or to sell at higher prices elsewhere. He joined his friend Robert McCary on horse rides throughout the town and into the countryside, looking for adventure or relaxation. McCary was also a free man of color and a barber, though not as successful as Johnson. The two were inseparable for much of their lives and enjoyed a close friendship. They gambled and competed against other free men of color, whites, and enslaved people, sometimes at large organized events like at the horse track, but sometimes with whomever they might encounter when out on a ride together. The men visited each other when sick or injured and helped when family members were ill.

Johnson eschewed some gambling outings once he purchased land and became a farmer. About eight miles from town, his farm began absorbing much more of his time and space in his journal later in his life. Johnson took up farming as another avenue to earn money to go along with his shop, but this also connected him to the dominant livelihood of most people in the region. Land ownership linked him to the same independence white men claimed, but farming also brought him into contact with new neighbors. Johnson's reputation as the town's most popular barber and his respectability as a businessman and someone who could cover his gambling debts did not carry any weight with his rural neighbors, many of whom fit into the category that historians call "poor whites." In this area that he called "the Swamp," Johnson found men who held different ideas about masculinity and were willing to take advantage of him based on Mississippi's racist laws. This new venture put him into a protracted verbal and legal battle with his neighbor Baylor Winn. Winn was known as a free man of color to some in the community, but he sometimes represented himself as and was considered a white man by others. In his diary, Johnson even describes Winn as a "voter," and hence a white man, but in another entry, he clarifies that he knows Winn was a free Black man. Winn had encouraged Johnson to buy the land that neighbored his farm, and though Johnson might have viewed this as a friendly proposition, it seems clear that Winn wanted Johnson to purchase the land because he thought he could take advantage of him.

Winn held a different concept of masculinity than Johnson, which historians have linked to poor whites living in rural areas and sometimes the planter class. This type of masculinity required domination; anything less than this signaled weakness, a lack of manliness, so its adherents viewed others as opponents to defeat at all costs.[20] Winn exhibited cruelty to his family and increasingly ignored Johnson's property rights by cutting timber irrespective of property boundaries. Despite repeated physical threats and other forms of intimidation, Johnson felt confident that he could handle Winn: he wrote that if attacked, he would respond in kind but expected Winn to be an honorable man and abide by the law. Johnson's business and personal dealings up to this point had turned on a shared expectation of men doing the moral and legal thing. Johnson was so confident that he could diffuse the problem between the two that he offered a generous deal to Winn after winning their boundary dispute. In response, Winn shot and killed him a few days afterward. For men like Winn, who viewed domination as the only acceptable form of masculinity, murder was not out of step with this form of manliness. After losing the dispute, Winn probably viewed it as the only way to salvage his reputation.[21] Winn faced three trials for murder but was never convicted. He escaped justice not by demonstrating innocence. Instead, Winn proved that he had participated in the community in ways that only a white man could, and as a result, the testimony that proved his guilt, offered only by Black witnesses, could not stand.

Of course, Johnson's death profoundly affected his family; however, his resources, example, and connections allowed his wife and children to maintain most of the lifestyle they had become accustomed to through the Civil War. Ann, his widow, took over the family's finances and made bold decisions to keep their position. The war and Reconstruction disrupted the family's finances, and their position as free people of color no longer possessed a special place in the postbellum South. The connections made by Ann and her husband continued to serve the family. They experienced multiple tragedies, including insanity, looming poverty, the murder of another family member, and the continued reminder that their lives would have been very different had their father not been taken from them. Still, Johnson's steps in life to protect his children paid off after his death.

CHAPTER I DEALS with Johnson's business dealings, particularly his barbershop. His shop was a way into a respectable trade and self-sufficiency for the biracial sons of white men in and around Natchez. Johnson stressed respectability as a man to his apprentices and even the men he enslaved in his shop. Johnson had different approaches with all of the men who worked in his shop, from educational lessons with some, deals with parents and enslavers, avenues for controlled amusements, and placing responsibility upon those who had earned it. Johnson was often disappointed with the choices these men and boys made and sometimes expressed that with violence. Johnson most especially concerned himself with his workers' interactions with women. While his biographers have suggested that Johnson's critiques of his apprentices stemmed from his sense of being superior to these younger men because of racial ideology, this explanation is not especially satisfying given that some of his apprentices stood to inherit substantial amounts of property upon reaching adulthood and all of them were of mixed race, just as he was. Given the entirety of Johnson's interactions, what is more likely is that he was critical of these young men for making poor choices of sexual or romantic partners that hindered the development of the next generation of free people of color in Natchez. His barbershop did not merely serve as a place to train these young men to become barbers; he also committed to educating them beyond the trade, including functioning as free men of color in a slave society. His apprentices and slaves sometimes accepted Johnson's model of respectable masculinity and sometimes rejected it in favor of other forms of manliness.

Chapter 2 shifts the discussion to Johnson's interest, maybe obsession, with gambling and contests. Johnson pursued these undertakings with the same vigor as his business interests, especially as a younger man. In these contests, Johnson showed how important he believed competition to be for men. His biographers describe him as perpetually lonely "at the top of his class," but his diary portrays the opposite. For most of his adult life, Johnson sought out and found companions with whom he gambled, hunted, and fished on nearly a daily basis. He discussed physical confrontations between other men and relished judging their prowess at dueling or fighting but only mentioned being drawn into such circumstances a handful of times, not including his punishments to apprentices or the men and women he enslaved. Johnson socialized and competed with whites, his apprentices, enslaved men, and other free people of color, including his sons, when they grew into teenagers, and was willing to make virtually any event into a competition. Winning was important to Johnson, but most important was the competition and the willingness to test skills and take risks. These contests established a public reputation that mirrored the ideology associated with combat and honor without leading to harmful or deadly consequences.[22]

Johnson's views on race and politics are the subject of chapter 3. Though his status as a free person of color prevented Johnson from voting, holding office, or serving on a jury, this does not mean that Johnson was disinterested or a casual observer of the world around him. Johnson believed that assertiveness and participation were critical traits of masculinity, and by engaging in Natchez's civic life, he could establish these behaviors. He read widely and took an interest in local and national elections, but he also considered the role of race in politics and expressed displeasure at removing or constraining the free Black population. When news of a robbery and murder in St. Louis in 1841 involving several free Black men reached Natchez, officials began demanding that free people of color get certificates signed by respectable white men testifying to their character to remain in Natchez. This event that he called "the Inquisition" disrupted the lives of Johnson's free Black associates and left him frustrated and angry. Even though he could not vote in elections, he engaged with politics as much as possible by attending speeches, following politics at every level, and making bets on elections with white men. Despite the popularity of the Whig Party in town, Johnson openly supported Democrats. Some of this interest might have resulted from national movements, but there is ample evidence that Johnson preferred the Democrats because of the favorable positions that several of them expressed regarding free people of color. Unlike many of the town's leading white gentlemen, he opposed the colonization of formerly enslaved people in Liberia. Additionally, he supported his neighbors' general interest by participating in local efforts like monitoring stray livestock, volunteering in the town's fire suppression efforts, and policing runaway slaves.

Just as he served as the nexus of the Natchez community, Johnson was the central connection for his extended family, which is the subject of chapter 4. In addition to his other masculine roles, Johnson took the protection of his family very seriously. Even though he appeared relatively secure in his position within Natchez, Johnson took several steps to ensure his family remained safe within a slave society. While he did not devote much space in his diary to his family, he frequently worried about his mother and her bad temper, which she often displayed in public. Free people of color always had to be conscious that minor legal transgressions could lead to their removal from town or possibly a loss of their freedom. Thus, limiting negative public attention was critical. Johnson made sure that his children received education to have every advantage. He had no way of anticipating the changes in the South after his death, but three of his daughters later became teachers. His three oldest sons trained to become barbers, just as he had, with the expectation that possessing a trade would be necessary for free men of color to maintain their positions in a slave society. The Johnson family took the precaution of having their children baptized in New Orleans at St. Louis Cathedral to provide a record of their freedom and connect them to the broader community of free people of color in that city.

Chapter 5 covers Johnson's dispute with his neighbors in "the Swamp" that ultimately led to his murder. Johnson's respectability that he worked so hard to earn in Natchez did not carry the same weight in his rural farming community. Baylor Winn, the man who murdered him, was in several ways Johnson's opposite; he had a reputation for being dishonest and immoral, cruel to his children, and threatened physical violence against those who challenged him in his shady practices. Winn kept his racial classification ambiguous. In this era, several free Black men in Mississippi petitioned the state to change their legal racial status from Black to white by demonstrating that they had participated in activities reserved for white men: voting, serving on juries, and marrying white women. Despite support from leading white men, none of those who petitioned the Mississippi legislature to change their status was successful. By murdering Johnson, Baylor Winn was able to change his categorization from Black to white. Rather than offering a defense that he was innocent of the charge of murder, Winn argued that he was not Black. Since the only evidence against Winn was the testimony of other Black men who witnessed the crime, if he could prove that he was white, the evidence presented against him would be inadmissible as Blacks could not testify against whites under Mississippi law. Since he confirmed that he participated in ways only white men were allowed and none of the juries that heard Winn's case could consider Black testimony against a white man, Winn could not be found guilty of the crime.

The epilogue deals with the repercussions of William Johnson's death on his family in the final years of the antebellum era, through the Civil War and Reconstruction. Natchez's newspapers acknowledged Johnson's reputation and mourned his loss, which was a testament to the respectability that he spent his life working toward, but it was the relationships and structures that he had created that most likely would have comforted him. His barbershop continued with his wife Ann's ability to take over the family's finances, his sons' management, and the skills of his apprentices and those he enslaved. As was true during his life, Johnson's example of respectable Black masculinity was not always followed perfectly by those under his tutelage. Johnson's friendships and connections with former apprentices allowed his family to draw on the same extensive network of free people of color from Natchez to New Orleans that he relied upon during his life.

CHAPTER ONE

Training Barbers and Men

GENERATIONS OF STUDIES have made it clear that enslavers purchased human property to maximize profit, and as Libra R. Hilde has written, "Paternalism and masculinity shaped slaveholders' self-conception, and both qualities involved a public performance that masked the actual conduct of masters and slaves within the institution of slavery."[1] William Johnson developed a form of paternalism with all of the boys and men in his household, free and enslaved. He expected all of them to conform to his example and obey his rules, but those in his charge often had other ideas. Sergio Lussana has written that Black men were collectively able to assert masculinity in the face of slavery, whereas others like Jeff Forret and David Doddington have maintained that masculinity was often a contest between men and that reputation and manliness could wax and wane depending on these contests.[2] Johnson's barbershop and household illustrate how these dynamics could play out among free people of color. For Johnson and the older generation of free men of color in Natchez, establishing respectability in business and their social lives was the key to creating their careers and establishing their households. Their conception of respectability rested upon their independence as businessmen, the wealth they generated, and how these characteristics made them distinct from the majority of African Americans in the region.[3] Whites in Mississippi and throughout the South made their hostility to free people of color well-known in law and custom, and as such, maintaining freedom and preserving livelihoods in a slave society had to be a priority.

Earlier scholars have focused on his respectability as evidence that Johnson aspired to adhere to white values, but deeper inspection reveals more complicated notions of how Black men viewed masculinity. While later chapters will clarify that Johnson recognized being a man required risk-taking and boldness, he also knew that self-control and learning the proper times to display those behaviors publicly were critical. Johnson's barbershop offers a venue to observe how these two aspects of masculinity sometimes intertwined and sometimes contradicted one another. The men and boys who worked in the barbershop, his friends, family members, and even those he enslaved were subjects to Johnson's example of Black masculinity daily. In some instances, Johnson expressed satisfaction and even admiration when Black men around him followed his path, but in others, he offered stern reprimands and violence when these very same men made other choices. As these men and boys decided to accept or reject Johnson's model, they demonstrated the various paths to black masculinity.[4]

Free People of Color in the American South

The first people of African heritage brought into British North America did not encounter a slave society as their descendants would. The man who took the name Anthony Johnson after arriving in Virginia in 1621, along with some of his African neighbors, carved out successful farms and even a kind of legal, if not social, equality with their white neighbors in the early Chesapeake. During his lifetime, colonial society shifted toward equating skin color rather than religion as the qualifier for slave status. The Virginia legislature established that even free people of color should not "be admitted to a full fruition of the exemptions and impunities of the English."[5] By the middle of the seventeenth century, colonial lawmakers had established a slave code and had begun removing free people of color from civic equality with whites, making whiteness a criterion for who was allowed to vote, hold office, serve in militias, and testify in court against whites in some places. As Winthrop Jordan wrote, the reasoning for these restrictions was that colonists assumed "that free Negroes were essentially more Negro than free, that in any contest between oppressed and oppressors free Negroes would side not with their brethren in legal status but with their brethren in color."[6] As slavery became firmly embedded, colonies took steps to prevent the expansion of the free Black population, restricting manumissions and requiring manumitted slaves to leave the area. Despite explicit prejudice against free people of color, not all colonies were consistent in their restrictions.[7]

The free Black population of the South remained small until three movements of the eighteenth century changed the ways Americans viewed liberty and slavery. The American Revolution directly led to freedom for some enslaved people who chose to fight in the war. The need for troops led American and British commanders to offer emancipation for military service. More indirectly, though, the ideals of the Revolution led some to question if slavery could play a role in a nation of liberty. Northern states, moved by ideology and demographic and economic changes, eventually concluded that slavery and the new American government were incompatible. Through outright abolition in some states and a more gradual approach in others, they ultimately banned slavery within their borders. Most slaveholders concluded that there was no inconsistency that an ostensibly free republic should hold 20 percent of its population in bondage. Enslaved people also took advantage of the upheaval of the war to run away on their own and move elsewhere to live as free people. Even as slave states worked to protect slavery, some enslavers determined to free enslaved people, usually in their wills, and as a result, the free Black population increased.[8]

Evangelical Christianity became the second movement that increased the number of free people of color in the South. Baptists and Methodists were at the forefront of this revival and brought a message that stressed the equality of everyone before God. Motivated by both this spiritual message and the ideology of the Revolution, some southern states relaxed restrictions on private manumissions. Upper South enslavers began emancipating enslaved men and women in their wills, indicating that the egalitarian spirit of the era moved them, but they intended to get a lifetime of service from the people they held in bondage. Thousands of enslaved people were released from bondage by these wills, including, most famously, 317 in George Washington's. Enslavers in the Lower South rarely followed this example despite the religious and civic movements in the new country and usually only freed their blood kin, those they believed had earned freedom from "meritous service," or the old and infirm who had become unable to work. These two denominations eventually took over southern churchgoing, only after dropping the antislavery message.[9]

Refugees from the revolution in Saint-Domingue created the third significant increase in free people of color in the South. While southern states welcomed white immigrants fleeing the revolt, they feared news of the fighting would lead to insurrection among their own enslaved populations, especially when they learned that some brought enslaved people with them. Along with whites, many free people of color looked to the United States for refuge, but not surprisingly, they encountered distrust and suspicion. Georgia and South Carolina banned their entry in 1793 and 1794, respectively, but still they entered Charleston and Savannah. By 1803, a group from North Carolina petitioned the US House of Representatives to ban free Blacks from the Caribbean. A bill was created to prevent "any negro, mulatto, or other person of color" from entering ports in the United States that banned them. Some representatives objected that this unfairly limited free Blacks' rights and changed the bill to exclude only those who were not "a native, a citizen, or registered seaman of the United States, or seamen natives of countries beyond the Cape of Good Hope." The bill passed. Discussion of the revolt and fears that enslaved or free people from Saint-Domingue might incite insurrection remained until the Civil War. Though the addition of free Black refugees from Saint-Domingue necessarily increased the population of free people of color, so did their example: as the free Black population grew, it became possible for enslaved men and women to run away and create new lives as free people. In the last decade of the eighteenth century, the free Black population of the United States increased by 82.3 percent, and the first decade of the nineteenth saw an additional increase of 72 percent.[10]

Even with these increases, free Blacks accounted for a small percentage of the African American population of the South. In 1800, free people of color represented 6.7 percent of the Black population of the South as a whole and only 2.1 percent in the Lower South. In the decades that followed, the free population rose in the South, mainly from natural increase and individual manumissions. Though abolitionists worked to create one, the nineteenth century had no movements that led to wholesale increases in freedom until slavery ended with the Thirteenth Amendment. The Mississippi Territory's first census data also appeared in 1800, and though free Blacks were 5 percent of the African American population, that only amounted to 182 people. Like the South as a whole, Mississippi's free Blacks increased in each decade until 1840, when legal restrictions against emancipating enslaved people and mandates to remove freed people led to a decline. Though some parts of the Slave South saw another increase in free Blacks by 1850, Mississippi's continued to drop.[11]

Though the number of free people of color grew in Mississippi, sometimes by large percentage increases, the numbers remained small because whites found them dangerous to slavery. Natchez and Adams County held the largest number of free Blacks in the state, but even at their highest point, there were only 258 free Blacks compared with 14,395 enslaved people in 1850. Through various laws and state supreme court decisions, the state's legal authorities clarified that "the laws of this state presume a negro *prima facie* to be a slave." In 1822, the Mississippi legislature passed a law directing manumission only if the legislature recognized that the individual had performed a "meritorious act" either for their owner or the state. In other words, releasing an enslaved person from bondage required a special act of the legislature. Convincing a lawmaking body composed of enslavers to emancipate enslaved people was no easy task; in 1823, only six petitions were submitted and only three granted. In the years that followed, petitioners received denials far more often than manumissions.[12]

State law defined a mulatto as "every person who shall have one-fourth part or more of negro blood," but this category did not by itself grant any special privilege or rights, nor did the law assume that a mulatto was necessarily free. Instead, the law made it clear that free Black people faced several restrictions based on race. Free people of color who met "with slaves, free negroes, or mulattoes at any unlawful meeting or assembly . . . shall be punished with stripes, at the discretion of the justice, not exceeding thirty-nine lashes," the same punishment enslaved people faced. Free Blacks could testify only against others of African heritage, not against whites. If a free person of color used "abusive or provoking language to, or lift his or her hand in opposition to any person, not being a negro or mulatto," they would be subject to thirty-nine lashes. Those who provided false testimony in court could have "both ears nailed to the pillory, and cut off, and thirty-nine lashes."[13]

Even those who became free did not receive equality with whites. Free people of color had to prove their freedom to the court and then be issued a certificate renewable every three years at the cost of one dollar before 1831 and three dollars thereafter. The certificate included a physical description of the individual and how they became free. If a free Black person could not produce their certificate, they could be jailed and perhaps sold into slavery. Mississippi law restricted free people of color from leaving the county they registered in unless they could prove they had secured employment; prevented the possession of firearms without a license; banned them from selling merchandise outside of established towns; and completely banned the sale of groceries and alcohol or operating "a house of entertainment." These limitations stemmed from the belief that free people of color threatened slavery, which most notably manifested in the ban on allowing anyone of African heritage, free or enslaved, to work in printing to prevent the creation or distribution of abolitionist literature. Those who employed Blacks in printing could be fined ten dollars per day for each individual; a Black person found working in this job could receive the death penalty.[14]

Along with these constraints, the state spelled out that people of mixed race could not expect treatment different from those with two African American parents. During the brief period of Spanish control of Natchez from 1779 to 1798, people of mixed race had greater access to freedom through self-purchase and higher status under the law than those with exclusively African heritage.[15] After the United States gained control of Mississippi, this practice ended, and the territory's laws became similar to those of the rest of the South, imposing restrictions on free people of color. Mississippi still expected free Blacks to have a means of supporting themselves. For enslavers seeking to free enslaved people, they would have to set them up with property or demonstrate that those who became free had learned a trade. The overseers and trustees of the poor were required to "make returns to the county and probate courts, twice a year, of all the poor free negro or mulatto children, within the same, whose parents, if they have any, they shall judge incapable of supporting and bringing them up in honest ways." To ensure that these children grew up in these "honest ways," the court authorized "said overseers and trustees to bind out all such free negro or mulatto children, apprentices to such person or persons whom the court shall approve, until twenty-one years if a male, or eighteen-years if a female."[16] As Ira Berlin has written, apprenticeship, when applied to free people of color, was another way to control their labor and place constraints on their freedoms. Though not enslaved, free Black apprentices were bound labor and thus not without supervision. Moreover, courts across the United States frequently placed free Black apprentices only into professions they deemed proper, sometimes not training apprentices in a trade and placing them as farmhands instead.[17]

In some cases, however, apprenticeship did work to establish free people of color into professions that would guarantee their freedom. Perhaps the most carefully explored life of a free man of color who transitioned from slavery to freedom through apprenticeship is that of William Ellison. Ellison was born into slavery in 1790, most likely the child of his enslaver, the white planter Robert Ellison, and an enslaved woman. By the age of sixteen, William Ellison became the property of Robert Ellison's white son and began to learn the trade of repairing and building cotton gins. As his biographers James Roark and Michael Johnson make clear, William Ellison earned a dual education as an apprentice, mastering the trade he was bound to and learning how to fit into a society in which people with any African heritage were presumed to be slaves.[18]

During his apprenticeship, Ellison learned the skills of a blacksmith, carpenter, and machinist as well as how to read and write, but at least as importantly, he learned that the key to achieving his goals was establishing a reputation for respectability among whites and other free people of color. Shortly thereafter, Ellison purchased his freedom and earned money to emancipate his wife and daughter. His skills in making and repairing cotton gins gained his white clients' respect. Still, Ellison also took other steps to link himself with whites in the South Carolina upstate, eventually becoming a cotton planter, owning almost nine hundred acres and enslaving sixty-three people. In joining the single high-status occupation in the South, Ellison showed his community that he was no more antislavery than whites were, which along with his wealth, helped him to gain social acceptance. As evidence of that belonging, the Ellison family eventually were allowed to sit among whites in their local Episcopal church rather than in the segregated gallery.[19]

Community and Respectability

While William Johnson never became as wealthy as William Ellison, he did become a central figure in Natchez. Unlike Ellison, Johnson was apprenticed to a free man of color and thus had a direct example to emulate. Johnson and several other free Black men who were his contemporaries found they could fit into Natchez society after passing through apprenticeships and learning trades or by offering services used by whites. Barbering and other professions allowed free men of color to interact with whites in ways that did not threaten the racial order: though they were free, they provided services to whites. This also allowed them to establish reputations of respectability, earning them some protection from restrictions faced by other African American men.

In Natchez, paths to freedom were gendered. Women had few occupations open to them that could create a path toward freedom and independence in southern towns. For women born into slavery, overwhelmingly, the only way to become free was to engage in a sexual relationship with a white man. The calculations enslaved women had to make to become free were often unbearable. Though scholars disagree over the influence Black women had in sexual encounters, the nature of racism and slavery has to be accounted for in any such case. Consequently, it is hard to view any relationship between an enslaved woman and a white man as consensual.[20] For boys and men, apprenticeship offered an opportunity for the dual education that William Ellison experienced in South Carolina: learning a trade while also learning how to negotiate being free and Black in a slave society. This was especially the case for those free Blacks who could do apprenticeships with other free Black men. Such a situation was potentially safer than apprenticing to a white man, who might use the indenture to hold him in bondage forever. It also offered an example for boys and men to establish a business and a reputation.

The Johnson family's emancipation exemplifies this gendered difference in becoming free. In 1814, a white man named William Johnson crossed the Mississippi River from Natchez to Vidalia, Louisiana, to free Amy, a woman he owned who was also the mother of his two children. After conferring with a judge, he posted a notice in English and French stating that William intended to free Amy and that anyone with any legal opposition to the act should come forward within forty days. When no one disputed the claim, Amy became free. Four years later, Johnson employed an agent to take the couple's daughter, Adelia, to Philadelphia, Pennsylvania, to emancipate her. While in Philadelphia, Adelia met and married James Miller, a free man of color, and the two returned to Natchez.[21] After freeing Amy and Adelia, William Johnson sought legislative approval to release his son, also named William. In his petition to the legislature, Johnson asked for permission "to make that disposition of his property most agreeable to his feelings & consonant to humanity," adding that emancipation would "give that Liberty to a human being which all are entitled to as a Birthright, & extend the hand of humanity to a rational creature, on whom Complexion, Custom, & even Law in this Land of Freedom, has conspirated [*sic*] to rivet the fetters of Slavery."[22]

The elder William Johnson freed his son differently than he had Amy and Adelia and in a way that would hold up much better in the event of a challenge to his legitimacy as a free man of color. Like most of the American South, the Mississippi legislature passed laws making it difficult to emancipate anyone, which explains why he took these two women out of the state to free them. Members of the state legislature and some of the townspeople of Natchez later complained of people of color who obtained freedom out of state. Eventually, the Mississippi High Court of Errors and Appeals used the *Dred Scott* decision to declare, "It is the policy of this State, as evinced by its legislation, to prevent the increase of free persons of color therein."[23] With his son, though, Johnson could prove a legal release from bondage and that the youngster was on track to establish himself as someone who would not become a burden on the state. Even though the petition did not address it, the newly freed William Johnson had been apprenticed to his brother-in-law, James Miller, and had begun learning the barber's trade.[24] The younger William Johnson came of age with the benefit of a state law declaring his freedom and a career that allowed him financial success and a secure position within the community.

Men of African heritage had a long history of serving as barbers to white men in the region that became the United States. During the colonial period, elite slaveholders often employed a "waiting man" who functioned as a personal servant. Waiting men might help run an owner's plantation, but importantly, they helped enslavers maintain gentility through their appearance, most notably through fashion and hairstyles. In some cases, this gave waiting men substantial influence over their enslavers. The American Revolution and subsequent economic and social changes opened opportunities for free Black men to become barbers, as white men who held those jobs in earlier times turned away from servile occupations associated with a lack of independence. Though some northern free Black leaders and certainly white men viewed barbering as a humiliating profession, these jobs also provided a niche for free men of color, North and South, to meet a "middle class" standard of respectability: material wealth, leisure time, the ability to have their wives remain at home, and to provide educations for their children.[25] Free Black barbers became public waiting men for their white customers, interacting with a wide range of men in their shops who trusted their barbers to make them fashionable.

As Douglas Bristol has established: "Black Barbers struck a bargain with white customers. The barbers assured white men that a barbershop friendship did not imply racial equality, and white men granted black barbers the right to pursue respectability without harassment."[26] Johnson's race might have prevented true friendships with most whites, but through his barbershop, he could establish respectability via his business dealings and by displaying masculinity that both white and Black men recognized. His shop was a distinctly male space: a clientele almost exclusively of white men served entirely by Black men. Visitors to the shop could consume products meant to enhance their appearance and witness Johnson as a business owner and a man who controlled the lives and labor of other Black men. For Johnson and other free Black men in Natchez, establishing respectability allowed them to become and remain free, distinguish themselves from the enslaved, and firmly assert their belonging in a community of men recognized by Blacks and whites.

After completing his apprenticeship with James Miller, Johnson moved to Port Gibson, Mississippi, to set up his own barbershop. However, he returned to Natchez shortly thereafter to take over Miller's shop as Miller and Adelia had determined to move to New Orleans. Johnson built it into the most popular barbershop in town, serving primarily white men as his customers. He also fashioned this shop to function in the same way that Miller's had for him: a path to freedom and independence for the area's mixed-race sons. Johnson cultivated a reputation based on high character and respectability to establish himself and build his business, which he knew was the key to financial success and maintaining his position as a free person of color in Natchez.

Though Johnson did not keep a diary as an apprentice and never wrote much about either his father or his time working in Miller's shop, it is clear that Miller had a more significant influence on the young man. After emancipating Amy and their children, the white William Johnson had a limited relationship with them. Amy established an independent household, and the younger William Johnson lived with Adelia and James while he trained as a barber. Whatever their relationship, Johnson might have thought of his father as an example of how not to live. In the few instances he wrote about him, Johnson referenced visiting his father's home and being, "Some what hurt at the sight of things &c." Johnson is not clear why he was hurt by how the place looked, though it might have been in disrepair. There are a few other references to "Capt. Johnson" in his records, but the only specific place where he names his father was in a record book where he recorded paying a seven-dollar debt for him. It may be that the younger William Johnson had other dealings with his father, but at no point does he spend any time or effort discussing their relationship as he did with so many other acquaintances, friends, and family members. The white William Johnson's unpaid debts led to lawsuits, and he might have struggled financially.[27]

In contrast, James Miller was considered a pillar of the Natchez community. In 1827, with the support of many of Natchez's leading white citizens and city council members, Miller petitioned the state legislature to remove his "civil disabilities" because of his race, with the exceptions of voting or jury or militia service. The petition cited Miller's nine years of residence in Natchez, his property, but also that he "has invariably afforded a good example to his brethren & that his conduct & demeanor are highly praiseworthy." The legislature denied the petition but did grant Miller the right to remain in the state regardless of any subsequent laws that required other free men and women of color to leave the state.[28] This petition shows that free men of color could cultivate respectability and recognition from the town's white men. During his apprenticeship, Miller served as a surrogate father to Johnson while the younger man learned the barber's trade, operated a shop, and navigated life as a free man of color. Johnson's diary does not begin until well after he graduated from Miller's tutelage, but it is clear that this is where he learned about establishing a reputation for respectability. Another of Miller's apprentices, Robert McCary, also started a barbershop in Natchez and became William Johnson's closest friend. Even though McCary was never as successful as Johnson, he seemed to have absorbed the same lessons from Miller about living as a free Black man in a slave state.

One scholar of Natchez has argued that the barbering profession "was but one step removed from that of servant and house slave."[29] During the nineteenth century, several prominent free Black men in the North shared this sentiment, arguing that service trades prevented African American men from countering racism from whites. David Walker wrote in his *Appeal*:

Understand me, brethren, I do not mean to speak against the occupations by which we acquire enough and sometimes scarcely that, to render ourselves and families comfortable through life. I am subjected to the same inconvenience, as you all.—My objections are, to our glorying and being happy in such low employments; for if we are men, we ought to be thankful to the Lord for the past, and for the future. Be looking forward with thankful hearts to higher attainments than wielding the razor and cleaning boots and shoes. The man whose aspirations are not above, and even below these, is indeed, ignorant and wretched enough.

25

I advance it therefore to you, not as a problematical, but as an unshaken and for ever immoveable fact, that your full glory and happiness, as well as all other coloured people under Heaven, shall never be fully consummated, but with the *entire emancipation of your enslaved brethren all over the world.*[30]

The journalist and abolitionist Martin Delany similarly complained that Black men working in service jobs hurt the cause of racial equality. In *The Condition, Elevation, Emigration, and Destiny of the Colored People of the United States,* Delany wrote: "How do we compare with them? Our fathers are their coachmen, our brothers their cookmen, and ourselves their waiting-men." The most vexing problem this created, according to Delany, was that such work forced African American women into working in similar types of labor, primarily as domestic servants, placing them at risk for sexual exploitation by the men who employed them. At the 1848 Convention of Colored Freedmen in Cleveland, Ohio, Delany said he "would rather receive a telegraphic despatch [*sic*], that his wife and two children had fallen victim to a loathsome disease, than to hear that they had become the servants of any man."[31]

Walker and Delany called for a collective resistance to racism that did not recognize that some free Blacks in the South had found their own paths to success even in one of the places most deeply committed to slavery. Eliza Potter, a free woman of color (and a hairdresser) who traveled to Natchez and New Orleans, found free Black enslavers behaved much as white slaveholders did and did not display racial solidarity with the people they enslaved. Her experience led her to criticize organized abolitionism since it did not acknowledge that some Blacks enslaved people.[32] Walker, Delany, and Potter did not consider that free people of color in the South had no room to speak out against slavery and found ways to advance that did not fit with abolition. Similarly, men like Miller, Johnson, and McCary exemplify that barbering was not a degrading profession though they served white clients. This trade allowed them to acquire wealth and support their families; none of their wives worked outside the home. Their barbershops also created a platform for other young men of color to demonstrate masculinity similarly to white men. All three men frequently spent their leisure time (stemming from the income that barbering provided) together hunting, fishing, and gambling, along with some of the men who were their clients. Even after their apprenticeships had long expired, Johnson and McCary remained close friends and business associates with Miller. They profited financially and socially from the lessons they had learned in his shop.

Johnson interacted with a small but vibrant, free Black community in Natchez along with McCary and others. In larger southern cities, white tradespeople prevented Black competition in some professions, but white men also shunned occupations that appeared to be servile. Material independence had become a critical marker of citizenship. Since only white men could be citizens, performing any job in which a white man served others could erode racial differences and prevent white men from asserting a critical public component of masculinity. As a Black barber in St. Louis wrote in his autobiography: "Should a white man attempt to wait on a southern country gentleman in the capacity of a barber, he would go into spasms. . . . It was not a white man's place to play the part of a servant."[33] This prejudice against these occupations allowed free Black men to find work and cultivate respectability as barbers, operating taxi services, and in other professions that white men in the South had decided were beneath them.

Most free men of color in Natchez had backgrounds similar to those of Johnson and McCary: they were born to enslaved mothers with white fathers and offered businesses that provided a service to whites. They understood the importance of maintaining a level of respectability in their work and public lives that allowed them to succeed in a slave society. Robert McCary's owner and father, James, freed Robert and his sister, Kitty, and granted each a town lot. Robert also received one thousand dollars from his father's estate and an enslaved man, who also happened to be his half brother, Warner. Warner was not James's son, so the white enslaver chose not to free him but instead left him as his children's property. Furthermore, the will provided Robert and Kitty funds for education, and at least five white tutors taught the siblings.[34] In many ways, McCary began his career in a higher position than Johnson had, as he had inherited wealth and property from his father, but McCary also was less ambitious and perhaps more cautious than Johnson when it came to business ventures. Like Johnson and other free Black men of their generation, he understood that men in their positions were under the scrutiny of whites. Their legal status was precarious in a society that equated any African heritage with slavery.

One scholar has labeled McCary "a role model and enforcer of white defined morality and discipline."[35] There is no denying that whites had all of the power of law and custom on their side in antebellum Natchez, but that does not mean that free people of color automatically deferred to whites on morality or discipline issues. While Johnson discusses whites throughout his diary, he discusses their immorality and destructive behaviors far more often than using them as exemplars for how to behave. Free men of color had different considerations than whites did. Though Johnson and McCary had white clienteles to whom they had to defer, that does not mean they did not witness frequent hypocrisy and immorality among whites. McCary joined the First Presbyterian Church of Natchez in 1856 and served as a spokesperson and role model for the church's Black members, ostensibly communicating their "wants, difficulties, or grievances" to the whites who ran the church. That the church leadership chose McCary for this role is evidence that he had achieved respectability in town with whites and Blacks.

In 1859, McCary leveled a misconduct charge against three Black churchgoers and called for a hearing. Of the three, one appeared for the hearing, but the other two did not and found themselves expelled from the church. One interpretation of this act is that McCary simply did the bidding of the church's white leadership. That implies that there were only two ways for a man to behave in McCary's position: he had to side with whites or rebel. As many recent scholars have demonstrated, there were many ways to assert masculinity, and holding a leadership role was undoubtedly one of them. In this case, the assumption is that whites generated the charges brought against these Black congregants, but McCary is the one who leveled the charges. These members did something that offended his sensibilities, which might have been in line with what the white leadership believed, but there was no order to go after them; he chose to do it himself. Like Johnson and Miller, McCary had strict ideas about public reputation and understood how important that was for Black people in town. These members' behavior could have undermined other Blacks' ability to remain in or join the church. Walter Johnson and David Stefan Doddington have argued that agency does not always equal resistance. To imply that McCary had no sense of what was right and proper for Black church members denies him that agency.[36]

Another free man of color from the same generation as Johnson and McCary, Nelson Fitzhugh, was born into slavery in 1807 and was enslaved by a baker named Adam Bauer. After becoming free, he learned to read and write and worked as a clerk in several stores in Natchez. Fitzhugh married and had seven children; one of his daughters married one of Robert

McCary's sons. He enslaved people and held real estate worth more than three thousand dollars. As the State of Mississippi increased pressure on removing free Blacks from the state in the 1850s, he was allowed to remain because, the *Natchez Weekly Courier* reported, "he and his family . . . were of good character and honest deportment, and . . . it is the wish of a number of citizens of this country that they be permitted to remain in the state."[37] After the Civil War, the same newspaper recalled Fitzhugh as "a bright mulatto lad . . . seemingly possessed of many virtues. . . . Citizens spoke of him as a proper man and named him in connection with such men as Wm. Johnson, the barber, and Robert McCary . . . both free men of color, both occupying honored graves . . . [and] all old citizens who knew them, all esteemed them." Nevertheless, this postwar paper lamented that Fitzhugh had deceived all of them and that "he never was more than a mask which concealed deformity and turpitude." After the war, the paper turned on him because Fitzhugh wrote a letter to the *Christian Recorder,* the African Methodist Episcopal Church newspaper published in Philadelphia, criticizing the *Natchez Weekly Courier* as "poor [and] contemptible."[38] The *Courier's* staff, angry over the attack in another publication, wounded Fitzhugh's public reputation among the town's whites and suggested that he was a "radical agent" rather than a friend of the South, which threatened his family's position in Natchez even after emancipation. The paper might have been correct that Fitzhugh had worn a mask of obedience while the institution of slavery still threatened his family's freedom, and he, like Johnson, was unhappy with the racism that constantly limited the success of his community. Still, the town's white population grouped these three men as exemplars of respectable free men of color before the Thirteenth Amendment changed the meanings of race and freedom.

Another contemporary free man of color in Natchez, Robert Smith, ran a taxi service. Smith was born free in Maryland and came to Natchez after living in New Orleans. Johnson's first recorded interaction with Smith had to do with a potential apprentice. In his diary, he listed the boy as the son of a man with the initials J. S., but Johnson intentionally obscured the father's actual name. Johnson wrote: "He [Smith] wanted me to take the Boy and Keep Him as Long as they were in this place which He supposed they would be Here about three Years—He said the Boy was not treated wright by Mr. S—— and for that Reason he wanted him away from thare." Smith brought the boy to Johnson on February 21, 1839. However, within a week, Johnson decided that he would not be a good fit for the shop, writing, "the Boy Peter that has been with me 4 or 5 Days went Home and his Mother Brought Him back again an I told Her that she had better keep him for I thought it impossible to Lern him the trade and she took him home again."[39] Smith had not been in Natchez for very long but had already identified Johnson's shop as the place for free boys of color to guarantee their futures. Johnson's rejection of the boy was not uncommon as he could afford to be selective since his shop had such a strong reputation for training barbers.

In spite of his dealing with Johnson, Smith's reputation was not universally flattering. When he died in 1858, the *Natchez Courier* published an obituary lamenting his passing and lauding his life, much as local papers did with other respectable free men of color who worked in service jobs. As the newspaper put it, "All our citizens—will regret to hear of the death of Robert D. Smith, a colored man of our city, but one who, by his *industry, probity of life, correctness of demeanor and Christian-like character, had won the favor and respect of the entire community.*"[40] Johnson, though, had a more complicated view of the man. Smith's arrival in Natchez created controversy as, like many free people of color in the town, he had to prove he was of good character, usually meaning he needed the endorsement of white men in town. Johnson learned that three men had signed on Smith's behalf that he should remain in Natchez. Mr. F. Taylor, one of the signers, had informed Johnson of this and claimed that "he believed Robt. Smith to be an Honest ad as correct a Coulurd Man as there was in Natchez." Certainly to the disappointment of Mr. Taylor, Johnson informed him that he "knew R. Smith Better than he did and I knew that at present time he was run off from New Orleans for Buying Goods from a Slave Negro and that when he came off he Left five hundred Dollars in Mr. Johnsons hands to pay his Bale for Johnson went his Bale."[41] A few years later, Johnson wrote in his diary, "Robert Smith and his Hacks and Horses All Sold to day at Auction, and they were All struck of[f] to Brevoort Butler which I think from what Smith told me, that it was no Sale, Intended to deceive Somebody I think."[42] Aside from these two entries, Johnson never explains the roots of his suspicions about Smith, though it is likely that he worried that Smith might do something that could hurt the status of free people of color in the city. It is also possible that when Taylor called Smith as "honest" and "correct" as any other free Black man in the town, Johnson found this an insult and intended to reduce Smith's reputation to raise his own.

These examples make clear that even if the white community believed that these free men of color were subservient, they did not always show their complete feelings or character. These distinctions seem to have been well-known among the free Black community. Even though Johnson had problems with Smith's character, he was willing to deal with him, taking on an apprentice on his word and later hiring Smith's carriages for his mother's funeral.[43] Johnson, McCary, Smith, Fitzhugh, Miller, and other free men of color of their generation were not merely grateful to whites for the ability to be free. They worked hard to clarify that they deserved their freedom through honest dealings and respectful, but not fawning, behavior toward whites. Like elsewhere across the South, most free people of color in town worked in the service industry and thus required white patronage to make a living, but they also had to rely upon whites to treat them reasonably within business dealings. Sometimes, Johnson had to go directly to his clients to collect money owed to him, and he rarely recorded problems despite the power imbalance possessed by white men. Indeed, other free Black business owners had similar experiences. They did not live at the margins of Natchez; they were firmly in its center. In creating these reputations for respectability, they were able to maintain their lives and businesses in a slave society and assert their masculinity in multiple ways, not just by cultivating a single reputation, but several, sometimes to display to whites, but in other instances, only among their community.

Apprenticeship and Freedom

Once he purchased the shop from James Miller, Johnson took on apprentices, just as Miller had, from the mixed-race sons of the area's planters and purchased enslaved men to be workers in the barbershop. As Douglas Bristol has argued, barbering had become a fraternity in which "the first generation of black barbers distilled their experience into a coherent tradition of African American barbering by which they transmitted their skills and social wiles to younger men."[44] Johnson never missed the chance to increase his earning potential, and bringing in apprentices certainly helped with this, but he could have chosen to use only the labor of enslaved men as some barbers in larger southern cities did.[45] Instead, he used these relationships with apprentices to pass on his notion of respectable Black masculinity to the town's next generation of free Black men. Natchez's white and Black residents sought to apprentice boys in his shop, indicating that they trusted Johnson's methods. By accepting these boys into his shop and home, Johnson acknowledged that he entered into contracts with their parents or guardians. He taught them the trade and how to live as free men of color in a slave society. While his relationships with most of these boys were complicated by their own ideas about masculinity, it is also the case that virtually all of his charges completed their apprenticeships and set up independent households. As a testament to his importance in their lives, most of these men remained connected to the Johnson family after leaving his shop and maintaining those associations even after Johnson's death.

Parents or guardians brought to Johnson prospective apprentices between the ages of ten and fifteen. Usually, these were boys freed by their enslavers, who were often their fathers, but sometimes he took them on while they were still enslaved with their freedom contingent upon completion of their training. Charles's enslaver, who likely was also his father, brought him to Johnson to learn the trade as a boy of ten or eleven as a condition for his freedom. Additionally, Johnson was to teach Charles "his books" and "to write also," which Johnson did with all of the boys in his shop, though he admitted in his diary that he was not always consistent with these lessons. While Charles was still a teenager, Johnson paid his enslaver $150 a year more than he paid his free journeymen. Despite his success as one of Johnson's most trusted and capable barbers, his enslaver/father expressed doubts about Charles's ability to either earn his freedom or function independently. Perhaps his enslaver kept Charles with Johnson because of how much he was paid for Charles's labor and wanted to continue the relationship to hire him out as an enslaved worker rather than a traditional apprentice. Charles remained with Johnson beyond age eighteen, when apprenticeships usually ended in his shop.[46] Though Johnson appreciated Charles's skills, the younger man was as subject as anyone else to Johnson's disapproval and discipline.

Johnson took on William Winston as an apprentice in 1836, when the boy was twelve. Winston was the son of Lieutenant Governor Fountain Winston and Rachel, one of the women he enslaved. Fountain Winston died in 1834 and, in his will, freed Rachel and directed William, sometimes called Bill, to live with his mother until he was old enough to be bound to "some reputable mechanic." His father's will read, "Believing Bill or William the son of Rachel to be too white to be continued in Slavery," that he would become free at age twenty-one. Additionally, the will granted Bill and his mother all of Fountain Winston's property, except his library, as long as his habits were good. Bill Winston had a considerable incentive to model himself on Johnson's example as his father's estate was worth more than three thousand dollars. Winston became Johnson's favored apprentice as he most closely followed Johnson's model as a free man of color.[47]

Johnson did not always accept the boys brought to him, and not all those brought to him wanted to become his apprentices. On May 4, 1841, Johnson recorded in his diary: "To Day I went by McCarys Shop and told Him that I had two Little Boys and was requested by Mr Hogatt to get situations for them to Learn a trade of some Kind—he wanted One of them and I gave him the Choice of the two, Jefferson and William. He Liked the Look of Wm Best tho. Wm told Him that He wanted to Live with me so Mc then said He would take the other—Accordingly I sent Jeff up to Him this Evening." Eight days later, Johnson reported: "This morning Shortly after Breakfast time The Boy William ran off and Took with Him Jeff, His Brother, that I had put with McCary. They Both went Out Home." Johnson blamed William for the incident because "I am Inclined to think that He is a Boy of no Kind of Energy." This lack of energy might have been Johnson's belief that he was lazy, but it is also possible that he simply believed the boy was not much of a boy. In the South, particularly in the Old Southwest, if a boy did not behave rambunctiously, it could signal that he did not have the qualities necessary to grow into a man.[48] Within that short time frame, Johnson had decided that William would not make a good apprentice, and the boy, whose family lived nearby, had agreed that the arrangement was not working for him either. Robert McCary attempted to catch the boys by riding on horseback but was unsuccessful. The two boys returned on May 14.[49]

Though his initial entries did not indicate it, Jefferson and William Hoggatt had reasons to feel uncomfortable with being uprooted from their family and placed in separate households. The two boys were the sons of William Hoggatt, a wealthy enslaver, and a woman named "Febe" or "Pheebe, a negro." The couple had seven children. Earlier in the year, William Hoggatt Sr. was murdered by an enslaved man named Isham. While their father's will offered all of the children and their mother a considerable inheritance, their mother no doubt understood that for the boys to be able to live as independent free men of color, they needed a trade and the instruction of men like Johnson and McCary on how to negotiate that path. Johnson had the boys' family over for dinner the following month. The barber and Pheebe agreed that William would stay with him, but one of his sisters also stayed in town, possibly with the Johnsons, as company for William.[50] Both Hoggatt brothers eventually worked for Johnson, and Jeff married Johnson's niece, Emma.

William Nix, yet another William in the household, who went by Bill, was a free person of color and joined Johnson as an apprentice in 1835 at age fifteen. Nix worked as a barber, but as he got older, he served as a hired-out body servant to whites from Natchez who traveled up and down the Mississippi River. He frequently delivered mail and packages to and from the Miller family in New Orleans, indicating that he must have been one of Johnson's most trusted workers. As a young man, Nix participated in much mischief with his fellow apprentices, leading to disapproval and discipline from the barber, but it seemed that Nix grew out of some of this as he aged. Johnson still criticized Nix for not following the barber's model for finding his way in the world. It appears that some of his troublemaking continued into his mid-twenties as Adelia Miller wrote to her brother, probably in a letter carried by Nix himself: "For William, you have the Most Negligent set of Boys About you that I ever saw. We could not get along with them one Month. Now those Mats that you Speak of. I gave [them] to William Nix and A Barrel of oysters for you and Mother and Beg him to give the Mats to [you] and the oysters to Mother to Be devided and he did not do it."[51] Johnson did not record any confrontation with Nix based on his sister's accusation, and Nix was still being sent out as a body servant to others just a few days later.[52] Nix eventually left Natchez to start a barbershop of his own.

Still another William, also named William Johnson, worked in the barbershop. This William, usually called "French William," "French," or "Old French," was the first of Johnson's workers to run his Natchez-Under-the-Hill shop. The town of Natchez was separated from the Mississippi River by a bluff. While under Spanish governance, the town was designed to have two sections: the part of town above the bluff was set out to be the residence of artisans and merchants, whereas the region underneath was for river traffic. This design fell apart almost immediately as the growing number of elite cotton planters who had moved to the area acquired huge town lots from Spanish authorities. By the beginning of the nineteenth century, they were constructing mansions as outward symbols of their wealth and power. One visitor remarked, "There is so much ground between most houses that it appears as if each dwelling was furnished with a plantation."[53] The river landing under the bluff, known as Natchez-Under-the-Hill by the late 1790s, remained the town's main economic center through the nineteenth century. Under-the-Hill represented a different neighborhood from the one above, intended to separate river travelers' vices from planters living in the upper part of the town. Of course, this barrier never truly worked, not because of a flaw in the town's design but rather because Under-the-Hill's indecent activities attracted respectable men just as it did the disreputable.[54]

French William was distinct from Johnson's other employees because he was the first to run a separate barbershop without direct supervision from the boss and because the two were probably related. French William's father was "Capt Johnson," most likely white William Johnson, meaning the two were half brothers. Like his other workers, Johnson expressed frustration with French William, though he did not apply physical punishment. On June 4, 1838, after paying French William his wages and collecting the money from the Under-the-Hill shop, "he showed me a Letter that Mr. Miller had wrote me and the substance of the letter was that Capt Johnson had requested Mr. Miller to write to me that he wanted me to Settle with Wm. It appears that the infernal Rascal has been writing to his Father himself." The white William Johnson must have sent French William to Natchez, hoping his other son would achieve similar independence and success. It also clarifies that the barbering William Johnson was not happy that his worker, who might have been formally apprenticed to him, was trying to escape his authority by writing to his father. On July 18, he recorded that "William Came up from New Orleans this morning and brought me a Receipt for two Hundred Dollars that I sent to his Father," indicating that French William's working relationship had ended, and he paid Captain Johnson the wages he owed him.[55] Johnson expressed no more emotion at the end of his time with his half brother than with other apprentices or enslaved men, and their relationship seems to have ended.

Johnson's reputation as a barber convinced various members of the Natchez community that his shop was the right site to place mixed-race boys to learn a trade and cultivate the respectability necessary to maintain freedom in a slave society. Their work and dual education enabled these young men to carve out lives for themselves and become independent men. Without that training and their ability to demonstrate respectability, these men could find themselves and the families they later formed either banished from the state or placed into slavery. Johnson's barbershop was billed by its owner and accepted by the community as a place to train boys to become free Black men. Johnson was never completely benevolent in his relationships with his apprentices as he profited from their labor, but he also set them all up for successful careers.

Apprentices and Paternalism

Johnson's shop became a space of connection between his personal and professional lives and a place where he developed his sense of paternalism centered upon helping free men of color guarantee their freedom. Eventually, the men who worked for him provided for their families in a broader society hostile to them. Sometimes his protégés accepted the lessons Johnson was offering, but just as often, they rejected them. Occasionally his response to his apprentices was similar to that of an enslaver doling out whippings for not conforming to his will. At other times, he reacted as a father might if his sons had been disobedient or made poor choices. Stephanie Camp argued: "Paternalism was also influenced by the early nineteenth-century ideal of affectionate family life and placed possessive and demanding fathers at the head of the plantation household. . . . This sense of intimacy partnered with a strong sense of license, and paternalists often intervened in the lives of their slaves."[56] Those interventions could include all kinds of intimate details. Johnson certainly felt this license with apprentices and the people he enslaved, controlling their labor, guiding their free time, and especially regulating their associations with women. Johnson's concern with his apprentices' personal lives contravenes any sense that he considered these men beneath him or in a separate social category. Rather than viewing himself as superior to the boys and young men in his shop, Johnson tried to mold them into his image.

Johnson was often judgmental, angry, and physically violent when his apprentices disappointed him or did not live up to his expected example of respectability. Much of his dissatisfaction came from their work habits, but he also found them wanting in other areas: their interactions with women, their behavior around whites, or general mischief that the young men might get into when out of his direct supervision. Johnson understood that the social distinctions placed upon people of color in Natchez by law and custom could result in his workers having their freedom taken from them, and their transgressions could hurt his reputation. Still, Johnson also believed that manliness required boldness and competition and was disappointed with his workers if they did not stand up for themselves or fight back when he thought it necessary. He was not always a cruel taskmaster and allowed his workers to attend parties, theater performances, or other traveling shows. He frequently brought them along to hunt, fish, and gamble with him. Johnson imparted the many-faceted aspects of what it took to be a man in the Slave South to his workers, much like the training he received from James Miller. That some of his charges resisted Johnson's rules is a testament to the many forms of masculinity that Black men displayed.

Johnson controlled his apprentices' lives at work, but they had opportunities to be out in the town without his supervision. Even when he was not present, he kept track of where they were and with whom they spent their time. For Johnson and other free men of color of his generation in Natchez, choosing sexual and marriage partners was a critical feature of establishing respectable masculinity. Marrying a free Black woman assured their children's freedom, thus allowing the free community to continue without fear of enslavement. Johnson married Ann Battles in 1835. Ann's experience was similar to her husband's: she was born into slavery and emancipated by her white father. Like Johnson's mother and sister, Ann's father took her and her mother to Ohio to secure records of their freedom. Mississippi courts later determined manumissions granted in other states were invalid, an attempt to circumvent state law, and an attack on the institution of slavery.[57] Johnson and other free men of color like his mentor James Miller, his close friend Robert McCary, and most of the other free Black men in town married free women of color. They encouraged their children and apprentices to do the same: one of McCary's sons married one of Miller's daughters, and one of McCary's daughters married the son of Nelson Fitzhugh. The number of free Blacks in Natchez between 1820 and 1860 began small and remained small, but the growth within this segment can be attributed more to family formation and childbearing than increased manumissions. The state legislature actively restricted the ability of enslavers to free the men and women they enslaved in 1831, 1842, and 1857. The small increase from 69 in 1820 to 202 by 1840 ended after this decade as the free Black population only grew to 214 by 1860.[58] If the free Black population's growth was slow, its ability to establish independent households was not. The percentage of free Black families living with whites declined each decade between Mississippi's admittance to statehood and the determination to leave the Union. Given the low numbers of free Blacks introduced via personal manumission and few free people of color moving into the town, the increase in numbers can only be a result of children being born free in Natchez, signifying the importance of marrying within this community for the last generation of free people of color born during the era of slavery in Mississippi.

Selecting romantic partners could be far more complicated for free men of color than white men. Even if, as one historian has noted, "attitudes toward male fornication were permissive" and "male lust was simply a recognized fact of life," for men in the South, slavery and slave codes altered what was considered "permissible."[59] Since slave codes made enslaved women property and they could not testify against whites in court in Mississippi, sexual relations between white men and Black women were implicitly sanctioned, whether they were consensual or not. Of course, the difference in power between whites and Blacks, enslavers and the enslaved, belies the notion that any relationship between an enslaved person and a free person could ever be consensual. At least among men, interracial sexual relations between white men and Black women seem to have been accepted tacitly as long as the white man treated the relationship as casual, remaining sufficiently superior in it so that no one could question who controlled the relationship. If that relationship became more serious, there might be social consequences. Adam Bingaman, one of the leading planters in Natchez and one of Johnson's closest white friends, began a relationship with a free woman of color named Mary Williams. The couple moved to New Orleans, where such relationships were more common than in Natchez, to raise their two daughters.[60]

Most scholars who have studied Johnson's life have attributed his criticism of his apprentices who had liaisons with enslaved women to the internalization of whites' racial prejudices. However, most of the evidence he left behind indicates that his real concern was that by associating or producing children with enslaved women, his free apprentices would slow the growth of the free Black community and create burdens upon themselves to free their children. After briefly leaving his barbershop one day in June 1837, Johnson returned and found "Bill and Charles had a Black Girl at the Shop Door" and disparagingly remarked: "oh what pupys [sic]. Fondling—beneath a Levell, Low minded creatures. I look on them as Soft." Of course, Johnson, being free and married and providing for a family, might not have shared the perspectives of Bill and Charles, and while he may have understood their competition for this Black girl's attention, he did not condone it.[61] Most likely, Johnson was disturbed that Bill and Charles were cavorting with a woman who was both "Black" and unfree and thus beneath their "level," though Charles was still enslaved. The criticism of the two came from Johnson's notion of respectable Black masculinity: any relationship that these two apprentices had with an enslaved woman would, in Johnson's mind and probably in the minds of other free people of color in Natchez, lower their status.

Bill Nix and Charles were two of his most trusted apprentices, but he was deeply critical of their associations with women. Johnson only rarely complained about Bill Nix's work as he proved to be a skillful barber and later opened a shop in Rodney, Mississippi, on Johnson's recommendation once his apprenticeship ended. Nix was frequently sent on trips up and down the Mississippi River to serve as a body servant for white men in Natchez. Johnson expressed admiration when Nix attended services at the Catholic Church to learn to sing and was pleased that he, like the master craftsman, had begun taking French lessons. Nix accompanied Johnson to hunt, fish, gamble, and locate the enslaved man Steven when he ran away from the shop. When it came to Nix's relationships with women, Johnson disapproved of his choices. In perhaps the most quoted line in Johnson's diary, he wrote, "Bill Nix is up to this Day a pure pure Negro in Heart and in action."[62] Most scholars have viewed the above entry as evidence that Johnson's mixed-race heritage led him to consider race in the same ways that whites did. Nix, like Johnson, was of mixed race and had a light complexion. Calling him a "pure Negro" mainly was a criticism of his relationships with Black women. Johnson rarely used this kind of racial language, and when he did, it was almost exclusively to describe his workers' sexual appetites. If Johnson subscribed to the same ideas as whites about racism, he would not have cared so much about policing the actions of his apprentices.

For both free and enslaved African Americans, choosing partners could be difficult. Enslavers often interfered in bondsmen's relationships, preventing enslaved men from claiming accepted masculine roles like husband and father. As Henry Brown wrote in his narrative, "the slave's wife is his, only at the will of her master, who may violate her chastity with impunity" and "suffice it to say, that no slave has the least certainty of being able to retain his wife or her husband a single hour; so that the slave is placed under strong inducements not to form a union of love, for he knows not how soon the chords wound around his heart would be snapped asunder, by the hand of the brutal slave-dealer."[63] Since enslaved marriages did not receive legal sanction, such unions could be broken at the whim of enslavers. Free men of color had other considerations. Marriage to an enslaved woman could mean taking on the financial burden of purchasing her freedom. Children born to an enslaved mother were not born free and were her enslaver's property, meaning they could be taken from their parents at any time. For free Black women, choosing a partner also offered a difficult calculus: there was no economic incentive to marry a man who did not own property. If a free Black woman owned property, then maintaining control of that property offered a reason to remain single. In Natchez, as in most other southern cities, free people of color practiced endogamous marriage rather than seeking partners outside their group, though free Black women occasionally married white men.[64]

Johnson made similar complaints when Nix and his other workers attended what he called "darkey balls," which were parties usually held in the Mississippi Hotel's ballroom. These parties were popular among some free people of color. Johnson allowed his workers to attend such parties as a reward for their work but restricted access when he wanted to punish them. Even when they were allowed to go to parties, Johnson found room to deride them. As one diary entry illustrated, "Bill [Nix] and Charles and Wellington all goes out to a party given by a servant of the Missis Evans out there at the residence—Butter, Butter will run in suitable weather."[65] The metaphorical "butter" was an insult he applied to various people in his diary, meaning that he viewed them as soft, in this case, giving in to their physical desires to go to these parties. Rather than assuming that Johnson did not go to these parties because he viewed himself racially superior to those who did attend, it makes more sense to acknowledge that Johnson had no interest because he was in a much different stage in his life than his apprentices. It seems unlikely that the older, married Johnson would find much amusement in attending a party with his workers and enslaved people much younger than he was. It is doubtful that he had much in common with them. He was bothered that these young men in his charge did not follow his example of respectability by avoiding these gatherings.

By the time Nix had completed his apprenticeship, Johnson felt that he had learned the ideas about respectability that he had been offering him since he was a young man. On March 27, 1844, Johnson discovered "that the Barber at Rodney is dead and the citizens wants another to Come up there, William Nicks is in a greate way to go up and take the Shop—I hope he may." In other words, when he learned that the town of Rodney needed a new barber, the first person he thought of to take the job was Bill Nix. Had he viewed Nix unfavorably, he had any number of other options to recommend for the job. The next day, Nix left for Rodney to take over the shop, and Johnson remarked, "I hope he may do well, I Know he can if He will Only try, for there is money to be made there and I Know it." Johnson's expression of confidence negates any sense that he thought Nix was a lousy worker or that the older biracial barber viewed the younger one as inferior. Ten days after taking over the shop in Rodney, Nix returned to Natchez to bring Robert Smith's son back with him as an apprentice.[66] Nix continued the tradition that James Miller had started with Johnson: bringing free boys of color into the trade to establish the financial independence required to be free and Black in Mississippi.

While Johnson was undoubtedly proud that Nix was carrying on his tradition, he still found room to criticize Nix for his choice of marriage partners. In May 1844, Johnson wrote in his diary, "Bill Nix and Henrieta Stut was married this morning Early and Left for Rodney Early this morning." Nix's wife was a free woman of color, which certainly met with Johnson's approval, but the day after the wedding, he conveyed: "It was today that I herd that Bill Nicks wife that he married yesterday had been once give to————and he made use of her. This it was Said was done for a House & Lot and afterwards he would not give it——So seys report Current."[67] The unnamed man in the report was white. Regardless of whether or not the relationship between this white man and Stuts was consensual, Johnson made clear in the diary that Nix had, once again, made a poor choice in companionship. In marrying a woman who had previously had a sexual relationship, Johnson made it clear that though Nix had succeeded professionally, he had not learned all he had been taught about respectability.[68]

Like Bill Nix, Charles was another of Johnson's workers who had considerable autonomy, running his Under-the-Hill shop without supervision. Unlike Nix, though, Charles was still enslaved in Johnson's employ. Charles's enslaver, "Major Young," had negotiated an agreement similar to those of Johnson's free apprentices, in which the young man would learn how to become independent. Based on Young's dealings with Johnson, it is clear that he intended to free Charles when he and Johnson agreed that the younger man was ready. Major Young met with Johnson in 1842 to renegotiate their deal for Charles's services. At the meeting, Johnson recalled, "He surprised me very much when he told me that the Boy's time has been out for some time &c." The surprise was probably Charles's age. He was over eighteen when most of his apprentices finished their time with Johnson. Whatever the case, Young wanted to know what Johnson thought Charles's time was worth for another year, implying that he could get a better rate to rent Charles out to someone else. Johnson drove something of a hard bargain, suggesting that he did not need Charles for six months out of the year because of slow business, though why that was the case is not apparent. The two eventually agreed that Johnson would pay fifteen dollars per month to Young, though he usually gave Charles more to recognize his work.[69]

Like Nix and most other young workers in his shop, Charles attended parties and sought out the company of young women, most of whom were enslaved. As his apprentices grew older, took on more responsibility, and in some cases, operated more independently, Johnson's complaints about their behaviors with women declined and shifted to the younger men in his charge. That did not mean that they stopped. In 1843, Johnson wrote: "Charles was over the River to day a fishing and came home Drunk—Wanted to marry an Old Black mans Daughter and told the old man to Refer to Wheelock & Sayers, A.L. Wilson, or Erhart & Foster if he wanted to know about his character."[70] Johnson does not record a response to Charles's desires here, perhaps because he did not take him seriously. The implication is that the "Old Black mans Daughter" was enslaved, as Johnson probably would have indicated if she were free. Whatever Charles's intentions toward this woman were, nothing came of the alleged interest in marrying her.

In 1848, however, Johnson recorded, "Charles disgraced Himself this Morning by Marrying Mrs. Littles Servant Girl May Known to the City as being a Buster."[71] "Buster" was a term that Johnson usually reserved for women, and it implied that these were women of ill repute and that he thought sexually promiscuous. According to Johnson, the "disgrace" that Charles had brought upon himself was twofold; not only was the girl "a Buster," but she also was enslaved. Of course, Charles was also still enslaved, but the expectation was that his apprenticeship with Johnson led to freedom. Johnson's condemnation of Charles's marriage signaled that it might hurt his ability to become free and that he had lowered his status.

Johnson met with Major Young again to pay him for Charles's time seven months later, and the two discussed the marriage. Johnson wrote: "He was Down on Charles about Getting married against his Orders—He told me that Charles Should have to give up that wife or Remain a Slave all his Life." Young's reaction confirmed Johnson's ideas about respectability for Black men in this era—by choosing his partner whom neither Young nor Johnson found agreeable, Charles had put his freedom in doubt. For Charles, selecting a marriage partner on his own was an assertion of his masculinity and a rejection of his father's and Johnson's notions of how he should live. Still, Young and Johnson's pressure was significant enough that Charles determined to end his marriage. On January 15, 1851, Johnson wrote in his diary: "I Saw Maj Young this Evening and he told me that he wantd to do something for Charles and that he wishd to give him a start in a shop for hisself. I told him very well and he spoke of Seting him free &c. and that if he did he thought it would be attened with Some Difficulty in regard to his Coming back here again &c."[72]

This entry explains much about the relationship between these three men. On the one hand, Charles probably ended the marriage as a contingency for his freedom, unless Young had a change of heart that Johnson did not mention. On the other, it seems that Charles had determined that he would not continue to work for Johnson as a free man. His feelings might have come from how Johnson had treated him over the marriage. In their meeting, Young made it clear that he intended to hold some kind of event announcing Charles's freedom and wanted Johnson in attendance. Johnson did not object, but he did not write anything about the event itself, either because he did not go or because he did not view it as worth his time to put it in his record. When Charles returned his key to the Under-the-Hill shop, Johnson only acknowledged in his diary that he had done so and had "Sent Gim Down in place of him."[73] Unlike other longtime apprentices or men he had enslaved, Johnson did not express any hope or confidence that Charles would succeed independently, possibly because he had rejected what Johnson believed to be the cornerstone of Black male respectability. Charles, Bill Nix, and other young men who worked in Johnson's shop likely understood their mentor's positions but also chose to find their own ways. Regardless of things they might have shared, these younger men wanted to establish their identities separate from Johnson, and though his model represented a successful one, it was not the only way to live as a free Black man. What is clear from the diary, though, is that despite his similarities with the young men who worked for him, Johnson viewed any deviance from the path he had taken to success as doomed to fail.

William Winston was the apprentice who followed Johnson's ideas about sexual propriety. Winston's arrangement was similar to Charles's in that he was still enslaved when he went to work for Johnson in 1836, but unlike Charles, Winston's father's will stipulated he became free when he reached the age of twenty-one. Charles's enslaver also intended to free him as an adult. However, since he was still living (unlike Fountain Winston) and had doubts about Charles's abilities and character, he did not have a built-in manumission date. Another significant difference was that Winston would inherit a sizable fortune when he became free as long as he maintained good habits.[74] It is possible that even as a young man Winston understood that his future wealth relied on his behavior, making him more receptive to Johnson's ideas about maintaining respectability.

Though Winston did not share his fellow apprentices' interests in cavorting with women, or at least did not get caught doing so, that did not mean that Johnson did not take opportunities to instruct him on behaving like a man. A few months after moving into the shop, Johnson noted, "To Day Bill Wilson & Bill Winston has a fight in the Back Room." In contrast with other behaviors that Johnson complained of as disruptive to work or discipline among his workers, he seemed to find this fight entertaining: "Winston has the Best of the fight tho. I Parted them Both and made a greate deal of fun of Winston. Second Fight took place in the Back of the Yard and Bill Winston whipped him Fairly and he hallowed to have Bill Winston taken off him. Winston had him down flat on the ground."[75] Johnson does not mention why he made fun of Winston, but he goaded the boys into fighting again. Bill Wilson was another boy who was probably free but not formally apprenticed to Johnson. It is possible that Johnson felt more attached to Winston and thus wanted to prove something to the boy about standing up for himself, but whatever his reasons, Johnson endorsed the fights and was pleased that Winston won. Winston might have taken this as a sign of approval. Johnson probably encouraged the boy to assert himself by fighting to fit into the shop, which was almost certainly a struggle for the boy who had grown up in a household with only his single mother. The following summer, Johnson explained in his diary: "To Day we had a first rate fight between Bill Rushelow & Bill Winston— They made a stand of[f]—Neither whipped."[76] Once again, Johnson was pleased with Winston's fight against another of the countless "Bills" and "Williams" in his shop.

Like all the young men in his shop, Winston challenged Johnson's rules and was punished. Over eight days, Johnson mentioned beating Winston three times. The first time Johnson "Gave Winston a very Seviere Floging to Day for impudence and other small offences that He Commited." Whatever offenses Winston might have committed that day, it was the first time Johnson had ever beaten the boy, who was around fifteen. In response, Winston left that night and went back home. Johnson responded by giving him "a comple[t]e Floging this morning for Going home Last night without Leave and for other small offences." Winston must have hoped to appeal to his mother to help get him out of his apprenticeship after the first beating. The teenager began rebelling against Johnson, the only male authority figure in his life. Winston ran home a few days later in response to yet another whipping. Johnson reacted with still another beating, writing in his diary, "I whipped Winston to Day again on account of his going Home and to tell his Mother Lyes &c." In 1841, Johnson discovered that Winston had bought a stolen pistol and was upset that the young man "after the best admonitions that I have been able to give, will disobey my orders."[77] Though Winston might not have resisted Johnson in the same ways other workers did by sneaking out at night to meet women, he still attempted to resist by placing his mother between himself and the master craftsman. Johnson does not mention the lies Winston told his mother, but it seems that his mother, Rachel, must have reached out to Johnson to relate what her son had told him. Johnson did not record Winston trying to do this again.

Winston was among Johnson's favorite apprentices despite these and occasionally other minor instances of resistance. In 1842, Johnson met with Mr. W. Burns, who served as the executor of Fountain Winston's will, to discuss Bill Winston's progress in the shop. Johnson told Burns: "He was doing very well tho I was not at this time Learning him much in the way of his Book. He wanted me to do so and he thought that Winston was now about Eighteen years old and that he wanted to have him Learn to Read and write, so that he might be able to Keep his Books or accts when he became older Enough to do Buisness for himself." Johnson agreed that this was a good idea for the young man. Burns also indicated that Winston should not receive wages as doing so exposed him to "Bad Habits." Not surprisingly, Johnson, the businessman, was more than willing to agree not to pay Winston for his work. The two concluded their meeting with a discussion of Winston's future. Burns told Johnson "that he thought that there would be something Left out of the Estate and that if he conducted himself well that he would give him a start some day," and Johnson replied that "Winston was a very smart Boy and that [he] liked him very much indeed."[78] Three years later, Johnson and Burns met again and agreed that Winston would start receiving wages now that he had reached the age of his promised emancipation. Johnson told Burns: "I would give him a Hundred & Fifty Dollars for him for a year, ie to the first of May next 1846, which was agreed upon, I promised to Learn him whatever I could during the year, ie to spell and to read, & write also—if I could."[79] This money was to go to Burns for Winston's work and was the standard amount Johnson paid to his advanced barbers, though less than he paid Charles.

Interestingly, Johnson wrote that he liked Winston very much. He never recorded a similar fondness even among his other workers who had been with him as long as Winston. However, Winston was distinct from his other workers because he did not challenge Johnston's model except for his minor rebellion as a teenager. Johnson did not complain about Winston drinking, attending parties, or mingling with enslaved women. Winston's last day in Johnson's shop was May 24, 1850. Johnson recalled that he spent "a good part of To day Looking up Winston's acct with me," which is not surprising after fourteen years. Despite his settlement with Burns, Johnson had paid Winston directly since their meeting but determined that he still owed him $217, which he gave him at the end of the day. Winston left "for the North" the next day, presumably to go to Cincinnati for a record of freedom, like so many other free people of color in Natchez. Winston and his mother were listed as "free negroes" in the 1850 census, and a special law was passed for him in 1854, allowing him to remain in Mississippi when there was much legal pressure to remove free people of color from the state. In 1863, Winston married Anna Leiper, part of a large and prominent free family in Natchez.[80] This marriage represented Johnson's preferred kind of pairing for all of his free apprentices and demonstrated that Winston had lived up to Johnson's example.

Enslaved Men Working in the Shop

Along with his apprentices, Johnson enslaved several men and women throughout his life. Before purchasing a farm, he split them up according to their gender: the women he enslaved worked in the home under the supervision of his wife, Ann. The men worked in his shop or were hired out for short terms to people who lived in or nearby Natchez, with the money going back to Johnson.[81] Johnson's interest in slavery was financial, though his treatment of the men he owned did not usually differ substantially from how he treated his apprentices. This does not mean that Johnson was kind to enslaved people; instead, he expected them to abide by his rules and punished them when they did not. Essentially, even though these men were not free like his apprentices (except for Charles and Winston, whose freedom was partly contingent upon completing their time with Johnson satisfactorily), he still expected them to use his example as a model for Black masculinity. Still, as with his free men workers, there were varying degrees of acceptance, illustrating that Black men found multiple ways of displaying masculinity.

Conflicting ideas about masculinity played out in Johnson's shop and household daily. Traditionally scholars have viewed slave masculinity as confined to rebellion—the idea that the only way that one could assert manliness was to reject the emasculating nature of slavery through violence. More recently, studies have indicated multiple ways of being a man while enslaved. Accepting a privileged role on a plantation or in an urban setting like Natchez did not mean that an enslaved man had given up all control of his life to his enslaver. Whereas some men accepted only rebellion or running away as a masculine response to enslavement, others might choose to use a privileged role like trustee or driver to gain power or respect within an enslaved community.[82] Perhaps more than white enslavers, Johnson's image of himself as a paternalist manifested itself in these contests within his household. While sometimes his free and enslaved workers fought among themselves, Johnson primarily recorded acts of resistance against his authority, and his responses usually ranged from mild anger to violent wrath.

The central historiographic question surrounding Black slaveholders is their motivation: did they enslave people out of benevolence, in other words, as a way to hold relatives or friends as slaves in name only, or did they do so to earn a profit, which is to say, for the same reason that whites owned human property? Carter Woodson first proposed the benevolence thesis in his 1924 book *Free Negro Owners of Slaves in the United States in 1830*. Since then, other historians have modified Woodson's position, arguing that the region of the South they lived in determined the motivations for enslaving others: making the case that Upper South enslavers tended toward nominal slavery whereas those in the Lower South were more inclined to purchase slaves for economic gain. Still others have asserted that Woodson was wrong and that African Americans who chose to become enslavers were no different from their white counterparts and driven only by the desire to exploit labor for their financial advantage.[83]

Eliza Potter, a free woman of color who worked as a hairdresser in Cincinnati during the antebellum era, published an autobiography in which she offered a critique of the idea that there was a sense of racial solidarity between free Blacks and enslaved people. In her introduction to the autobiography, Xiomara Santamarina wrote, "her experiences in of slavery in Natchez and New Orleans convince her, counterintuitively, that racial identity alone in the highly stratified Lower South . . . does not organize all southern behavior" and "instead, she contends polemically that 'color makes no difference' in the social relations between slaveholders, slaves, free blacks and poor whites." As an example, Potter recalled a free woman of color who moved to New Orleans and became an enslaver who was "the most tyrannical, overbearing, cruel task-mistress that ever existed; so you can see color makes no difference, the propensities are the same, and those who have been oppressed themselves, are the sorest oppressors." To Potter, the point of slaveholding was to earn money for the slave owner, regardless of race.[84]

Understanding why free people of color chose to purchase enslaved people is a challenging endeavor for historians in the aggregate, but some of the most prominent African American enslavers have left records indicating why they decided to invest in human "property" that bear out Potter's observations. John Stanly, born into slavery in North Carolina in 1774, had several similarities to William Johnson: he was born to a Black mother and a white father, was trained as a barber, and was emancipated. Also, like Johnson, he began buying enslaved people to work in his barbershop and diversified his portfolio by investing in urban real estate and farming. Unlike Johnson, though, he became enormously wealthy via cotton planting, eventually owning 2,600 acres spread out on three plantations and enslaving 163 people. One of Stanly's white neighbors described him as a "hard-task master" who "fed and clothed indifferently."[85] Based on the size of his holdings and the descriptions of him as an enslaver, it is clear that Stanly purchased enslaved people for the same reasons his white neighbors did.

Several free men of color across the South left behind enough records that historians can reasonably infer why they enslaved people. After training to repair cotton gins, William Ellison of South Carolina purchased enslaved men to help run his gin shop and eventually work on his cotton plantations, ultimately owning sixty-three slaves. The numbers alone indicate that he bought more than just family members, but further evidence suggests that he split up enslaved families and could be harsh in punishments.[86] Born free in New Orleans, Andrew Durnford enslaved seventy-seven people whom he put to work on a sugar plantation. Durnford left no ambiguity in his thoughts toward the enslaved: when punishing a man named Jackson, he "ordered five rounds to be given him." In response to the whipping, when Jackson ran away, Durnford wrote: "I wish to lay eyes on him once more. I will fix him so the dogs will not bark at him." After running away again, Durnford expressed anger that the man had left with "all the irons I had putt on him." Additionally, Durnford spent as little as possible to feed the people he enslaved. While he might have believed slavery was a moral evil, he freed only one person: a boy he fathered with an enslaved woman.[87]

That these three men held enslaved people for the sake of profit is by no means a definitive statement on why all African Americans who owned slaves chose to do so, and though these exceptional cases point toward favoring profit, other similarly situated individuals had the opposite motivation.[88] In exploring the number of people enslaved by African Americans in the South, some historians have concluded that Black slaveholding, especially among those with relatively high numbers of enslaved people, might not have been substantially different from white slaveholding. In their study of Woodson's data, David L. Lightner and Alexander M. Ragan argue that Black enslavers with relatively few slaves, fewer than four, might have become enslavers to keep their families together and behaved with benevolence toward them, but the preponderance of Black enslavers who held a larger number of slaves were most likely moved to invest in human property for profit. They also found that people enslaved by Blacks in the Lower South were more likely to live in households or plantations with considerably more than four slaves, whereas Black enslavers in the Upper South tended to have fewer slaves and could more reliably be expected to be benevolent owners.[89]

Regardless of the statistics, William Johnson's life indicates that individuals could have various motives for enslaving people. In the main, there is no doubt that Johnson was a profit-maximizer who enslaved men and women for his advantage. Still, it is also the case that Johnson's treatment of these individuals was not always static: he expressed rage and violence toward them but also, with less frequency, kindness and compassion. Johnson was also motivated as an enslaver by other nonpecuniary benefits. In a town like Natchez, enslaving people was not just a way of earning money: it also was a means of protecting his family and their status by belonging to a group of slaveholding men. Paternalism for Johnson was not just about getting the men and women he enslaved to do what he wanted. He likewise thought about his reputation and expressed legitimate concern for individuals in rare situations. As was true of Stanly, Ellison, and Durnford, Johnson dispensed abject cruelty just as white enslavers did, but unlike some of his white or Black contemporaries, he also recorded instances of kindheartedness.

None of the men he enslaved or apprenticed during his lifetime more fully embraced Johnson's notions of what it meant to be a Black man than Jim. Johnson purchased Jim at auction on February 29, 1844. Jim had been enslaved to a Natchez shopkeeper and was put up for auction when that man died. Johnson noted in his diary that he was concerned that if he showed up to the auction to purchase Jim, white men in the crowd would run the price up on him, forcing him to pay more, or more generally, to torment a free man of color at one of these auctions. It seems that this was a treatment that Johnson had experienced before. To avoid this, a white man named "Mr. Canon" stood in for Johnson at the auction, and while the price that he arrived at for Jim, $790, "Tis thought to be high," he also noted that "I am very well pleased with him." Jim was nineteen years old when Johnson bought him, and it is possible that Johnson already knew him from his time with his former enslaver, which seems likely as he gave Jim a pass to attend a party two days after he purchased him at auction.[90]

Jim worked in the barbershop and later on the farm alongside Johnson's free apprentices, others he enslaved, his white hired hands, and his family. Though he used his diary to complain about the others, Johnson never mentioned Jim stepping out of line or not completing his work or that Johnson whipped him for any offense. When Charles's owner set him free, and he resigned from Johnson's employ in April 1851, Johnson put Jim in charge of the Under-the-Hill barbershop. Johnson chose Jim to run the shop over several apprentices who had been with him longer. A few days after Jim took over, he noticed that business in the shop had improved. He wrote: "This is getting a little Better, I now See how I have been Humbuged. I Notice that Charles Can Get under the Hill now as Soon as Any One. Thus I find out Considerable in take a Little notice."[91] Johnson observed that Charles seemed to have been not as honest a broker as he had assumed. Jim had the same type of autonomy as Charles, thus indicating that Johnson had enormous trust in him.

On October 24, 1849, Johnson wrote that he "Gave Gim (Jim) Permission to Marry this Evening in a note to Mr. & Mrs. Hunter." This permission came two years after Jim had separated from a woman named Hanah. Jim and Hanah were to be married, apparently with Johnson's approval, but the enslaver discovered that "They are variance because Jdg.——— tis Said has taken the 1st chances." In other words, the couple had broken off their engagement because Jim believed Hanah had an affair with a white man. In his diary, Johnson reported: "Hanah Came to me this morning and made her Statement in regard to her visits to Certain places &c. She Said that She had went thare twice and she went thare on business for her Cozen Mary and that the man had never Said a Dispectfull word to her in his Life." Her cousin Mary corroborated Hanah's denial of the relationship.[92]

Johnson's discussion with Hanah and her cousin Mary clarifies that the two disputed that Hanah had slept with the unnamed white man. Jim seemed to believe Hanah and that he had misunderstood the nature of the relationship, if there was one at all, as two days later, Johnson wrote "Gim Sends Hanahs Ring back to her," but also "She refused to acept it but returns it to him." Some enslaved men used sexual exploits with women to establish themselves as more masculine than their peers.[93] Johnson wholeheartedly rejected this path to masculinity for those who lived under his roof and disapproved of the men in his household when they engaged in sexual relationships with women who either were not free or had questionable histories. Unlike in other instances with free men in his charge, Johnson did not mock Jim or label Hanah negatively after this breakup. Perhaps because Johnson believed Hanah, or maybe it was the right thing to do to call off the wedding if there was even a suspicion that Hanah might have had an affair with a white man first. Johnson did not record the name of the woman Jim married in 1849, but he approved of this relationship.[94] Given how Johnson wrote of Jim throughout his diary, it is clear that he respected Jim—of all those who worked for him, Jim is the only one spared criticism for work or personal habits, and he never recorded any punishments. Notwithstanding the comparative esteem for Jim, Johnson never considered freeing him. Jim was still with the Johnson family in September 1864, even though the Union had occupied the town over a year earlier.[95]

If Jim represented the ideal enslaved man to Johnson, others embodied the opposite. In 1835, Johnson purchased a man named Walker, about thirty-seven years old, at auction for fifty-five dollars. Johnson described him as "a very black man who smiled broadly and was usually confused when addressed."[96] Like most men and boys who worked for Johnson, Walker took advantage of Natchez's urban location and his enslaver's willingness to allow the men he enslaved to move about the city with some frequency. In January 1836, Johnson wrote: "Last night Walker Came Home Drunk and sliped off again. I then went under the Hill to Look for him—I intended to mall him well but I could not find him and to night he Came home the Same way—I did not strike him but came very near it."[97] Natchez had become a center for cotton production and the domestic slave trade. Like other cities across the South, it became a hub for people of various classes and ethnicities to interact in ways unavailable in the countryside.[98] This urban space created a forum for Black men to assert their place in the town's community of men. For Walker and other men and boys who lived in Johnson's household, that meant taking opportunities to escape the control of his enslaver and to drink illicitly with others. Johnson frequently complained of his workers, free and enslaved, sneaking out and night and getting into trouble.

By July 1837, Walker had used his relative freedom of movement to run away from Natchez and Johnson. Johnson wrote on July 23, 1837, "I herd to day that my Negro man Walker had ran away On Bourd of Some Steam Bourd [boat] that left here on Friday Evening, 21st." He discovered three boats had left that day and believed someone onboard one of them had stolen Walker. The next day, Johnson sent a letter to the sheriff of Louisville "with a Discription of the thief and the Negro" and an "advertizement to the office of the Courrier [one of the local newspapers] to [be] published in the daily One week and to be published in the weekly until forbid." He also sent a letter to his sister telling her he believed, "he was stolen by a Fellow—under the hill—I never expect to see him any more."[99] Though Johnson assumed someone stole Walker, it seems he chose to run away to get to Kentucky for a reunion with his wife, from whom he had been sold away.[100]

Like other enslaved men throughout the South, the domestic slave trade separated Walker's family, and also, like many other men, he tried to reunite with his loved ones. While some enslaved men ran away and left their families as an expression of masculinity, sometimes because of humiliations rendered by enslavers and the denial of their roles as husbands and fathers, in Walker's case, it appears that he ran away to return to his family.[101] Perhaps Johnson did not believe that Walker would run away from him either because he viewed himself as a good enslaver or thought Walker could not pull this off and assumed that a third party must have stolen him.

Several weeks later, Johnson received notification that Walker had been found and arrested in Paducah, Kentucky. He went to the office of Jacob Soria, who sold general merchandise in town but also held slave auctions, to get a bill of sale indicating that he had purchased Walker, as he had lost his original. Afterward, he boarded a steamboat to Kentucky. Though he does not explain what happened, Johnson did not return with Walker and recorded his "disappointment," likely resulting from a case of mistaken identity. It is unknown if Walker actually found his wife, but Johnson's steps to either bring Walker back to Natchez or offer him for sale in Kentucky do not make sense based only on finances. It is doubtful that Johnson was upset at losing an investment of fifty-five dollars from two years prior, especially since he was willing to lose far more than that on games of chance. Instead, Johnson likely went to the trouble and expense to recapture Walker because it might have hurt his reputation as a slaveholder not to do so. Though he never expressed it directly, enslaved men taking advantage of a free man of color might have made it appear to whites that he was either incapable of enforcing discipline or perhaps in league with enslaved people.[102]

Running away offered a rejection of Johnson as an enslaver, but other enslaved men found different ways to challenge Johnson's ideas of manliness. Drinking, especially among southern white men, was a way of asserting masculinity: buying drinks for others was a form of hospitality, and consuming alcohol was a demonstration of stamina. Drinking could lead to challenges, insults, and debts to others, all behaviors that white men used to perform masculinity to the public.[103] Johnson did not have a problem with drinking per se; instead, he found it distasteful when men drank excessively and committed acts they would not otherwise have. One enslaved man he called "Old Middleton" was the property of Adelia and James Miller but was allowed to remain in Natchez after the couple moved to New Orleans.

Johnson and the Millers agreed that Middleton would give Johnson a portion of his earnings, sending them to his sister and brother-in-law. In a letter to Adelia, William asked, "[W]hat must be done with Old Middleton—he is now lying. . . . [T]he old fellow has killed himself—drinking—he has not paid me a cent for I can't tell when . . . he says he [can't] work nor walk." Johnson wanted to send Middleton to the Millers since he had become a burden, but the enslaved man remained in Natchez. In 1841, Johnson loaned him money to purchase a house for himself and his wife.[104] In Middleton's case, Johnson denounced the behavior, but he was not interested in changing it since he was not in his household. Still, he lamented the man's inability to control his drinking. When the men he enslaved or apprentices drank, Johnson viewed this as revealing a lack of restraint and respectability. It could subject them to arrest, which might endanger the freedom of apprentices or hurt their chances of establishing independent households, but when enslaved people drank, it could challenge Johnson's reputation as a businessman and a slaveholder and his income.

If Middleton and Walker represented challenges to Johnson's ideas about respectable Black masculinity, Steven, another man Johnson enslaved, defied it completely. Jim represented Johnson's ideal enslaved man, and Steven was the opposite. Johnson brought Steven into the barbershop to learn the trade on January 2, 1836. Six days later, he recorded in his diary: "Steven went Out—The patroll caught him and whiped him and I whiped him myself the morning afterward." Given Johnson's willingness to teach Steven the trade when he turned away free apprentices, it is clear from the start that Johnson saw something in the younger man that was promising, but Steven had his own designs, whatever Johnson's plans were for him. Perhaps recognizing that Steven might not fit in with being a barber full time or maybe just because he saw opportunities to make money from his labor elsewhere, Johnson hired Steven out to others in Natchez to do various types of work. As with most slave hiring situations, the agreement was that Steven's wages went to Johnson. Steven did not always hand them over. In September 1836, Johnson wrote: "[It] makes precisly three weeks since I Received any wages from Steven. I found Out this Evening by whiping prety severely that he had Received his wages from Messrs Spraigue & Howell and made away with the whole if it." The same day, he heard a complaint from "old Mr. Christopher Miller" that Steven had been "Coming Out to his House after his girl &c."[105] Steven's behavior was vexing for Johnson for multiple reasons: he was out without permission, drinking, stealing wages, and cavorting with enslaved girls. These activities challenged Johnson's respectability and public image as a businessman and enslaver. In response, Johnson's punishments were severe, not just because of Steven's behavior but also because it could damage the enslaver's reputation.

The ability of enslaved people in Natchez to sneak out and drink resulted in complaints and legal attempts to prevent them from acquiring alcohol. In 1839, the state legislature passed a law to suppress tippling houses and the "odious vice of drunkenness" and "to put down the evil practice of retailing liquor to negroes." The act stated, "if any person, either with or without license to retail, shall sell any vinous or spirituous liquors to any slave, without the permission of his or her master, mistress, owner or overseer . . . they so offending . . . and upon conviction thereof, shall pay a fine of five hundred dollars, and shall be imprisoned in the common jail of the county for not less than thirty and not more than ninety days." If a person sold liquor to a person proven later to be "negro or mulatto, that fact shall be received as prima facie evidence of his or her being a slave."[106] However, the practice continued despite the hefty punishment. For those accused of selling liquor to the enslaved, the issue of the owner's permission became the difference between determining guilt or innocence. Some of those brought to court for selling to enslaved people contended that when an enslaved entered their shop to buy liquor, the possession of money implied an enslaver had given consent. Technically, it was not illegal for enslaved people to purchase alcohol; it was unlawful for free people to sell it to them.[107] Slaveholders could give permission to retailers orally or provide the enslaved with alcohol; enslaved people could acquire it through theft or have a free companion purchase it for them. As the court noted, this traffic was "hard to detect."[108]

In Natchez and cities across the South, citizens routinely ignored the law forbidding alcohol sales to Blacks. In a letter to the *Natchez Courier,* one writer identifying himself only as "Law and Justice" complained that despite the law, "hundreds of negroes are nightly drunk in consequence of the attention paid to them by the grogshops on the roads leading out of Natchez." These roads also led into Natchez, which seemed to be the more significant problem for the writer, who protested the dangerous practice of drunken Black men riding "through the streets of Natchez at the rapid rate of 12 miles an hour." The town's night guard was also blamed for this early practice of driving while intoxicated, which "Law and Justice" argued "was not worth a baubee."[109] As with others associated with alcohol, the author's complaint was not the act of drinking but the racial problem it fostered and the inability or unwillingness of authorities to address the issue.

Steven continued to escape and drink despite the law and Johnson's punishment. On March 19, 1838, Johnson complained that Steven "got drunk last night and was not here this morning," and then "he ran off 4 times in about three hours," presumably to drink more and keep from doing his prescribed tasks. Eventually, Johnson "gave him a pretty severe thrashing with the cowhide" and remarked, "tis singular how much good it does some people to get whipped." Whatever good this was supposed to have done Steven, he ran away eight days later, and this time Johnson vowed to "hurt his feelings" should he be fortunate enough to catch him again. Steven heard of Johnson's intentions through other workers in the shop, possibly through Bill Nix, who Johnson frequently sent out to find him when he ran off. In his diary two days later, Johnson wrote, "He sent me word that if I would Only Let him off without whiping him that he would never runaway again Durring His Life."[110] Johnson agreed to the terms.

Steven's promise lasted nearly two years. When he relapsed, Johnson did not seem surprised that Steven had run away again to drink, but rather than just expressing a desire to whip him, Johnson wrote, "I hope I will be able to put Him in a Safe place yet if I dont mind." On the first reading, it might sound that he intended to help Steven remain safe, but Johnson did not mean to keep Steven safe; he meant to keep his investment in Steven and his reputation safe. The next time Steven came home drunk, Johnson "Hand Cuffed him and Floged Him," ostensibly believing that the handcuffs prevented Steven from leaving, but they did not, and he managed to escape to drink more on the same day. The next time, Steven was put "in Chains, waiting for better times." The following day, he was flogged again, then released for work. Johnson put him in chains again the next time, but Steven somehow escaped while still wearing the chains and was discovered by Robert McCary. The following two times, Steven was arrested and confined in the city's guardhouse and then caught by a young man named Phelps, who required Johnson to pay him for capturing and returning him. These last attempts involved whites capturing Steven, which appears to have established a breaking point for his tolerance of Steven's behavior as the next time that he ran away, Johnson "rode out to the Forks of the Road [the site

TRAINING BARBERS AND MEN

of the largest slave auction house in Natchez] to try to swap Stephen off for Some One Else, But could find none that I would like."[111] Once whites and the authorities had gotten involved in Steven's situation, this became a public problem, potentially threatening Johnson's reputation.

Between 1841 and 1843, Steven continued to drink, evade work, and occasionally get arrested by the city guard, and finally, Johnson determined that he had to sell him rather than continue to allow the public to witness his inability to control the younger man. In December 1843, Johnson wrote: "And what is the Cause of my parting with him, why it is nothing but Liquor, Liquor, His fondness for it. Nothing more, Poor Fellow. There are many worse fellows than poor Steven is, God Bless him. Tis his own fault." On New Year's Eve, the two went to the Mississippi River to put Steven on a boat to take him to his new owner. Johnson recorded an uncharacteristic level of emotion in his diary, writing, "Today has been to me a very sad day; many tears was in my eyes today on acct. of my selling poor Steven." They missed the boat, and somehow Steven escaped Johnson's notice and got drunk. When Johnson found him, he "took him home & made him sleep in the garret and kept him safe." On the first day of 1844, Johnson got Steven on the boat, gave him several gifts, and shook his hand as he departed. Johnson wrote, "I would not have parted with him if he had only let liquor alone but he cannot do it I believe."[112]

Johnson's relationships with Jim, Steven, Middleton, and Walker reveal that Black men, enslaved and free, chose different ways of expressing masculinity. Even though Johnson found Jim to be the most capable and trustworthy of his workers, he never wrote about him in the ways he did about Steven. Steven rejected virtually all things that Johnson held to be important for a Black man, and he wrote about him with more emotion than anyone else who worked in his household. Johnson never avoided noting in his diary when he was unhappy with his workers' efforts on the various jobs he had them do, but his only complaints about Steven stemmed from Steven running away to drink. It seems likely that Steven was an alcoholic, and though this was not a condition recognized in the antebellum period, Johnson eventually was sympathetic but not forgiving, as he still sold the man. On the other hand, Steven might have simply taken advantage of Natchez's spaces to reject his enslaver's morality and model of Black manhood. Johnson's apprentices and other enslaved men who were closer in age to Steven might have admired his willingness to break the rules and defy their owner, and this respect motivated him to continue to rebel. It certainly is the case that Johnson's free Black apprentices challenged Johnson similarly during their time in his household and shop. In spite of their troubles, Johnson found himself impressed by Steven's intelligence and craftiness. In one case, Steven was arrested and charged with theft but was able to clear "his own self before the Jury in about a minute," which was no small feat in antebellum Mississippi, where all juries were made exclusively of white men and the law wholly against African Americans.[113] These men who resisted or rejected Johnson's ideas about how to be a man not only represented different masculinities, they forced Johnson to recognize them, though he only respected his own.

Conclusion

Representing Johnson as a class elitist or merely a receptacle of white men's racist values negates Johnson's roles within Natchez's free Black community. Johnson and the other free men of color of his generation learned trades and how to operate within a slave society as young men via their apprenticeships. Johnson was particularly concerned about transferring his lessons from James Miller and his life as a businessman to his apprentices and even the men he enslaved. His relationship with the boys and men in his shop was complicated. Even though he represented a successful example of achieving respectability within a slave society, the younger men in his shop had other ideas about masculinity, and asserting those differences frequently conflicted with Johnson. His reactions to these challenges sometimes demonstrate a similar mind-set that a white enslaver might have, imposing physical punishment for disobedience, but on other occasions, he reacted as a father might when a son made poor choices that could hurt his future. Johnson had developed a form of paternalism when dealing with his workers, extending kindness and sympathy sometimes and cruelty and disapproval in other cases. His concern with how his workers interacted with women counters the notion that he held himself separate from the free Black community. Johnson did not only train his apprentices to become barbers; he passed on how to live as free men of color in a slave society. Despite his frequent disappointments, most of his apprentices married free women of color and remained in the region, maintaining connections to the Johnson family even decades after the barber's death.

Interestingly, neither Johnson, his family, nor the free men of color who worked for him appear to have considered moving to the North. Certainly, they knew that such a move offered no escape from racism, but it presented a less restrictive environment in which Black men, especially those with a trade, could make a living without daily fears of enslavement. For Johnson, it is clear that he was too attached to slavery to consider the move, both in terms of the wealth it provided and the sense that owning enslaved men and women differentiated him from the enslaved in the minds of whites. Eliza Potter had a similar position to Johnson in Cincinnati, where she served as a hairdresser for privileged white women and, through her knowledge and skills, helped them to learn what it meant to be a "lady."[114] However, because of racial and gender conventions and the simple fact that she worked to earn a living, Potter was an outsider who could not be considered a lady. Johnson's shop also helped clients achieve the desired look, but unlike Potter, he could connect with his patrons through shared gender conventions, which required a more public display in the South than in the North and will be discussed in the next chapter.

CHAPTER TWO

Manly Competition

GAMBLING, HUNTING, FISHING, AND FIGHTING

JOHNSON UNDERSTOOD and taught his workers that maintaining respectability was critical, but it was not the only aspect of masculinity he
modeled to the men and boys in his household. Though his workdays were
full of dealings with whites in his shop, collecting debts, or buying and
selling items at markets and auctions, usually with an eye for profit later,
his free time was absorbed with various "manly pursuits" like gambling,
hunting, and fishing. These were not just casual amusements for Johnson.
They were opportunities to display manliness differently than he did in
his regular business ventures, as these events allowed for competition and
assertiveness. Barbering allowed him to achieve respectability and maintain his freedom, but it was also a job that required subservience to whites.
His participation in competitions with others permitted him to engage
with men differently than he had to at work. As one historian of American manhood has written, "There were hundreds of conduct-of-life books
aimed at young men praising self-controlled manhood[, and] . . . there were
very few authors writing that men should get drunk, should fight, should
gamble," yet these homosocial behaviors, along with hunting, fishing, and
sometimes dueling, were crucial ways in which American men, especially
southern men, asserted their manliness among one another.[1] These behaviors were bound to the cult of honor for southerners, which ultimately
amounted to a reputation based on status and public performance. Real
men accepted challenges to compete, and to turn down a contest might
result in the question and insult, "are you a man?" A loss in a competition
could hurt one's status, but a failure to accept the challenge marked one as
a coward or unmanly. These activities were not only the domain of white
men; Black men, too, engaged in these contests to assert manliness, elevate
status, make friends, and establish camaraderie.[2]

60

When Johnson went to the race track with his friends or shooting with his apprentices or men he enslaved, he wrote of these competitions and pursued them with the same vigor and importance that he assigned to his various business dealings. Like anyone who engages in these activities, Johnson wanted to win, but the competition was essential. Sometimes Johnson won competitions and earned sizable material awards. On other occasions, he lost substantial amounts of money or property, and though he wrote in much greater volume about his victories, he did not omit his losses and understood that taking a defeat with equanimity was just as important as not being overbearing with a win. Contests also allowed Johnson to bond with a broad group of men within Natchez, expanding his business and social circles. Free Black barbers needed to be engaged in pursuits that their white customers cared about, as being able to entertain them while in the shop was good for business. These behaviors also incorporated men like Johnson into the same pastimes as the town's most powerful men, leading to his acceptance in a community of men outside of the job and helping to distance him from the enslaved in the minds of white men.[3]

Johnson casually remarked in his diary that he was "always ready for anything" when it came to any competition, and it is clear that he was also willing to put money on his ability to win. Johnson wagered on his marksmanship, cards, horse races, toy-boat races, elections, and sometimes his ability to outrun or outjump others throughout his life. Besides fighting, these contests were the most public ways men could measure their skills and manliness against others. The idiom "may the best man win" was more than an expression for Johnson; he always looked to compete and rank his abilities against others. His competitors ranged from his apprentices and men he enslaved to some of the town's wealthiest white plantation owners and political figures. Given the amount of space his diary devotes to competitive activities, there is an impression that the diary itself was a testament to his manliness. Just as he enforced his example of respectability to the boys and men in his charge, he also stressed the importance of competition with others to establish masculinity.

Gambling vs. Gamblers: Social Distinctions in Wagering

Gambling was more than a recreational diversion for southern white men; it was also a way to display masculinity. Gambling allowed aggressively facing someone else without resorting to violence. Games of chance demonstrated that a man had faith in his abilities and skill, and, at least as importantly, that men did not fear losing money or property, even if the sums were considerable. Gambling offered this opportunity for men, but it did not do so irrespective of class or race; though men of different social standings might have played a game against one another, both participants and observers remained keenly aware of the social standings of players. In other words, the game was not a "closed world" since distinctions between players outside of the game remained important to the game, even if a player of lower status won. Still, choosing to enter into a game of chance with other men of different status did offer a public appearance, at least during the game, of a sense of equality, which no doubt appealed to men of lower social position.[4]

City "gaming" ordinances, like those against alcohol, were much more concerned with regulating the practice than ending it. Popular Under-the Hill games, like roulette, were outlawed, whereas horse racing and the betting that went along with it, fashionable among planters in the upper town, remained legal. In some cases, town magistrates resorted to trickery to catch those at the landing in gambling schemes. Christian Schultz, who visited Natchez in 1808, witnessed a boat hand arguing with another man over some "trifling dispute." The two decided to settle the issue by a coin flip, and though "the boatman lost his wager fairly . . . what was his surprise when he afterwards found himself arrested upon the information of this very villain and fined either twenty or thirty dollars for gambling."[5]

The gambling itself was not the problem; instead, who gambled and to what end troubled some Natchez officials. Local men, especially planters, had stakes in society, and though losing significant amounts of money might have been irresponsible, they also might be admired for the manly quality of taking the risk. Professional gamblers, however, were viewed as just as unmanly as those who were unwilling to play games of chance because they risked nothing but money and took nothing but profit from a winning game. One southerner explained to Harriet Martineau that a man "may game, but not keep a gaming house."[6] Planters might gamble as John Nevitt and forty of his friends did when they "sat up all night" playing "brag," but these men were the town's elite and did not have to worry about being fined or jailed.[7] However, town officials complained that vagrants and professional gamblers arrive in town "with every *fresh* of the Mississippi."[8]

Regardless of how much money planters won or lost, they remained bound to Natchez because of their societal positions and ability to earn livelihoods in acceptable ways, unlike professionals described as parasites.

Some complained that professionals sought to corrupt, took advantage of locals, and did so boldly and perhaps violently. A person known only as "Z" wrote to the *Mississippi Herald* that "one miscreant had the insolence to fix his table in the open . . . with a pair of loaded pistols to protect it—a fracas ensued between several of these vermin . . . to the great danger of the lives of several citizens."[9] William Hall, a traveler to the town, noted the eagerness of locals to join in with boatmen and professionals in these games. After entering the first open establishment he found in Under-the-Hill one morning, Hall found men and women, both Black and white, drinking, dancing, and gambling together despite the early hour. He noticed several men playing faro in a backroom, some betting "with silver coin, some with bank notes, and a few of the largest betters, with 'checks' or counters." Some of the men bet with "counters," demonstrating that they were either established gamblers or locals of well-known means. Hall noted that one of the men who bet with counters seemed indifferent to the amounts wagered as he won "several large bets in succession without lifting his money from the table. . . . The large amount now pending induced the banker to ask the bettor whether he 'went' the whole amount. 'Yes by——, I'll pile my paralee to the ceiling.'" Though Hall described this man as a "desperate gambler," in many ways he demonstrated the traits that the elite prized in gambling, even if professionals had taken advantage of him.[10]

Professional gamblers were repeatedly marked as the dregs of society looking for any opportunity to harm or cheat the unwary, and as a result, their stories became popular reading material. The exploits of gamblers in Natchez-Under-the-Hill became legendary throughout the United States and furthered rumors that gamblers operated outside society's rules. According to these stories, professional gamblers prowled the town looking for unsuspecting marks. William Hall related that he fell victim to one such scheme. While in a tavern, he noticed a man who appeared very drunk, offering to wager five hundred dollars on any bet he could take, regardless of the odds. He then took out a deck of cards and bet five hundred dollars that he could "name and turn any of the three cards, or he would bet the same amount no one else could do so." A "gentleman" approached Hall and asserted that the only charitable thing was to take the bet, beat the drunken man, and return the money when he sobered up. The gentleman said he would do this himself but left his "pocket book" at the hotel because he was afraid of being pickpocketed in Under-the-Hill. After putting up the money, Hall lost to the man who suddenly appeared sober, and the "gentleman" turned out to be his partner. While Hall sets this story up as a cautionary tale, it also seems he expected his readers to admire the gamblers secretly.[11]

James Green, who billed himself as a reformed gambler, offered another instance of how professionals took advantage of the unsuspecting in Under-the-Hill. Green explained the practice of "Spanish Burying," which was common among "the brotherhood" of gamblers in Natchez. Green described this custom as "one of those plays, or exercises, which the gamblers use partly to make their victims afraid to give them further trouble, and partly to gratify their own cruel and hellish passions." It usually involved ten to twenty men approaching an unsuspecting victim and proposing a simple game with a wager of alcohol that the ringleader promised to buy. After the victim agreed to the seemingly risk-free match, they performed a confusing ceremony in which participants "saluted the dead man," who happened to be the largest and strongest of the crew, lying flat on the ground. When the victim approached the "dead man," he was seized and then hit by the rest of the band with their "handkerchiefs, which have been tied full of knots on purpose, and twisted so as to be almost as hard as cow-skins." After the beating, the victim learned that he had won the bet, but he needed to become a group member to collect, requiring additional beatings. Green explained to his readers:

> Such is the thirst of gamblers for unnatural excitement, that when tired of cards, they often seek it in such brutal sports as this. In order to kill time, they are ready to sacrifice the last vestige of principle, or of human feeling in their hearts. And when their interest is concerned in the result, as is usually the case, it gives their fiend-like sport a double relish. The reader may like to know to what class of gamblers this applies. I have known those who are upheld as respectable sportsmen, or gentlemanly faro dealers, to engage in such brutalizing scenes; and I warn every inexperienced youth to beware how he comes within the circle of their influence.[12]

Green warned his readers that professionals might appear "respectable" and "gentlemanly" but only wanted to swindle and harm the unsuspecting.

Labeling professional gamblers as outsiders and devoid of humanity made it far easier for people in Natchez to distance themselves from their vices. Though the legislature outlawed gambling in taverns, inns, other "public houses," and streets, these laws were never consistently enforced. This lack of prosecution resulted from planters' desire to use Under-the-Hill as a public venue to display manliness and the riverfront's crucial economic function. Though Under-the-Hill was the center of vice, it was also the town's immediate access to trade. The entertainment and lodging offered at the landing ensured that boatmen stopped. These men acquired bad reputations for their rowdy behavior in Natchez, but they also brought manufactured goods from the North and took locally grown cotton to New Orleans for sale in England.[13]

Ordinances against gambling did little to curb the gambling habits of Natchezians, nor did they change the tendency to view professional gamblers as a specific group. The first gambler caught breaking the law in 1806 promptly escaped the jailhouse and took his gaming table with him. Authorities believed that he was bound for New Orleans, where he could continue to ply his trade and was described as having "a downcast, uninviting look." When several of the town's most respected citizens gathered at Steele's Spring in Under-the-Hill to celebrate the Fourth of July with dinner and toasts, a collection of "gamblers" crashed the party, allegedly because they had not been invited to the festivities. These uninvited guests "armed with clubs and poniards . . . assailed the company with threats and insulting language" and were repulsed only after "attempting to assassinate several gentlemen." Most of these party-crashers wound up in jail, but it is likely that many among the revelers also styled themselves as capable, if amateur, gamblers.[14]

Responses against professional gamblers only occurred when conditions suggested that they were attempting to subvert the racial order. The first genuine attempt to remove professionals from Mississippi occurred in Vicksburg in 1835, when an Independence Day fight led locals to believe that gamblers might be involved in a rumored slave revolt. Allegedly, the uprising was organized by white "steam doctors," whose strange remedies and close relationship with enslaved people made them suspicious to local slaveholders. Professional gamblers had similar relationships with Blacks. When one of these professionals started a fight in a July Fourth barbeque, citizens at Vicksburg became convinced professionals might incite a slave revolt. Authorities ordered professional gamblers to leave the town of Vicksburg by July 6 or face serious consequences. Though most did go, six professionals remained barricaded in a house. A shoot-out occurred when a mob attempted to remove them forcibly, resulting in two deaths and five gamblers' public execution.[15] In defense of the extralegal punishment, the Committee of Safety declared, "We are proud of the public spirit and indignation against offenders displayed by the citizens, and congratulate them on having at length banished a class of individuals, whose shameless vices and daring outrages long poisoned the springs of morality, and interrupted the relations of society." These professionals, outsiders without family or property in the area, were described as "destitute of all sense of moral obligation—unconnected with society by any of its ordinary ties, and intent only on the gratification of their avarice."[16] While the alleged slave insurrection plot in nearby Livingston did not directly involve the professional gamblers executed at Vicksburg, one local man, Thomas Shackelford, made a connection between the two events, suggesting they were related in the sense of "the state of high excitement that pervaded the whole southern country at that time, which had led the citizens to deal more rigorously with all offenders; and more especially with those of an abandoned and dissolute character as all professional gamblers are."[17]

If Natchezians, in general, had a problem with professional gamblers, they certainly did not have a problem with those who gambled on horse racing. The Pharsalia Course, located just outside the town at St. Catherine's Creek, became the elite's primary nonfarming focus from the territorial period through the Civil War. The Mississippi Jockey Club owned and operated the track and its members included some of Natchez's wealthiest families, including the Bingamans, Minors, Duncans, and Surgets. The latter two may have been the most prominent slaveholding families in the United States. David Burney, one of the founding members of the Jockey Club, was "the first breeder of fast horses and gamecocks in the Territory and a great patron of the turf." Those who had the means did not purchase their horses locally; instead, they looked abroad for the world's finest horses. For some planters, like William Minor, horse racing seems to have been at least as important as maintaining his plantation. Some planters maintained private racetracks on their plantations. One visitor to the town testified, "The horsemen appeared to me more skillful than those at New Orleans and in [other] parts of America I have seen."[18]

The main competitors in Lower Mississippi Valley horse racing between the 1820s and the 1850s were two planters in Natchez: William Minor and Adam Bingaman. These men were horse breeders and major sponsors of races from Natchez to New Orleans. Bets made on racing dwarfed those made on card games, either in Under-the-Hill or in private contests. The Minors and Bingamans bet up to ten thousand dollars on races. However, by the 1850s, both families had become disenchanted with horse racing in Natchez. Bingaman left the town for New Orleans, as the track at Metairie had become more popular and commanded higher prize money. William Minor's problem stemmed from a different source: "I consider that the 'Pharsalia Course' has been desecrated by this mule race. If the Club . . . [survives] it is immortal." The reference is to the track's practice in the 1840s of allowing less well-to-do whites and free Blacks to race horses and mules. Though these groups had been allowed to place bets at Pharsalia and the quarter track in Under-the-Hill, this more prestigious track had previously catered to the wealthiest owners. Minor chose to relocate his horses and interests to Louisiana, where only Thoroughbreds could compete and only whites could take part.[19]

Planters' interest in gambling explains the differences between those who gambled and professional gamblers. Planters who bet thousands of dollars received admiration instead of condemnation that they were "desperate" or morally bereft. The differences had to do with the unspoken code separating professionals from amateurs. Professionals were labeled as transient, suspicious characters who cared only about profiting from the unsuspecting and causing disorder. For amateurs, particularly those of high status, gambling displayed masculinity to cultivate a reputation. These views of professional gamblers are similar to how enslavers described slave traders. Southerners did not vilify slave traders because they treated enslaved people with physical cruelty and split families at will but instead denounced them because of "the dishonesty and the avarice with which he [the slave trader] threatened to poison social relations among white people." Slave traders' goal, according to most southern planters, was to unload enslaved people who had been sold because they had committed crimes or were "diseased" to unsuspecting buyers.[20] Like slave traders who allowed enslavers to expand their fortunes, professional gamblers enabled the elite to compete in games of chance but took their profits to their next stop when the games ended and could leave ruin in their wake. Planters used Under-the-Hill to display masculinity, and without the taverns and brothels, the boatmen who operated trade on the Mississippi were less inclined to stop at Natchez. By imposing a difference between professional gamblers and those who gambled, elite white men in Natchez separated themselves from vices. They blamed their problems on the "frontier" nature of these professionals who traveled the Mississippi River.

Competition and Black Masculinity

The mix of urban and rural spaces in and around Natchez and an active community of avid but not professional gamblers allowed Black men ample opportunities to use these contests to assert their manliness publicly. William Johnson seemingly never missed a chance to find some action to bet on, and he was willing to place or take bets with anyone: other free men of color, white men, his apprentices, even enslaved men. Johnson was especially interested in horse racing, which became a growing form of entertainment in Natchez just as the barber had begun establishing himself as a businessman. Adam Bingaman was the first of the town's wealthy white planters to become deeply involved in horse racing, breeding and racing horses, and operating the town's racetrack with one of his family members. Johnson probably began his relationship with Bingaman through his barbershop, but he frequently attended and bet on races at the Pharsalia Course. Johnson bet with Samuel Gossin, Bingaman's farm manager, at these races. Gossin might have served as a go-between for Johnson and Bingaman, maybe because Bingaman did not think he should publicly trade bets with a man of color. Still, given that he later married a free woman of color and frequently wrote to the Johnson family after the barber's death, that might be unlikely. Moreover, despite criticism from his rivals, Bingaman allowed nonelites, including Black men, to attend and bet on the races.[21]

On a typical day at the racetrack, Johnson went out with Robert McCary, perhaps with James Miller if he was in town, or sometimes with some of his free apprentices, especially Bill Nix and William Winston, both of whom picked up an interest in the sport and betting from Johnson. In some weeks, mostly when he was a younger man, Johnson recorded multiple days in a row of attending and betting on races. Johnson bet indiscriminately with men in the crowd. On one good day at the track, he recalled: "I came off winr to day $13 I won $5 worth of gold from Mr McFadgin & I won $5 in cash from old Mc [McCary] & I won $2 from Mardice & I won $2 from St. Clair $5 from St. Claire on another race and I lost &6 with H Cobler." He and McCary went to the track the next day with mixed results. They placed bets for a more significant race that was coming up between one of Bingaman's horses and one of William Minor's. Johnson did not fare well in this one, losing two pairs of boots that he valued at fourteen dollars, another seven dollars that settled a shaving bill or paid for a shaving bill later with a Mr. Wiswall, and another twenty-six dollars for his part of a larger bet he had placed with a partner.[22]

Johnson also raced his horses. In December 1835, Johnson mentioned taking two of his horses out for a race, presumably at Under-the-Hill's quarter track. He noted: "John rode the sorrel Horse and Bill Nix wrode [*sic*] the Bay horse, Paginini—They won two heats a piece."[23] A few months later, he wrote: "My Horse Rob Roy Ran a Quarter agains St. Clairs grey Horse. Rob Roy won the Race very easy—it was for $20 only." This second race seems to have been at the Pharsalia Course, as it allowed public participation between the elite races. The purse for these lower-stake races remained below fifty dollars.[24] Johnson used his free apprentices as jockeys in these races, but it is unclear if he rewarded them when they won. Johnson certainly enjoyed racing his horses on the same track as the elite did, though the stakes for the big races could reach several thousand dollars, and the side bets were occasionally five thousand dollars or higher.[25]

Though Johnson punished his apprentices when they violated his ideas about respectability, he often rewarded good behavior by bringing them along to the racetrack, which no doubt helped them understand how gambling between men functioned. Johnson lost more often than he won at most of his trips to the track but paid his debts and never seemed to lose more than he could cover, though he did make one reference to doing that in 1836: "I Borrowed from Ann to Day $10 which I lost on the Races." Over four days in November 1847, Johnson recorded losing every day, with his losses totaling $105. Notably, he lost to William Winston several times over those days and paid his apprentice thirty-eight dollars. On the last of these trips, he recalled, "I was out at the race track, Betting away money Like it was nothing . . . and I Lost Every Bet that I made.[26] Johnson did not treat the loss to Winston any differently than his other losses on those days to various others at the track. Even if he did not generally treat "money like it was nothing," his willingness to risk money and lose offered an important lesson to his young apprentice: making bets and losing money was a viable way of asserting manliness. As Johnson knew from both his moneylending business and his experiences with gambling, paying off debts was also critical in the Slave South, but gambling debts were different from borrowing money. Delay or failure to repay a loan was not uncommon in this economy based on the cotton season, which left even the wealthy cash-poor for periods of the year. In failing to repay loans, men might draw on their reputations or relationships to put off the obligation, but a gambling debt was more immediate and could hurt the status of the defaulter by signaling a refusal to acknowledge the loss. Debts could lead to dependency upon others, eroding a claim of manly independence for whites and threatening Black men's freedom.[27]

Cockfighting was another "sport" that drew the attention and money of men in and around Natchez. Like horse racing, owners took pride in these animals' characteristics in the same way they did their own. If the horses or roosters were fast or exceptionally skilled fighters, their owners treated them as extensions of themselves, but of course, if they were not especially good at these contests, owners discarded them. On a trip to buy supplies in 1837, Johnson spent five dollars on a "game Cock" but afterward was disappointed when he "put him down in the yard and the Frizeling chicken whipped him So I find he is not much." Apparently, after this experiment, he determined not to use the bird in an actual match because not only would it be killed, but its performance would damage his image in the minds of those present. He does mention attending a cockfight in 1849, but wrote: "I wrode [sic] out this Evening To the Tract to See a fight of Chickens and I saw 3 fights and Lost 2.50 and it is a Sport that is to me Disgusting in the Exstream [sic], I shall not go to See any more I Promise."[28] There is no evidence that Johnson ever attended another. Still, it is telling that despite how disgusting he found the practice, he was willing to take part, both through betting and the attempt to raise a bird for fighting, because this was a pursuit that other men engaged in and, as such, another way for Johnson to compete against them.

Even though Johnson was an avid follower of horse racing, his favorite form of competition involved shooting contests, hunting, and fishing. Some of these contests included wagers of money, cigars, liquor, or other items of value, but in others, they simply involved testing his skills against others for bragging rights. Nicholas Proctor has argued that hunting allowed men "to create a varied but coherent image of the hunter as a masculine ideal" by enabling a hunter to exhibit traits like "prowess, self-control, and mastery." Mastery, he identified, as a trait distinct among southern hunters "representing control over other people, animals, nature, and even death," and by displaying this while hunting, others who witnessed this kind of mastery attributed the same traits to these individuals in the world beyond the hunt. Most significantly, hunting, and maybe to a lesser degree, fishing, gave men the chance to compete and rank each other's skills in competition.[29]

Johnson's excursions usually involved his friend Robert McCary, whom he often referred to as "Mc" or "Old Mc," and his workers, but often some of his white friends, white employees on his farm, and, when they were old enough, his sons. Usually, he recorded the numbers of animals killed and fish caught on hunting and fishing outings, indicating that Johnson kept score even when no wager was involved. Unlike in his gambling ventures, Johnson intended to display dominance over his companions. On one hunting trip in 1836, he and McCary went out with Mr. Reid and encountered Mr. Barland, who was already out in the woods and joined them. Reid was probably a white man, and John Barland was a free man of color, one of twelve mixed-race children released from slavery by their father, William Barland. Johnson noted that "Old Mc killed one Duck and one squirrel Mr Reid did not kill anything that he got, he said that he killed two Ducks, but did not get them. . . . Mr Barland killed three squirrels." Johnson, on the other hand, recorded his tally as, "I killed 7 Large snipe and five Small Ones, two Large Squirrels, One Duck, two Loons, one yellow Hammer and One very large alligator," and he noted, "I Beet the Crowd by a Large Deal."[30] Maybe the others had a foul day shooting, or perhaps they did not understand that this was a competition, but it was for Johnson, who made sure to note his superiority.

Johnson took his apprentices on some hunts to compete with them and use their labor. In September 1836, Johnson and McCary went out to hunt with Bill Nix. He beat McCary soundly but did not record letting Nix hunt; instead, it seems he brought the younger man with them to collect the animals they shot. When they got back to town, Johnson noticed, "the Little Rascally Bill Lost all my Birds . . . and the way I whipped him was the Right way." What Johnson meant by "the Right way" is not entirely clear, but it was a phrase he used throughout his diary. It probably meant that he did this to correct behavior and impart a lesson rather than doing it out of anger, though he was also irritated. Despite his annoyance, Johnson took Bill Nix, Charles, and another worker named Simpson out shooting shortly afterward and had the boys engage in a horse race. Later, he took Bill Winston out with James Miller and McCary to hunt with him. Winston and the others performed well, but Johnson determined that he "was the Captain On the Hunt."[31] Johnson took these young men on trips for companionship and likely viewed the trips as a reward for their work. Of course, it is doubtful that the apprentices could turn down these invitations, but Johnson does not record any resistance from the boys, and it seems to be the case that they generally enjoyed these outings.

Johnson's diary indicates that he favored William Winston above most other workers in his household, partly because the younger man mimicked Johnson's sense of respectability and shared interests. Still, Johnson was angered when Winston acquired a gun of his own. At one point, Winston purchased a stolen firearm. Johnson discovered that Winston and John, another apprentice, left town without permission to go hunting. Johnson wrote: "I took my Horse in the afternoon and wrode up there and Caught Both of them and gave them Both a Floging and took away their guns—I threw away Winstons as far as I could in the Mississippi." Even though he was angry at him, Johnson still took Winston out for hunts, maybe because Winston enjoyed this more than his other workers.[32] Johnson's penchant for guns and hunting had rubbed off on his workers, but he could not abide them shunning work, being away without permission, or possessing firearms. Once again, the workers found ways to assert their masculinity, and though Johnson also enjoyed guns, he did not appreciate that distinction and instead punished the disobedience.

One of Johnson's frequent shooting, gambling, and fishing companions was John Jacquemine, sometimes referred to as "John the Greek," a white man born in Greece who moved to Natchez in the 1830s. In one contest, he challenged Jacquemine "to shoot 25 yards with a Riffle [sic], 3 best in five for One Qtr. Box of Segars and I lost the Cegars—I shot afterward with him and Mc and Beat them both—they both shot with my Riffle." Johnson lost the first bet but seemed to insist that they shoot again, if not to get the wager back, at least to prove that he was the better shot and maybe his rifle's quality. In another instance, when he, McCary, and Jacquemine went to shoot again, he referenced beating the white man, "Oh I beat him Bad—Shure—Shore—Shuree." It is possible he was excited to have defeated Jacquemine because of the racial difference, but since he never mentions that, it appeared that Johnson viewed him as one of the worthier opponents that he routinely faced. Jacquemine shared Johnson's interest in competition and operated an amusement center outside of Natchez, making him more of a professional than the other men with whom Johnson usually competed. On another hunt with Jacquemine and McCary, Johnson noted in his diary, "I always Beat the crowd that I go with and no mistake." The level of competitiveness between the two men is probably best illustrated by an entry Johnson made in his diary in 1844: "I made a Bet with Jaqumine to day or proposed a Bet and we bet another bet which was 1.50 that he would back Out. That taken, he did back Out and refused to pay the 1.50. He must pay it or I Shall think hard of Him, and will get Even with him when it may be Convenient &c."[33]

Johnson and McCary often associated with Winslow Winn, often referred to as "Young Winn" or "Little Winn." Winn was the son of a free man of color named George Winn, who, upon his death in 1831, left Winslow and his two sisters a cotton plantation of almost 1,200 acres and twenty-two enslaved people. Though Johnson has garnered more attention, this inheritance made Winn the largest free Black enslaver and likely the wealthiest free man of color in Mississippi. The three men often fished and hunted together, but the older men did not view Winn as their peer. Age played a role, but Winn's taste for alcohol did as well. In one instance, Winn stayed at the Johnson family's residence for several days to get over an "illness," but the diarist also wrote, "Poor creature, I Pitty him very much indeed—I am Sorry that he drink So much."[34] Johnson and McCary both drank and sometimes even gambled for liquor, but they distinguished the way they drank from the alcohol problems many of their contemporaries shared.

Johnson was much more willing to bring his workers to fish than to hunt, perhaps because he was uncomfortable with his apprentices having firearms. As with hunting or horse racing, fishing was a competitive venture for him, and even if others were not keeping track of how many fish they caught, Johnson was always paying attention. On one outing in 1837, Johnson wrote: "There were a number of us went Out to St. Catherine to fish Mc Caught 8 Small fish, Sterns One and I Caught One None of the Boys caught a single One and there were 7 of them in number I made them Run Races for meat and Bread I had good many Races out of them."[35] On this trip, Johnson and McCary seem to have taken all the boys and young men who worked in their shops out to fish, but as Johnson noted, only Washington Sterns caught one. Sterns worked in McCary's and Johnson's shops in the 1830s and 1840s. Like most of the other free men and boys of color on this trip, Sterns's white father freed him and left him property, but unlike the others, he was closer in age to Johnson and McCary and had known Johnson before he had opened the shop. In a letter he wrote in 1829, Sterns asked, "Old Jim wrote to you the other day did he not what does he say about letting you have the shop now?" Based on the letter, the two seemed to regard one another as peers in 1829, but their fortunes increasingly diverged as Johnson eventually took over James Miller's shop, and Sterns later worked for him.[36] Like many of the men whom Johnson knew, Sterns seems to have had a drinking problem, which might have been why he was not as successful as his two contemporaries. McCary told Johnson of one instance in which "Sterns got Drunk and went out into the yard to Sleep and he fell off of the chair that he was setting On. Made water in his pantaloons."[37] Johnson did not include Sterns as one of the boys here; the men had caught fish, whereas the boys had not. The races that he had them run probably did not serve as punishment but rather as a way to mock the boys for their poor performance and to continue the competition between them for his amusement.

Like other events, Johnson used fishing to assert his dominance in a competitive activity. In August 1840, Johnson took Wellington West, a free man of color who occasionally worked for him but most often worked for his brother-in-law in New Orleans, fishing "at the Concordia Lake" across the Mississippi River in Louisiana. He reported: "I Caught I think about thirty and Wellington about 25. I Know of no man that has Ever Fished over [there] that Ever Came Home with more Fish than I for the same length of time—I Fished for about 24 hours and no Longer."[38] If he recorded this sentiment in his diary, he probably let everyone else he came into contact with know about his assumed record for the most fish caught at the lake. Of course, it is hard to imagine that a man as busy as Johnson had committed twenty-four hours to fishing. He did not do this over several days, only one, which implies that he fished all night, maybe with the point of catching more fish than anyone else, especially West. In other instances, when he did not catch the most fish, he could find excuses: "I went down in the Swamp to fish and I caught three Doz and 11 fish. Mr. Walker, the Tinner, Caught Eighteen. Wins[ton] Caught Five [doz] and 5 I was Hunting part of the time or I would have Caught more." Most fishermen probably would be satisfied catching forty-seven fish in one outing, but Johnson thought it necessary to explain how one of his workers surpassed him. Johnson recorded catching ninety-four fish on another excursion, the most out of the large group of men with him. Johnson claimed to have caught 231 fish on yet another trip and remarked, "I as usual Caught more than any other person in the company."[39] Certainly, fishermen tend to exaggerate the sizes and numbers of fish, but if Johnson's numbers are correct, the Natchez area seems to have been one of the best places for fishing imaginable.

Johnson's competitive nature went well beyond horse racing, hunting, and fishing; he took virtually any opportunity to place a bet, take a bet, or engage in some game of chance. For example, one evening, Johnson and McCary shot marbles, and he recalled, "Mc and myself played Sixteen Games at Marbles this Evening and He won ten Out of 16 and I have not been so tyred from some time as I am now from playing those Marbles.[40] It is hard to imagine a man who crammed as much activity as possible into every day could find himself so exhausted from playing marbles, but it might have been his inability to win that made him this tired. After complaining about a terrible day of business at this shop because of the economic downturn resulting from the Panic of 1837, which continued into the 1840s for Natchez, Johnson took a break to pitch quoits with John Meshio, a white man who rented shop space from him. However, he was disappointed that "he Beat me Easy. I lost 5 15cts worth Cigars at the Game."[41] He did not say how long it took him to lose that many cigars, but he felt compelled to keep playing despite being bad at the game. One night in March 1845, he wrote, "I was up very early this morning, for the Simple Reason that I did not go to bed Last night at all," because he and Mc had stayed up gambling all night with two other men.[42] He and McCary competed over racing toy boats, noting: "I sailed Boats this Evening with Mc and the Boys and Mc Boat Beat the old Shark at Last. It was a new one that he built." Johnson challenged his nephew to shoot his hat, not while on his head, "from 10 paces" and then "from 5 paces," but he missed the hat, so Johnson won.[43] He entered raffles and contests to win watches but almost always lost.[44] He bet his white farmworkers on corn-shucking and how many cords of wood they had.[45] Even when he bought a sofa and felt that the seller cheated him, he vowed, "Very well, I must get Even with him if I can."[46]

Johnson had all the marks of a compulsive gambler, but these contests were opportunities to assert his boldness, competitiveness, and masculinity to his opponents and other onlookers. Gambling and competing in these ways were safe ways for a man of color to demonstrate these traits in ways that did not challenge the Old South's racial order. These competitions never leveled the significant legal restrictions he had because of his race compared to his white opponents, but Johnson never records any white men's attempt to challenge his victories based on racial distinctions, nor did he ever blame any loss he had on his status. Beyond the social aspect of these contests, Johnson seemed to take deep personal satisfaction from performing better than others no matter the standing of his opponents. Given the amount of space he devoted in his diary to these contests, it is clear that being the best at shooting, hunting, fishing, or whatever other game he could imagine informed how he thought about himself and how he ranked himself against others.

Fights, Duels, and Other Violence

By any measure, Natchez was a violent town in the antebellum period, but Johnson's diary makes it hard to imagine that anyone could have survived it. His barbershop was situated in a prime location for business and witnessing what happened in the streets. The shop was an almost exclusively masculine space where men traded stories and shared gossip about their neighbors. Johnson's favorite stories were about physical confrontations, either those he witnessed or those related to him by his white customers. He judged the manliness of the men based on how they performed in these fights and how they behaved before and afterward. He noted that some of these men fought well or at least fought bravely, whereas others ran away or fought in dirty or unfair ways. In one such instance, Johnson described a fight in the courthouse between "Mr. McClure and Col. Sanders." After leaving the courtroom, McClure attacked Sanders "and was gouging Him in an instant," and though his actions led to a fine and four days in jail, Johnson remarked, "Good many Persons was Surprised to find McClure So much a Man."[47] Notwithstanding the nature of the fight or the punishment received, Johnson and others celebrated McClure for his manliness.

These fights, which often led to severe injuries and death, were considered part of "men's nature" by large swaths of the American public in the nineteenth century, especially among southern men. Some newspapers in the Old Southwest contended that increased fighting, gambling, and drinking resulted from a shift in parenting techniques compared to those practiced along the Eastern Seaboard. One writer in *DeBow's Review* argued: "In some countries, as long as the parent lived, the child was not free from his control," but "in our country, partly probably from carrying to excess our notions of liberty and restraint, partly from the newness of the country . . . and partly from the facility with which any person can support himself and thus become independent of others—we have gone to the other extreme. The child, at an early age, throws off all control."[48] Joan Cashin noted a gender difference between how parents viewed rebellious sons: mothers worried their sons' rambunctious behavior might signal a lack of character, whereas husbands often celebrated when their sons aggressively misbehaved as an early sign of "manly independence." One Mississippian took pleasure in his son's outbursts, and despite his son's damaging property and potentially himself, the father determined that his son was "a great boy." Another resident of the region wrote to his brother, imploring him to move west because "you can live like a fighting cock with us." The implication was that moving to the Old Southwest offered a better chance of exhibiting the unrestrained masculinity stifled in the Southeast.[49]

Beyond just an acceptance that men fought, though, these contests functioned as entertainment for onlookers who judged the manliness of the participants among one another as a part of local gossip. Regardless of how savage a fight could be, participants and even spectators understood there were basic rules. Only elite men engaged in dueling and only with someone they viewed as an equal, but regardless of social class, accepting a challenge to a fight or a duel was especially important in a society that made it clear that manliness was a public performance. Slavery made social distinctions even more crucial in the South than in other areas of the country that were also violent. Refusing a challenge could identify one as unmanly and relegate his status to that of a woman, a child, or a slave. Though white men did not view Black men as possessing manliness in the same ways they did, Black men viewed these confrontations as opportunities to rank masculinity.[50]

Johnson never recorded any violent confrontation between himself and someone he considered an equal; he only mentioned dealing violently with his apprentices or with the men and women he enslaved. Once he purchased land and began farming, he received several threats from men who had no interest in his reputation within Natchez, including from the man who eventually murdered him. Still, when he heard of these threats, he expressed confidence that he could defend himself with no problem or that they were not serious. Those challenges are the subject of a later chapter, but from the violence around him, Johnson made it clear that he viewed these confrontations as another form of competition between men. Like gambling or other competitions, Johnson believed that the willingness to participate in the contest was the most critical measure of manliness.

One fight in November 1836 offers an interesting example of the physical confrontations Johnson regularly encountered in Natchez. Johnson wrote: "[L]ast night . . . several gentlemen were in a conversation about a duel that was fought in South Carolina. When Mr. Charles Stewart stated that those gentlemen who fought actually fought with bullets, Mr. Dahlgreen said that they must [have] fought with paper bullets." Stewart became enraged at the contention that the two duelists were not committed to maiming or killing one another and exclaimed, "if any man would say they fought with paper Bullits that he is a Damed Lyar and a Dd Scoundrel & a Dd Coward." Dalhgreen responded to the insult by jumping up from the table and "Slaped Mr C. Stewarts Check one very hard slapp," at which point bystanders separated the two men. Stewart vowed they would settle it the following day. The fight the subsequent day began with sticks and umbrellas, then knives, and finally pistols as the two men exchanged shots resulting in Dalhgreen taking a bullet in the side, and eventually Stewart being shot in the face (after Dalhgreen missed with his first shot) and killed. Afterward, several other men joined in and left Dalhgreen seriously wounded. One of Natchez's newspapers reported the event and lamented that "such a disaster would never have occurred but for the abominable practice of carrying arms" but also tried to deflect the bad publicity of the event by pointing out that these men were not natives of the city but "strangers" and that "these street fights always occur between men recently from the north." The article, however, expressed that they "should have let the event pass in silence" rather than report it and damage the character of the city, but the author felt the need to speak out against carrying guns. The following week's edition featured a call for a public meeting held in Natchez committed to "destroying the false notions of honor, the pretexts of self defense, or the indulgence of violent passions, which has hitherto introduced the practice of carrying dirks, pistols, or bowie knives, of engaging in duels, of endangering the lives of peaceable citizens by street fights and of taking the execution of the laws by mobs into their own hands." Johnson, though, simply commented, "It was one of the gamest fights we have Ever had in Our City before."[51]

Though the newspaper might have wanted to push a more genteel image of Natchez, men in town like Johnson found the fight entertaining, and this was not even the only fight that day. Johnson wrote: "Mr R. Bledsoe and Mr Hewit has a small fist fight. After a Blow or two past, Mr Bledsoe went and got his Pistols. I am told as Soon as Mr Hewit saw the pistols he Said whoorer and ran Down the street and got in a Store and Mr Bledsoe made him retract what he Said in writing before he would Let him go—this he did from fear."[52] What made the first one of the "gamest" for Johnson was not just that it was more gruesome and deadlier but also that it was one in which both men fought with equal vigor. Even though Stewart died in the fight, he fought bravely and was willing to risk his life over the insult, which Johnson admired. On the other hand, Hewitt ran when faced with Bledsoe's pistols and backed down from the insult he had given out of fear of losing his life. Of course, both fights stemmed from minor disagreements that did not require anyone to die as punishment, but in terms of how men viewed masculinity in the antebellum South, Stewart and Dalhgreen were manlier than Hewitt. For Johnson and other men of the era, the notion was that if Hewitt was willing to make the insult, he should have been willing to die rather than retract it. Historians have offered many reasons why the South was more violent, ranging from the persistence of frontier conditions and a lack of official law enforcement to conformity to a code of honor to the institution of slavery.[53] In all of these situations, though, the importance of a public assertion of masculinity is present—to back down from a fight, retract an insult, or apologize for an offense hurt one's reputation of manliness. Johnson's note that Hewitt took back his words in writing out of fear was an insult to Hewitt and an example of something that a man should not do, whereas Stewart's murder and the maiming of Dalhgreen was the correct way for a man to behave.

Two discussions of the visit of a traveling theater company to Natchez in 1835 demonstrate the distinction between how the press and townspeople viewed violence. The *Mississippi Free Trader* reported: "Mr. Parsons has again returned among us with an excellent stock company. . . . We learn arrangements have been made for a succession of STARS heretofore unequalled on the Natchez boards." The actors put on several plays, including *Romeo and*

Juliet and *The Irish Tutor*.[54] Johnson noted the company's arrival and attended some of the plays, but instead of describing the event, he discussed a fight between Parsons and an actor: "Parson and one of his actors by the name of Chipp has a fight. Parson takes him by the hair of his head and throws him Down and Choakes him." After referencing a few more shows at the theater, Johnson described another fight: "Two Irishmen commenced boxing in fun and then they began to fight. The one kicked the other in such a seviere manner that he broke his gaul [jaw?]. His head was bruised also—He Died in 8 or ten hours after the fight His name was Russell he was killed by [blank]."[55] Indeed the people of Natchez, including Johnson, were excited about the theater company's performances, but Johnson appeared more interested in the fights that took place simultaneously.

Duels were of particular interest to Johnson and the general public of Natchez. Of course, dueling was exclusively for the upper class, but the practice served the same purpose as fights did for those who could not claim the status that allowed for the trappings of honor—they were public displays of masculinity. Seargent S. Prentiss, a member of the US Congress for Mississippi and attorney, expressed a standard view of dueling for men in his era in his memoir: "I am no advocate of dueling, and always shall from principle avoid such a thing, as much as possible; but when a man is placed in a situation where if he does not fight, life will be rendered valueless to him, both in his own eyes and those of the community, and existence will become a burden to him; then I say he will fight, and by so doing, will select the least of two evils."[56] Still, Prentiss wound up in two duels with Henry S. Foote, a US senator and governor of Mississippi, who also held "disapproval of the practice of settling individual disputes upon the field of honor" but fought several duels himself. These two leading men disparaged dueling in their memoirs but had found it necessary to answer insults with potentially deadly violence at multiple points in their earlier lives. At one point, Foote advised Alexander McNutt, another governor of Mississippi, to duel a man who had slapped him in public, as his only other option was to "attack him on the street-side with weapons." The duel, he suggested, would be safer for bystanders.[57]

Unlike spontaneous fights, men scheduled duels, giving spectators a chance to watch them. In April 1838, Johnson recorded: "To day was spent in Talk about the Duell that was to have Taken place this Evening between Col. Nikolds and Dr Booye They were to have fought between 4 and 5

Oclock this Evening—There was a Greate many Person assembled to see the Expected fight." The duel between Nichols and Bowie was to have taken place on the Louisiana side of the Mississippi River, and Johnson and many others crossed the river to watch while several others remained on the Natchez side, trying to see as well. Once across, several prominent men spoke out against dueling and had "resolved to follow those Gentleman and prevent there fighting on any part of the Ground—Well the time had passed when they were to have fought and still there was no preparations made that I could see for the fight."[58] A sheriff from Louisiana showed up shortly afterward to keep the peace, and the two would-be combatants never faced off. Johnson expressed disappointment and noted the next day: "The Large Town Meeting that was to have Taken place to day on the Subject of Dueling appears to have been Neglected by the partees as there was no meeting at all. No person to Open the meeting. Tis well enough."[59] In other words, after the planned duel, the men who prevented it from taking place had called for a meeting, probably to denounce the practice of dueling, but no one showed up for it, not even those who called for the meeting. To Johnson, the lack of attendance presented the public's view that dueling was not a problem and should be allowed.

Despite newspaper articles reviling violence, they still allowed men like Bowie to use the paper to call out other men's behaviors they thought had wronged them and issue challenges to duels. In this instance, Johnson found Bowie's frustrations significant enough to transcribe his entire article into his diary. Bowie wrote: "After the outrage that was offered to my person, I demanded of Col. Nichols that satisfaction to which I was entitled. In reply to my note he objected to the language in which it was couched, but professed his willingness to respond to the call when made in a proper form." After some back-and-forth involving other parties, Bowie explained that he "considered the challenge still in force" even though Nichols apparently "considered the affair at an end." Bowie, remaining incensed, told the newspaper's audience: "It is certainly difficult to understand how a response to a call which resulted in an ineffectual meeting is a satisfaction to an injury. Yet by this subterfuge, which in effect amounts to a refusal to accept my call, I am left as I originally stood after the insult offered. And it is impossible to elevate this man to the dignity of a gentleman. I shall leave him in the situation in which by his own conduct he has placed himself."[60] In copying the article in his diary, Johnson seemed to endorse Bowie's position that Nichols had evaded the challenge through others' work. Moreover, Johnson and the others who had attended the proposed duel were probably unhappy that they could not witness the event. While southern ideas about honor might not have required anyone to be shot or die in a duel, they needed an agreed-upon resolution. In airing his grievances in the newspaper, Bowie had declared that Nichols was not a man, and Johnson appears to have agreed.

In Natchez, just as elsewhere across the South, the public's desire to see or participate in violence led to vigilante activity. In 1838, Johnson observed: "The Irish Turned Out pretty strong to Day, or this Evening, after a Fellow by the name of McCabe who tis believed Killed a man Last night and threw him over the Bluff so as to make it appear that he had fallen over the Bluff Himself." The alleged murderer, named Spielman, was targeted by the Irish for retribution, and to get revenge they "threw over the House that he Lived in and Let it fall Down the Bluff The Guards and Fencibles had to turn Out to Keep them from Linching him."[61] Johnson did not venture any kind of judgment on whether Spielman deserved the attack, but law enforcement in Natchez was not especially attentive during the antebellum period. The "Guards" were the town's watch, who worked on a volunteer basis until the late 1830s, at which point the town's selectmen authorized two officers and seven other watchmen to patrol the town and "to apprehend and detain, for examination in the morning before a magistrate, all disturbers of the peace, and all persons concerned in nocturnal uproar," as well as to confine all enslaved people found in the streets without permission to the city's watch house.[62] Johnson and apparently most of Natchez did not think very highly of the men who joined the guard. In one instance involving "8 or 10 wild Irishmen," Johnson observed that they "Beat one man by the name of Roundtree—a guard he is for the City. He Hallowd Like a Clever fellow." Johnson found the whole event "Laughable indeed," mocking Roundtree's ability as a law enforcer but also his masculinity. It was not just that a large group of men beat him, but that he "Hallowd," or cried out, during the beating, probably asking for them to stop or for help, which Johnson found wanting. He also saw two other fights that night and noticed that the behavior was "Just like such people."[63] His judgment against these men might have had a basis in class, but it certainly was not merely for fighting, as clearly Johnson found fighting to be a component of masculinity.

Other examples indicate that Johnson found the city's watch dishonest and unmanly. Roundtree, the captain of the watch in 1842, was jailed for "assault and Battery" and was later "fined fifty Dollars—all for fighting."[64] In another instance, referring to a member of the guard that he found problematic, he wrote: "To night as I came home from sup[p]er I Herd a fuss in the Tremont House Down stairs and it proved to be Mr young Ephram Harrison in a chace after Mr James Kidney He ran across the street and got into some French Ladies Room to Keep young Harrison from getting Hold off Him. . . . He is a member of the Natchez Guards and to run in that maner does not become him."[65] On another morning at the market, he encountered an exchange between some members of the guard and wrote: "Found Dr Wright cutting up and Swearing and Defying all of the officers of the Place to take him to the Guard House He cursed Mr Benbrrok [one of the guards] in Particular and threatened to cow Hide him &c. He cleared all of the officers out for none of them would tuch him."[66] As these three events show, Johnson found that some guard members were prone to criminal activity, which made them unfit for enforcing the law. Others were cowardly, running away from a confrontation in the street and backing down from a belligerent man in the market.

Given southern men's insistence that manliness had to be performed in public settings, even an effective city guard would have been hard-pressed to limit the fights and duels in Natchez. As much as Johnson enjoyed watching a good fight, he also enjoyed watching bad ones where one of the men experienced humiliation. In June 1841, Johnson saw a skirmish between "A Mr Turner and Mr Miderhoff." Though he did not know what provoked the fight, he wrote: "It Commenced in this way, Turner Commenced on Miderhoff with a Cow hide, fell by accident, at that time, M Jumped on him but the other was too Strong for him. Miderhoff Jumped of[f] and ran away." Johnson noticed that Miderhoff left his hat behind as he ran, which he found amusing, but also observed: "He fought prety well for a very Short time and at the close of the fight he made a Splendid run It was a very good time that he made the Run."[67] Johnson, who enjoyed watching horses run fast, also enjoyed watching men run, and in this case, Midderhoff was lucky that he was so fast, as he was in danger of being badly beaten. As much as he enjoyed watching men display bravery, he also enjoyed mocking cowardice.

Word of Midderhoff's speed must have traveled around town quickly as well. To avoid being publicly labeled a coward, Midderhoff published a "Card" in one of the local papers proclaiming: "I hereby denounce N. E. Turner as a base poltroon and an arrant Coward, This Scoundrel made an assass[i]nlike attack upon me the night before Last at Dusk when I was unarmed & did not Expect an attac[k]. When yesterday a friend of mine Called on Him to Cross the river, he basely sculked from responsibility by saying that 'he was not a fighting man.'"[68] Johnson transcribed the card into his diary almost certainly to mark the irony of a man running from a fight calling another a coward. Midderhoff gave the impression that the attack had no provocation, which might have been true, but he used the code of honor to turn the tables on his assailant by claiming that Turner had turned down a challenge to a duel to erase his humiliation in the fight. Johnson appreciated the whole exchange.

Sometimes men issued challenges and planned duels, but they did not happen as the two parties, unlike Turner and Midderhoff, could come to a resolution without the need to shoot at one another. Johnson recalled a planned duel between "a Mr Duncan of New Orleans and Capt Page" that was to have taken place, as many of these seemed to, on the Louisiana side of the river. Johnson did not make the trip across the river to watch, but his apprentice Winston did. Johnson referenced, "They Came over in the night and Left the old Dr asleep."[69] Johnson might be referring to himself as the "old Dr" as he did not seem to know that Winston had gone until he came back late the following day. Johnson encouraged Winston to fight as a young man. He seemed to have taken quite an interest in fighting with other men throughout his time in Johnson's shop but also appears to have taken on Johnson's interest in watching others fight duels. Contrary to other times when his workers went out for the evening and did not return until the next day, Johnson did not record any anger or punishment for Winston, perhaps because he understood the attraction of going to the fight even though it never occurred.

Johnson was glad to see a duel called off in at least one case. In 1837, Johnson discovered that his friend Adam Bingaman had been challenged by "Col Osburn Claibourne." Johnson wrote that Bingaman "Came in very Early this morning and got shaved He seemed to be wraped up in thought, he had nothing to say." The silence resulted from the pending conflict. As Johnson noted, "The Roumer Says that they are to fight with Riffles," which was out of the ordinary since most used pistols. Since rifles are more accurate than the more traditionally used pistols, this might explain why Bingaman was concerned about the duel and was less talkative than usual in the shop. For his part, Johnson expressed: "I am very Sorry to heare that they are agoing to fight—I only wish that they may be preventd from fighting for I like them Both." Johnson did not detail the conflict that led to the dispute between the two men but recorded that "Col. Clabourne had 40 of his Slaves put up to be Sold at auction, Report Seys they are sold for debt." Given how Johnson wrote this, the impression is that the debt and the duel were related. Tension over the duel lasted for a few more days until the barber reported: "The Difficulty that was to have taken place to Day was very Hansomely arranged, the matter was Left to a Committee of Honor—I was never more glad that to hear it."[70] In this case, whatever insults between the two men had been settled by others, and Johnson did not think less of either man as a result. This might be because Johnson knew and respected both men. It might have resulted from the two playing by the code of honor rather than displaying cowardice or taking to the newspapers to make excuses for their behavior. The two men had agreed to the duel and decided not to fight it, meaning both had met the requirements of honor and manliness.

Conclusion

In a rare expression of melancholy in 1848 following the death of his sister, Johnson wrote in his diary: "And I have sined most grievously, by giving vent to a passionate temper, In allowing my Lips to give utterance to angry words. O, the misery that is entailed on one by an ungovernable temper."[71] Johnson's free and enslaved workers would definitely agree that he had a bad temper, but despite claiming that it was "ungovernable," Johnson kept that temper in check most of the time in public. Johnson was violent and cruel to the men who worked in his shop and the enslaved women in his household, but he did not express his bad temper toward his customers, those he did business with outside of the shop, or even the men with whom he gambled, hunted, and fished. While Johnson enjoyed watching others fight, he did not engage in such conflicts. His insistence on maintaining a reputation for respectability in public explains why he might not have fought with others, but his ideas about masculine competition also support this choice. Johnson believed that men had to compete with others and that there were winners and losers. Still, the important thing was the competition and handling the victories and defeats without losing one's cool. Johnson might have been addicted to gambling as he always kept score in every contest he had with anyone, but what was important was taking the risk. When Johnson won, he often boasted about his prowess, but when he lost, he accepted that, too, whether it was a few cigars or a sizable sum of money. Johnson's ideas regarding actual fights or duels are well understood—a man had to accept the challenge and could not back down from it. Men who ran from fights or abused the honor code to escape duels were less masculine than those who stuck with the challenge, even if it meant injury or death. Antebellum Natchez offered Johnson plenty of opportunities to judge the masculinity of those around him. Even though he was never in a fight himself, he expressed confidence that he would not back down if confronted. Johnson eventually faced challenges from men who did not share his ideas about respectability and did not care about his reputation in town, and he responded with confidence that he could defend himself and his sense of masculinity.

CHAPTER THREE

Politics, Race, and Masculinity

ON JANUARY 31, 1836, William Johnson and Robert McCary met at Johnson's barbershop in the evening. After cutting McCary's hair, Johnson read aloud a speech entitled "The Natural Slavery of the Negro" by George McDuffie, the governor of South Carolina. In the speech, McDuffie declared: "That the African negro is destined by Providence to occupy this condition of servile dependence, is not less manifest. It is marked on the face, stamped on the skin, and evinced by the intellectual inferiority and natural improvidence of this race. They have all the qualities that fit them for slaves, and not one of those that would fit them to freemen." The irony, in this case, is not only that the two men reading the speech by McDuffie were Black men who were free and possessed the "qualities" that would "fit them" to be such since they were reading it, but also that Johnson's only remarks on it were, "We both got tyred of it before I finished."[1] McDuffie's speech was very much in keeping with the proslavery rhetoric of the South in the antebellum period, most especially that of his fellow South Carolinian John C. Calhoun. Johnson and McCary, two men born into slavery, were well acquainted with this mode of thought and lived in a town, county, and state whose commitment to the institution and the racism behind it were best expressed in Mississippi's declaration of secession in 1860: "Our position is thoroughly identified with the institution of slavery—the greatest material interest of the world. . . . These products are peculiar to the climate verging on the tropical regions, and by an imperious law of nature, none but the black race can bear exposure to the tropical sun. These products have become necessities of the world, and a blow at slavery is a blow at commerce and civilization."[2]

In the nineteenth century, one of the expressions of racism throughout the United States was denying African Americans the right to vote and keeping the franchise explicitly only in white men's hands, which became a qualifying feature of masculinity. During the colonial era, some southern legislatures allowed Blacks to vote, but after the American Revolution, suffrage became a marker of citizenship, and as states decided only white men could be citizens, they purposely excluded free people of color from voting. By the nineteenth century, property requirements for voting disappeared, making all adult white men eligible to vote and the only people who could be full citizens, confirming the United States as a "white man's country."[3] In this formulation of masculinity, men were to be the public voice for their families and could best express that by voting. Enslaved people counted as dependents, and keeping the franchise out of the hands of Black men removed African American men, even free men like Johnson and McCary, from one of the essential features of manliness.[4]

However, just as Black men could exert agency in their lives in ways not tied to overt physical resistance against enslavers, political participation is not just voting. Northern Black men, and some Black women, pushed back against the idea that skin color should determine citizenship. Some claimed that birthright citizenship did not rest upon color and that immigrants who could gain access to the franchise just by being included in whiteness were far less deserving than they were. Enslaved people held their own politics and exercised them individually and collectively from the colonial era through the Civil War.[5] William Johnson's politics shared some of the features of those of his northern contemporaries, especially the idea of citizenship for all free men regardless of race, but unlike these movements based on abolition, he supported slavery. On the one hand, Johnson's politics represented his individual interests rather than those shared by most northern Blacks. Still, on the other, he championed ideas and politicians who supported free people of color in the South. Johnson, and no doubt, other free people of color in Natchez and elsewhere, offer a counterexample to the notion that all African Americans shared the same political views. Johnson viewed assertiveness and participation as essential traits of masculinity. Though he could not vote in elections or serve on juries, he still engaged in his community and politics in multiple ways. Johnson kept track of politics, was conscious of and interacted with the law and courts, and was a firm Jacksonian Democrat, despite never being able to call himself one formally.[6] In some ways, politics functioned similarly to gambling for Johnson: it allowed him to compete with other men, participate in civic causes, and helped to further his reputation for respectable manhood. He made bets on elections, attended rallies and speeches, and worked for the causes he supported and against those he disliked. Beyond purely political causes, Johnson established himself by fulfilling what he saw as his civic duties in multiple ways.

"Sold Down the River": How the Enslaved Viewed Natchez

One of the founding historiographic debates on the institution of slavery, initiated by U. B. Phillips at the beginning of the twentieth century, is the debate over how slaveholders viewed the institution. The dispute mainly considered how committed enslavers were to profit from slavery versus some other kind of motivation based on ideas of paternalism, social status, or other nonpecuniary benefits that slavery allowed. Regardless of the questions historians have posed, it is difficult to argue that those who moved to the American Southwest, including Natchez and its surroundings, were interested in anything other than the wealth that slavery and cotton could bring them. Though paternalism might have motivated older generations in the Southeast, those ideas seem to have been considered old-fashioned and outdated to Mississippi, Louisiana, and Texas settlers during the antebellum period.[7] Like other enslavers in and around Natchez, William Johnson bought men and women to improve his finances. Sometimes he expressed the sense that enslaved people owed him familial obligation, and he occasionally showed sympathy along with punishment and cruelty. There is no evidence that Johnson considered manumitting any of the people he held in bondage as a reward for their services, though he did express a sense of surprise and confusion that the enslaved man Walker chose to run away or when others misbehaved or defied him. In these ways, Johnson identified with white enslavers in Natchez, supporting slavery within his household, doing his part to regulate the behavior of enslaved people in town, and performing just the kind of behavior that white men expected of one another in a slave society.

Johnson lived during a massive expansion of slavery in Natchez. The number of people living in Natchez and the rest of Adams County proliferated in the first half of the nineteenth century, but the free population remained nearly static. By 1860, the county had 5,648 whites and 14,292 slaves, along with 225 free people of color. Of course, the enormous influx of enslaved African Americans resulted from the cotton boom of the early nineteenth century. Though cotton prices shifted because of vagaries in the textile industry of the Northeast and England, the crop had effectively become king in Natchez as early as the first decade of the century. As a result, Natchez became second only to New Orleans as a market for human property and the final destination for many brought to the market from other parts of the South.[8] Not surprisingly, the region's enormous demands for enslaved workers shaped the political leanings of its inhabitants.

For their part, enslaved people believed the Old Southwest was home to the nation's harshest slaveholders driven by profit alone. When asked, "why do slaves dread so bad to go to the South—to Mississippi or Louisiana?," Lewis Clarke, a formerly enslaved person, replied, "because they know slaves are driven very hard there, and worked to death in a few years." Jacob Stroyer claimed the Old Southwest "was considered by the slaves a place of slaughter, so those who were going there did not expect to see their friends again." The Reverend Josiah Henson held that enslaved people in the Upper South associated the area with "perpetual dread."[9] While growing cotton required vast amounts of labor, the work necessary to produce the crop paled compared to more dangerous work environments such as the malarial rice swamps of the lowcountry or the human-consuming sugar plantations of the Caribbean and Latin America.[10] Nevertheless, among enslaved people in the Upper South, cotton-growing regions like Natchez inspired fear and anxiety. This tension was not because of the work's danger but rather the way African Americans believed enslavers viewed enslaved people in the Old Southwest, that the bodies of Blacks served merely as commodities to be bought, sold, and worked to death.

Nineteenth-century slave narratives offer rich evidence of how the enslaved viewed the journey to Mississippi and expectations of treatment from owners once they arrived. These narratives often portray slavery in the Upper South (Virginia, Maryland, Kentucky) as far gentler by comparison. William Anderson wrote of his experience in Natchez and sale to a cotton planter versus his life in Virginia in biblical terms: "When I remembered old Virginia, the place of my birth, my mother's house, the cabin, the grove, the spring, the associates, the Sabbath enjoyments. I felt that I was like the children of Israel when they were taken down into Babylonian captivity." In Natchez's slave pens, Anderson described the scenes of many who experienced sale to the Old Southwest. He specifically noted the behavior of enslavers themselves at auctions, where it was not uncommon to "see a large, rough slaveholder, take a poor female slave into a room, make her strip, then feel of and examine her, as though she were a pig, or a hen, or merchandise. O, how can a poor slave husband or father stand and see his wife, daughters and sons thus treated?"[11] Such treatment supported claims that enslavers in Natchez were among the worst and prevented enslaved men from protecting their families, divorcing them from a crucial masculine role.

It was not only the long journey to the Old Southwest and the separation of families that made these people apprehensive; it also was the type of owners to be expected. In the biography that she wrote of her father, Josephine Brown noted, "In the cotton districts, the picking season is always the most severe for the bondman, for when they gather in the cotton, the slaves are worked from fifteen to twenty hours out of the twenty-four."[12] William Webb, forced by his master to move from Kentucky to Mississippi, noted a striking contrast between the enslavers in the two states. While traveling through Mississippi on his first journey to the state, he observed: "We passed through many large plantations during our travels, and the same cruelty was going on in every one of them. The whip and whipping post were used as an every day occurrence." This contrasted strongly with Kentucky, which he felt was "better than any state" regarding the treatment of the enslaved. Still, human commodification due to the market made available in the cotton-producing Old Southwest struck him powerfully. In Bowling Green, he noticed "something different here, than I had ever seen before. The speculators went round buying colored people—even little children. They had large plantations of them and when they got a large drove of them together, they shipped them down South." Webb described Natchez as "a sea-port where they raised colored people and shipped them to other States." When his master decided to relocate to Mississippi, it did not take long for Webb to notice a difference in the treatment of the enslaved. He observed, "It seemed as though people were free in Kentucky, when compared with Mississippi."[13]

In the nineteenth century, African American newspapers often used Mississippi and Natchez as evidence of the most barbaric treatment within the Old South. Frederick Douglass reported to his readers that an enslaved man had been burned to death in Natchez, and though the local newspapers disputed the date that this happened, they did not challenge that the act took place.[14] The *North Star* described another instance in which authorities in Natchez separated a white man and his wife from traveling up the Mississippi to Indiana because they suspected the woman was a runaway.

The woman was then confined to jail until the husband could prove that the woman, who might have had mixed ancestry, was legally his wife. The reporter noted, "I could not myself detect anything in her countenance or conversation that would condemn her in the North from walking in the highest circles of society."[15] Natchez was represented as the home of especially malicious people who made it difficult even for those who could travel freely.

Abolitionist newspapers furthered Natchez's image as the home of some of the cruelest masters in the South. One northerner who had relocated to Natchez in the 1820s found that though many of his neighbors suggested that he would "soon wear off [his] northern prejudices, and probably have slaves of [his] own," he could not resolve to "make injustice appear justice."[16] In other instances, runaway slave ads ran in papers stressing the harsh punishment faced by enslaved people in Natchez. One such ad, published in the *Natchez Courier* and reprinted in the *National Era,* listed a runaway named Mary with a description highlighting the malicious nature of enslavers: "[She] has a small scar over her eye; a good many teeth missing. The letter A is branded on her cheek and forehead."[17] The copyeditor assigned the whippings, brandings, and other tortures to the "character of those who direct their labor." For the most part, he spoke of overseers, who commonly worked in Natchez, where many of the wealthiest planters owned multiple plantations while living in town, as being "abandoned, brutal, and desperate men." Despite the attack on the overseers' character, all of the vignettes of cruelty described in the letter place the blame squarely on masters, who, while they may have been less abandoned and desperate, appear no less brutal in their descriptions.[18]

It is impossible to know how the men and women Johnson enslaved felt about him or if they shared the sense that so many had that Natchez was perhaps the worst place they could have lived. Johnson's feelings toward the men and women he enslaved, though, are available, and, not surprisingly, they are complicated. Like all slaveholders, Johnson accepted that people could be owned as property, but enslavers had to come to terms with the fact that the enslaved were never only extensions of their wills. As Frederick Douglass observed, enslavers "had to deal not with earth, wood, and stone, but with men; and by every regard they had for their safety and prosperity they had need to know the material on which they were to work."[19] For Johnson, the racial difference between himself and whites placed him at a legal and social disadvantage. By enslaving people, he could establish a distance between himself and other African Americans and use this as evidence that he supported the slave society in which he lived. Like most other slaveholders, how he treated his slaves or how much trouble they got into outside his household could affect his reputation. As a result, Johnson extended opportunities to these men and women and offered violent punishments if they violated his rules. Establishing a sense of "mastery" was a part of masculinity for slaveholding men, and Johnson was conscious of that, but it also was true that as a slaveholder in a city, Johnson participated in the civic responsibility of keeping his human property under control. Like his white neighbors, Johnson supported city and social ordinances to control enslaved people.[20]

Johnson witnessed the ways that other enslavers behaved toward enslaved people firsthand. In one case, he discovered that one of his horses was missing, and he later found it "in possession of a Black man belonging [to] Mr Barber. The Boys name was Patrick." Johnson does not report any confrontation with Patrick; instead, he took the horse and rode it back home, but before doing so, he alerted Mr. Barber to what happened: "After having showed the Horse to his master he promised me that he would pay any Damage that I seen proper to Charge him for the Horse."[21] The following day, Johnson found that Barber had sold Patrick and that "he Sold him on that count alone," in other words, he sold him because of the theft. In another case, Johnson discovered: "Mr Braziers Boy Norman was caught up in a tree I understand stealing of Chickens Last night They took him to Jail and Kept him there untill Late to day and whiped him then turned him Out." Johnson relates both of these instances without telling how he felt about them, but given how he treated the men and women he enslaved, he appears to have agreed with both punishments.

Johnson was hesitant to sell the men and women he enslaved as punishment. In fact, of the sixteen men and women he enslaved during his life, he only sold Steven as a direct result of his behavior, and even then, only after years of other kinds of reprimands, including whippings, confinement, and bargains between the two. When he finally did sell Steven, his diary entry appeared to contain genuine remorse for doing it, probably understanding that wherever he wound up, he would find a worse situation: "Today has been to me a very sad day; many tears was in my eyes today on acct. of my selling poor Steven."[22] Even with that expression of regret, though, Johnson did not hesitate to inflict physical pain on Steven in the years leading up to his eventual sale. As his entries on Steven show, he recognized Steven's humanity, but that did not stop him from trying to impose his will.

Other similar instances show these contradictions in how Johnson treated these men and women. For example, in 1836, he wrote: "Steven [a different one than the one discussed above], Belonging to Mr Nickols came to me and asked my permission to Let him have Sarah, which I agreed to it if he would always behave himself properly in my yard." Though this entry reads as if it is an attempt by Steven to buy Sarah from Johnson, Steven asked Johnson's permission to marry Sarah, a woman he enslaved. Johnson agreed to the arrangement, assuming Steven's good behavior, and presumably, the two married. A man approached Johnson "at the auction Room" two years later and said "he wanted to buy my Girl Sarah. I told him he could have her for twelve Hundred Dollars in cash. I intend to see about it To morrow and if I can find out about him I will do something." Although Sarah was married to the local man, Steven, Johnson was willing to sell her away from her husband. Like other slaveholders across the South, Johnson was not bound by law to recognize marriages entered into by enslaved couples. Though Steven and Sarah undoubtedly intended to remain together, Johnson was more than willing to separate them for $1,200.[23] Johnson did not sell Sarah, not because he respected her marriage, but because he believed the man who approached him was trying to steal her.[24]

Residents of Natchez always concerned themselves with limiting the movement of enslaved people when away from their enslavers. One of the primary reasons the town created the city guard was to police enslaved people who moved about outside the watch of enslavers. Stephanie Camp labeled enslaved peoples' usage of space as a "rival geography," which though accessible to whites, allowed for "private and public creative expression, rest and recreation, alternative communication, and importantly, resistance to planters' domination of slaves' every move." In Camp's work, this mainly consisted of rural areas, but towns like Natchez offered these spaces as well and invoked frequent complaints from whites.[25] The townspeople of Natchez complained that "the license given by many owners of slaves to go at large, hire their own time, and trade as freemen in the county of Adams, is in direct violation of law and dangerous in example and practice. The condition of slavery cannot be maintained with such license. The indulgence of them in one liberty above their condition, but creates the desire of another."[26] Johnson and many other enslavers, white and Black, hired their slaves out in Natchez. Before he purchased a farm, Johnson mainly purchased enslaved people to work in his shop and hire them out. Also, in keeping with the practice of Natchez's slaveholders, Johnson wrote passes for them to travel in the city to see amusements or, in a few cases, to attend church services. On one evening in 1840, Johnson recorded: "I wrote some passes Last night, One for Phillip, 1 for Sarah [and] One for Lucinda to Go Out to Brackets to a Preacher and neither of them Came Home at all Last Night." Johnson recognized that even if this was technically unlawful, it was also a common practice and usually was ignored by law enforcement as long as there was a pass. The enslaved knew this and used passes to go places without authorization or stay out longer. Even if the city guard did not pick them up, they could expect retribution from Johnson. When the group finally returned the following day, Johnson whipped them.[27]

Even if he focused on the local custom of allowing enslaved people to be out without supervision rather than the law, he was willing to help enforce the law in instances involving others. In his diary, Johnson wrote that one of Robert McCary's apprentices ran away, and he sent one of his enslaved men, named Dick, out to find him. As McCary discovered, "Dick ranaway [sic] himself," and Johnson noted, "I caught him this night and Took him home to Mc."[28] Johnson might have been simply aiding a friend in returning Dick, but in doing so, he was taking part in what he saw to be his civic duty to the broader community of Natchez.

Civic Engagement

Participation in causes that benefited the city and its residents was another way Johnson could assert his belonging to a larger body politic, even if his racial status kept him from engaging in the same ways that white men could. One of Natchez's residents' most significant concerns, as in all urban areas in the nineteenth century, was fire. Uncontrolled fires could ruin businesses and cause deaths for those living and working in town. Alerting others to danger and helping suppress fires required the community to pull together, and Johnson was always ready to pitch in to help. One evening in 1836, Johnson recalled: "Just before Day this morning I herd the cry of a fire I jumped up almost Naked and ran over to Mr Bells with a bucket of water the fire was then Burning in Mr Harris's ware or cotton yard, I worked at Mr bells until after Day light. I then went over to the City Hotel & worked there with the water at the pump until 12 Oclock and then the Engine quit work." The *Mississippi Free Trader* reported, "The fire is believed to have originated in a kitchen occupied by negroes, in the rear of the Barber's shop, on Wall street," which is to say, right behind Johnson's shop and home. Though no one died in the fire, "two negroes were severely injured by the falling of a wall." The paper also noted that despite the damage, estimated to be around fifty-two thousand dollars, the destruction would have been far more severe, and through "the most praiseworthy exertions of our citizens with buckets, the main buildings were saved."[29] Though the fire began very close by, Johnson and his neighbors prevented damage to his shop.

Nine days later, another fire broke out in town, caused by a suspected arsonist. In his diary, Johnson wrote: "Between 8 and 9 Oclock to night, the fire Broke Out in a House next door below the Barber shop ocupied by John Williams, Barber—He was taken and his wife and children and put in Jail." While fighting the blaze, he noted, "I worked very hard at the fire, tore my coat all to pieces in the Back, spoiled my Boots also."[30] The *Free Trader* did not mention John Williams or blame him for the fire but claimed that "some villain" was responsible. The newspaper's reporters hoped it was enough "to induce a general call upon the City Council to adopt such measures as will insure the organization of an energetic police or night watch, so that our citizens may sleep under strong assurance of safety." Johnson did not sleep soundly after the incident and instead, "Loaded [his] Gun and garded [his] yard until ½ after 2oclock."[31] Williams and his family were investigated and released with the finding that the fire had been an accident.[32]

Johnson's concern was well-founded as yet another fire destroyed twenty-eight houses in Under-the-Hill a few days later. One of the town's newspapers reported hearing residents shouting that the fire was "a plot to burn us up" and "Take care of your own property." As a result of an arsonist on the loose, "every man turned out, almost every one with fire-arms, and regular patrols were established. Every square was guarded during the whole night, and every stranger stopped. Several persons were apprehended and lodged in jail."[33] Johnson joined in with his neighbors, noting: "I was Out on Gard in my Yard until 10 Oclock precisely. It then Commenced raining and I went to bed."[34] Yet another fire was discovered a few days later at the home of a Mrs. Dunn. Johnson recorded, a "Mr Sweney was arrested and put under the gard at the Gard House he was supposed to have Either set fire to Mrs Dunns House or Else he knew something about it—The fire was discovered in the Room of Mrs Dunn—The Gard took Nancy Latimore and Cut her all over her Back, whiped her very much." Nancy Lattimore, a free woman of color, was blamed for the fire. In addition to a severe whipping, they confined Lattimore in the guardhouse, and upon her release, "She went through the Market the next morning with her Cloathes hanging all of at Each Shoulder. Her back was very much whiped It was thought that Dr. Lattimore made her walk in the Streets that way." Even though Nancy Lattimore had been free for at least four years, she must have been bound to Dr. David Lattimore somehow, as Johnson suggested that he had imposed this walk as additional punishment for the woman.[35] When still another fire broke out at the house while a guard was on duty, Johnson offered, "it is my Candid Opinion that Mrs Dunn must have done it Herself or had it done—public sentiment is very much against her."[36]

Johnson pitched in to help his neighbors throughout his life when fires broke out and to guard against arson. Fighting fires with buckets of water, aside from being a difficult physical task, was also dangerous and could result in severe injury or death. Johnson knew the risks and acknowledged them, but that did not dissuade him from participating in his civic duty. When his niece, Lavinia, heard that Johnson had become ill from helping to fight a fire in 1850, she wrote to Ann Johnson: "[I] was very sorry to hear that uncle was unwell. Tho it was very imprudent on his part to go to that fire and work so. They would not do so much for him."[37] Johnson might have disagreed that his neighbors would not come to his aid in a similar situation, but he also might have recognized that not helping in these circumstances could hurt his position. Lavinia's assertion that his white neighbors would not help him if the situation were reversed is likely based on racism rather than on specific instances where Johnson or his family experienced animosity. Johnson never recorded any disputes with his neighbors in town that indicated hostility, but it is possible that the family did have these experiences even if they were not written down.

Johnson generally relied on Natchez's broader community, white and Black, to do the right thing regarding obligations like fire safety and his business dealings. Given the imbalance of legal power between whites and Blacks, he might have expected his customers and clients to take advantage of him, but that rarely was the case. Besides his barbershop, Johnson's most frequent dealings with whites was as a moneylender. For the most part, the amounts he lent out at any one time were small, usually less than one hundred dollars, but they amounted to substantial sums when taken together. In one year, he lent out a total of $4,700. He charged interest rates from 5 percent per month to 6 percent per year to a diverse clientele ranging from the poor to business owners and wealthy plantation owners such as John B. Nevitt and George Poindexter, one-time governor of Mississippi. Johnson was persistent in collecting debts and rarely had a problem doing so, at least partly because he was cautious about the people to whom he extended loans. On the rare occasions when his clients did not pay, Johnson might transfer the debt to a trusted white associate; in other circumstances, he sued his debtors in court.[38]

Along with loaning money, Johnson also was a landlord. His financial success enabled him to buy and improve upon several town lots. From 1836 to 1838, Johnson purchased two lots and constructed two new buildings, which he then rented out. The tenants of these buildings were P. McGetterick, a white man who operated a coffee shop called "The Southern Exchange," and a business called Green & Blake. Johnson also rented out his "Fancy Shop on Main Street," located in the same building as his primary barbershop. The "fancy shop" was rented to several different tenants from its completion in 1839 through Johnson's death in 1851 and included two storekeepers, a druggist, a bootmaker, and a bowling alley. These tenants were white men; some were immigrants newly arrived from Europe.[39]

Johnson's tenants lived up to their agreements with him in the main, even though Johnson's legal status as a free man of color might give them an advantage. Johnson never complained that any of his tenants attempted to use his race against him, but in one case, one of his tenants decided not to honor his contract. In 1837, Johnson wrote: "Adoph M. Flecho Ran off from this place To Day—I hold a note of His that He gave me for Rent that was Due to me for $180.00. . . . The note is past Due and was not protes[t]ed."[40] Flecho, a jeweler and engraver, bought land from Johnson in 1835 and had been his tenant for more than a year. Another man named Seureau had endorsed the note that Flecho had given Johnson, and since Flecho had skipped town without paying, Johnson intended to collect from Seureau. When he found that Flecho had gone, rather than going directly to Seureau, Johnson hired a lawyer, G. Baker, "To Collect the money if He could possibly do So and I told him could [he] collect it that I would give him $40 of the money."[41]

Rather than simply accepting that Flecho cheated him, Johnson relied on the law to rectify his problems. Baker could not collect the money from Serueau, so Johnson filed suit against him. The court met on January 28, 1837, to settle the case. Johnson wrote in his diary: "To day I had a Suit in Court and I Lost it. . . . I Lost the money by not having the note protested when it fell due." Additionally, Johnson believed that he had made a few other mistakes. Specifically, he noted that "L David," a witness for Serueau, testified that he had heard Johnson say that he "Expected to loose the money for I had neglected to have the note protested when it fell due." The most significant count against him, he believed, was that "He [Serueau] acknowledged the promise of Paying the debt if it Could not be made Out of Flecho, but my having but the One witness and the law reqquirrs that there shall be two witness in such cases." Johnson attributed the loss not to prejudice under the law because of his race but to his own mistakes. This entry illustrates that Johnson trusted Flecho to abide by the agreement, and when he failed to, he also trusted that the law would render a fair verdict. In this case, even though he lost, he did not argue that it was unfair, but instead that he had made miscalculations that led to the loss in court. Johnson's faith that individuals and institutions were impartial proves his sense of civic duty and engagement. If he had no faith in others, he would not have loaned money or become a landlord in the first place. Just as whites in town expected Natchez's people to conform to established law to deal with one another in good faith, Johnson participated in the body politic by relying on the law and filing suit.

Elections and Politics

Andrew Jackson's political movement drew nonelite white men into politics in an age where the property requirement to vote had been dropped, thus creating universal white man suffrage and a notion that, at least at the ballot box, all white men were equal. Despite Adams County, Mississippi, being named for John Quincy Adams's father, the county and the rest of the Old Southwest chose Jackson over Adams in 1824 and 1828. Jackson's policies and popularity carried the region again in 1832, but even with his endorsement of Van Buren as his successor, the Whig Party made serious inroads into the state and even carried Adams County in the presidential election of 1836. Mississippi's political division resulted from a schism between the older, more established southern counties and the new northern counties carved out of Native Americans' lands. Like national ones, those divides had roots in class differences as many, but not all, of the wealthy planters in the Natchez area began drifting toward the Whigs, whereas the less affluent adhered to the Democrats. The split between the two regions led some to suggest that counties like Adams should secede from Mississippi and join Louisiana because at least there "rule by gentleman" was still in place. As one newspaper put it, "There is scarcely a reason why we should remain linked (like the living to the dead among the Romans) to the dead carcass of Northern Mississippi."[42]

William Johnson overtly supported the Democratic Party. This support might have come from broader national or state interests, which he wrote about frequently but most likely emerged from more personal concerns. Johnson's political stances offer further evidence that he agreed that participation in politics was a way of demonstrating manliness. Even if he could not vote as white men did, this did not mean he had no stake in the system. Further, Johnson's support of Democrats counters his biographers' contention from the 1950s that he aspired to be like the white gentlemen he so admired. Johnson's most powerful white acquaintances and friends were Whigs, and several ran for office. Johnson supported Democrats because he identified men within the party who, at least in his mind, took stances favorable to free people of color.

One of the local Democratic politicians whom Johnson supported was John D. Freeman. Freeman ran for and won the office of attorney general of Mississippi and later a seat in the US Congress. What drew Johnson to Freeman was his support for allowing free people of color's testimony in court against whites. In a speech delivered in the town of Port Gibson, Freeman defended the court-martial of a naval officer based on the testimony of free people of color. President Martin Van Buren chose to uphold the officer's conviction based on this testimony, which drew censure from southerners. The *Mississippi Free Trader* contended that local Whigs had "grossly and outrageously vilified" him "at the 'log cabin' on the bluff" mainly on the assumption that Freeman's support made him an abolitionist. The *Free Trader* tried to correct the record on Freeman's stance on slavery, making it clear that, "when Mr. Freeman delivered his speech, that there were more than fifty slave holders who heard him, and so far from finding fault with his remarks, unanimously voted a resolution of thanks, and requested him to furnish his speech for publication." In a contradictory fashion, though, just below their defense of Freeman, the newspaper included an article about "the late trial of the celebrated Dr. Hines in New Orleans. . . . Upon his trial 'a free negro man and free negro woman' were permitted to testify against him." The paper expressed the "outrage" of the citizens of Natchez over the case and also noted that "the Judge must be a democrat, or he never would have obeyed the law."[43]

Regardless of the whiplash of supporting Freeman's position on allowing the testimony of free Blacks and immediately following that with a denunciation of the same idea, the newspaper continued to defend Freeman in its next issue. The paper insisted: "The whig party, orators and press, have taken great umbrage at Mr. Freeman's able exposition of the *legality* of free negro testimony in the case of Lieut. Hooe, and have denounced him as an abolitionist worse than Garrison, Tappan or any of the horde of northern fanatics." To counter this, they published one of Freeman's speeches given in New York with several abolitionists in the audience. In that speech, Freeman claimed that abolitionists had "forty thousand votes" and "that the party who will support their abominable doctrines, are to receive the bounty." Freeman argued that Whigs were already working to secure those votes for themselves and hoped "no Judas Iscariot will be found in the democratic ranks, base enough to receive such a bribe." Further, Freeman clarified his position on abolitionists: "I would rather see the whole party crushed for years to come, than witness the crown of abolition placed on the head of its triumph. Abolition is the child of phrenzy—the illegitimate offspring of bigotry and base ambition—it was conceived in sin and born in inequity."[44] The *Free Trader* was Natchez's Democratic newspaper and contested with the *Courier*, which favored the Whigs for the town's readers. The *Free Trader* published Freeman's position against abolition and showed that he spoke against abolition to both northern and southern audiences. William Johnson was no abolitionist, but neither were Democrats and Whigs in Natchez. Any sympathy toward abolition would have resulted in an assurance they would lose and expose themselves to attacks by angry mobs.

The case that caused so much controversy for the Natchez newspapers was Lieutenant George Mason Hooe, an officer in the US Navy. Hooe was charged with several counts of disrespect, disobedience to his superior officer, cruelty, insubordination, and sedition. Hooe was convicted of many of these charges and sentenced to removal from his squadron. After the verdict, Hooe appealed directly to President Martin Van Buren to review and overturn his conviction. Within his letter to Van Buren, he mentioned several inconsistencies in the testimony of many against him, but he specifically noted: "There is one other point in the proceedings of the court . . . to which I incite the particular attention of your excellency. It respects a matter as to which all southern men are deeply sensitive, and if not overruled by your excellency, will assuredly drive many valuable men from the navy." The matter was: "In the progress of the proceedings of this court two negroes—one the cook, the other the private steward of Commander Levy—were introduced as witnesses against me." Because this occurred in the territory of Florida, which banned African Americans from testifying against whites, Hooe argued, "This I charge as a proceeding illegal and erroneous on the part of the court." Van Buren turned to Francis Scott Key to review the case, who determined that the court was bound only by laws passed by Congress, not the Florida Territory, and thus "Till they [Congress] enact the disqualification [of free people of color], it cannot be enforced. The court could not do otherwise than admit the testimony." Moreover, Key concluded that the verdict would not change even with these free Blacks' testimony omitted. Van Buren then concluded, "The President finds nothing in the proceedings of Lieut. Hooe which requires his interference."[45]

Others used this case to claim that Whigs, not Van Buren and the Democrats, were abolitionists. Amos Kendall, a Kentucky Democrat, used the case to attack John Botts, a Virginia Whig. In his defense of Van Buren, Kendall pointed out: "You will find, sir, that four out of the seven members composing this court belonged to the slaveholding States. It was THEY, sir, and not the President, who admitted the colored witnesses." Kendall echoed Key's defense that only Congress could determine who could testify and for Van Buren to try to allow otherwise was illegal and an attempt to usurp the power of Congress. Kendall claimed that his attack on Van Buren over this case was rooted in "THE EXISTING POLITICAL ALLIANCE BETWEEN THE WHIGS AND ABOLITIONISTS!"[46] The local and national discussion of Hooe devolved into a partisan fight charging each party of being in league with abolitionists when no southern politician of either party supported ending slavery anywhere. For Johnson, the partisanship over which party was more committed to slavery was not relevant; instead, he was simply impressed with Freeman's support of the position that free men, regardless of race, should be able to testify in court, which would have allowed a measure of equality to free men of color.

Another Democratic politician William Johnson admired was Richard Johnson, Martin Van Buren's vice president. In 1837, Johnson transcribed the following short passage by Richard Johnson, explaining why he supported the Democratic Party:

THE BASIS OF OUR FREE INSTITION

No Priviledged orders—Liberty of Speech—Freedom of the press— The rights of conscience—Strict Construction of the federal Constitution—Universal Sufferage—Responsibility to the people—No Imprisonment for debt—And a general Diffusion of Knoledge among all classes of the People

Richard M. Johnson
By William T Johnson

For a free man of color like William Johnson, there is no doubt that the virtues that Richard Johnson listed here appealed to him. He knew that there were privileged orders as he lived that experience every day of his life. While it was not the Democratic Party's policy to remove the racial laws that restricted Johnson's access to all of the freedoms that the United States guaranteed, the expression of such an idea was something that appealed to him. Unlike most other politicians of his age, Richard Johnson did not view the United States as a republic for whites only; instead, his career indicated that he believed that African Americans and Native Americans could be incorporated and "walk the great path of 'civilization' that would lead to citizenship." In recording this piece in his diary, the barber set out his ideal notion of the United States, which mirrored Richard Johnson's position.[47]

Richard Johnson was born in Kentucky in 1781, trained as a lawyer, and served in the Kentucky legislature, the US House of Representatives, and the US Senate. Most of his fame, though, came from his military service, especially as an Indian fighter, which put him in the mold of Andrew Jackson, something that men from both political parties tried to claim and mimic for the remainder of the antebellum period. At the beginning of the War of 1812, Congress charged Johnson with raising a volunteer army to fight against the British and their Native American allies. His deeply hagiographic biography described Colonel Johnson's time as an officer as both discipline-focused and democratic, claiming, "The officers never forgot that the men were their brothers and their equals; nor did the men lose the spirit of Independence, while they yielded a willing obedience to the officers of their own choice." At the Battle of the Thames, Colonel Johnson and his men faced off against Tecumseh, and according to his biography and others present at the battle, Johnson charged at the Shawnee Chief and killed him despite Johnson's being wounded several times. There is some dispute about whether Tecumseh was actually the man Colonel Johnson killed. Even his biography acknowledged that this might have been a case of mistaken identity, but, whether true or not, the legend certainly helped Johnson's fame and political career.[48] Tecumseh's death at Johnson's hands has been memorialized in paintings, a frieze in the rotunda at the US Capitol, and a political slogan used in the presidential election of 1836, "Rumpsey Dumpsey, Rumpsey Dumpsey, Colonel Johnson killed Tecumseh."[49]

No doubt, this fame appealed to white men who could view Richard Johnson in the same mold as Andrew Jackson: a westerner who embodied the kind of experience they valued, but he also had a common-law wife who was a woman of color. Richard Johnson inherited an enslaved woman named Julia Chinn from his father. Contemporaries described Chinn as an "octoroon," a person with one-eighth African heritage. Because she was enslaved, Johnson could not legally marry her, but instead of freeing her or trying to challenge the law, the couple had a common-law marriage. As William Johnson and many free people of color could attest, sexual relationships between white men and Black women were not unusual, but what made Richard Johnson's out of the ordinary was that he openly referred to Chinn as "my bride." Chinn operated Johnson's household while he was away, including directing the men and women he held in bondage. The couple had two children Richard Johnson acknowledged, and they carried the name "Johnson." When Chinn died in 1833, he began a relationship with another woman he enslaved, and when that woman left him for another man, Johnson sold her at auction and started a liaison with her sister, also enslaved.[50]

Though it seems that Richard Johnson's open association with Chinn and other enslaved women did not hurt his reputation locally, it did follow him when he sought national office. Andrew Jackson supported Johnson as Van Buren's vice president because of his experience in the War of 1812, but others thought he was a liability because of his relationships with enslaved women. In a political cartoon for the 1836 election, an artist mocked Johnson with the portrayal of an African American woman under the slogan

"Carrying the War into Africa." The woman, who probably was supposed to represent Julia Chinn, though she had been dead for three years, said in the cartoon, "Let ebery good dimicrat vote for my husband, and den he shall hab his sheer ub de surplum rebbenu wat is in my bag." The cartoon, titled *Jinnoowine [genuine] Johnson Ticket,* was created by Ohio Democrats who opposed Johnson's candidacy for vice president, not by Henry Clay's campaign, the Whig candidate for the presidency.[51] Though Richard Johnson's relationships with enslaved women might have driven some white supporters away from the Democrats, it did not move William Johnson's support.

Another political cartoon mocked Richard Johnson's connection to African Americans in a similar but more direct way. In the cartoon, Johnson is in the middle of a group of people with one hand covering his eyes in despair while the other holds a copy of the *New York Courier and Enquirer.* In the caption, Johnson exclaims: "When I read the scurrilous attacks in the Newspapers on the Mother of my children, pardon me, my friends if I give way to feelings!! My dear Girls, bring me your Mother's picture, that I may show it to my friends here." Those surrounding Johnson attempted to console him, but all in a way that was either self-interested or exposed Johnson's racial sensibilities as incorrect or radical. On the left, a Black man tells Johnson, "Colonel, I pledge you de honor of a Gentlemen dat all de Gentlemen of Colour will support you." Of course, men of color could not vote, which is understood, but the main point portrayed Johnson as someone who sympathized with African Americans. To his right, an abolitionist reassures him by saying, "Be comforted Richard, all of the abolitionists will support thee." Support by abolitionists, viewed as radicals by both southerners and northerners, would have doomed the Van Buren/Johnson ticket, and that was the point. Farther to the left are two African American women, representing his two daughters with Julia Chinn. The one closest to him says to her sister, "Poor dear Pa show much he is affected," while the other hands Johnson a portrait of a Black woman in a turban and tells Johnson, "Here it is Pa, but don't take on so." Another man in the background ridicules Johnson's emotions, declaring, "Pickle!! Pop!! And Ginger!! Can the slayer of Tecumseh be thus overcome like a summer cloud! Fire and furies, oh!"[52]

Johnson's positions on racial equality continued to be used by politicians well after his death in 1850. In one of his famous debates with Stephen Douglas in 1858, Abraham Lincoln defended his stance on inequality between whites and Blacks by saying: "I will add to this that I have never seen to my knowledge a man, woman, or child who is in favor of producing perfect equality, social and political, between negroes and white men. I recollect of but one distinguished instance . . . Col. Richard M. Johnson." Lincoln's reference to Johnson resulted in roaring laughter from the audience.[53]

Trying to paint Johnson and Van Buren as radicals who supported an end to slavery or rights for African Americans would almost certainly have led some white men, maybe even Democrats, to turn their support to Henry Clay and the Whigs. Though William Johnson does not mention reading about Richard Johnson's personal life, given his political news consumption, it is reasonable to assume that he knew about his relationships and positions on African Americans. While it is not the case that Richard Johnson or the Van Buren administration was any more favorable to Blacks, free or enslaved, William Johnson might have been hopeful that the vice president had a more open view about race than his opponents, given his public statements. The Democrats dropped Richard Johnson from the ticket for the election of 1840. Still, the barber's admiration for Richard Johnson is evident in that he noted the politician's death in his diary in 1850 and named his second son, born in 1837, Richard.[54]

Even after the Panic of 1837 had taken a severe toll on Natchez and his own business, William Johnson expressed his support for Van Buren and the Democrats in 1840. In August 1840, Johnson wrote: "The Good Whig Citizens of this place is very active in Building a Log Cabbin on the Bluff this Evening, getting it ready for to morrow, for to morrow is the Grand Log Cabbin day. The town is all Excitement, oh what regoiceing."[55] This was a part of William Henry Harrison's "Log Cabin and Hard Cider" campaign, in which he tried to capture the same kind of political support that Jackson had: presenting himself as having grown up as an average American, living in a log cabin, and having similar tastes as ordinary people, although Harrison was from a wealthy family in Virginia. Johnson found the local expression of Whig support annoying and paid close attention to their sentiments in their meetings. The day after the construction of the log cabin, Johnson wrote: "Of all the Pomp of Nonsense and Splendid Foolishness that I Ever have seen, this Day exceeds all I am sory to see the Ladys Join in the Foolery. I have One wish and that is that the Democrats will Get a Large majority in Every State."[56] Even with this dislike for the Whigs, Johnson attended parts of their meetings and listened to their speeches. Some of the speeches he enjoyed, noting that one speaker gave "the Best [speech] that I have Ever Herd by a Wig" and that "The Language was Beautifully and Every Charge he made was I thought well Explained." Others he found disappointing, especially one that mocked "Poor Van Buren" as a "King, Lord, Master, Tyrant, Usurper, Rober, and Every thing that Could be Conceived or Imagined. I was much Disappointed in the man and I have very Little Doubt but what the argument made use [of] changed many to the opposite side."[57] Though he disagreed with the Whigs, Johnson appeared willing to hear their points at least and was ready to concede when they made a good case for their side. Even though he was not allowed to vote, he engaged with the process to the degree he could.

After the Log Cabin event, Johnson witnessed the political effect the speeches had on some of those in Natchez who could vote. The next morning, probably in his barbershop, Johnson heard, "Mr. Dobins this morning State and If Mr Van Buren was [reelected] that He was willing to Shoulder his musket and wage war against Him and His Party." Dobbins then asked "Mr L. Pitcher" if he agreed and was willing to take up arms against the government in the event of a Democratic victory. Pitcher replied: "no, not unless He was fraudulently Elected. He might then if it was required." Dobbins suggested that Pitcher might need to do so by comparing Van Buren to "George the Third." Johnson observed that other men nearby who heard the discussion and the Log Cabin speeches were "disgusted" and "half Left the Whig Ranks and will vote for Van Buren."[58] Johnson did not mention participating in this discussion between these white men. He almost certainly did not, as doing so might have hurt his business and would have been viewed as out of place for the free Black barber. Still, he was a shrewd observer of the political scene who understood the issues and had ideas about which party would be better for the country.

A few days later, Johnson reported that the Democrats had held a meeting at the courthouse after yet another session by the Whigs at the Log Cabin. Johnson had heard that "The Speech by Mr [Claibourne] yesterday is said to be very good and Eloquent, the Best that has been in the Court House for many a day and tis said to be the Best that Ever has been deliverd in the Court Hous."[59] The *Natchez Weekly Courier,* the Whig newspaper, was less complimentary of the courthouse meeting and reported: "The standing army, sub-treasury, silk-stocking spoilers held a meeting at the Courthouse yesterday, and as usual with said party, nothing was heard but vilification of Gen. Harrison and a cormorant senseless cry about bank! bank!" They also confirmed that Claibourne's speech was good because it did not attack Harrison. The Whig-supporting *Courier* republished an article from a Louisiana paper describing Van Buren as a supporter of "negro suffrage" and rejected the idea that he was a "northern man with southern principles." Moreover, they contended Van Buren had promoted rejecting Missouri's statehood unless they "would agree to liberate all slaves" and "to restrict the introduction of slavery in the Territory of Florida."[60] However untrue these positions were, Johnson favored "negro suffrage" though not on restrictions of slavery. Again, the coverage of the election that Johnson read about and experienced from locals drove him to support the Democrats.

After Harrison's victory, Johnson expressed his disappointment but still kept up with politics on the national level. Harrison's death complicated the most significant issue that the Whigs had run on, creating a Third Bank of the United States to improve the economy they argued Democrats had destroyed. In a move that confounded his fellow Whigs, the new president, John Tyler, vetoed the bill that would have created the bank. On August 27, 1841, Johnson noted: "Today has been a day of much interest to the Citizens of this place. The Veto of the Bank Bill reached this place to day and the Whigs are very much Disappointed whilst the Demmcrats are rejoicing at the veto— The people have something to do to day in the way of Talking Politics."[61]

In addition, Johnson kept up with other events relating to national issues and sometimes openly discussed his thoughts with white men. In 1842, Johnson wrote: "Mr T. Rose Came in the shope to night and we began and ta[l]ked untill After ten Oclock—The Subjects, Banks & Banking—prospects of war—money Loaning—insolvent people, England and the English—Slavry—Texas & Mexico."[62] Unfortunately, Johnson only gives the topics, not the details of the conversation. Still, unlike most southerners, he opposed Texas's annexation and, later, the Mexican War, complaining that the conflict had made his business "dull," but does not offer further explanation of why he disagreed with so many of his neighbors on the issue.[63]

Even though Johnson professed to "care very Little who is Elected" in the presidential election of 1844, he became more engaged as he found a way to combine his interest in politics with his primary hobby: he began betting on elections. Though most scholars have suggested that free men of color had to be silent regarding their political ideas, Johnson was confident enough to disagree with the men he bet with and put money on it. This was another way that Johnson asserted belonging in the body politic; he could not vote but could express himself through these bets. In putting stakes on these elections, Johnson engaged with white men politically but in a way that did not threaten the social order. In 1844, he wrote: "Clay Party [the Whigs] trying to get up a Strait Out party to be composed of Mechanicks, I made a bet with Mr Morgan of twenty five Dollars viz. He bets me that those ten states viz. will go for Mr. Clay as follows . . . and if One Single One of those did not he would Loose the Bet &c."[64] At first glance, it seems that Johnson had a much better chance of winning the bet since only one of the ten states named would have to go for James Polk, and he would win. Interestingly, Morgan was very accurate in selecting which states preferred Clay, but Johnson won the bet as New York chose Polk, the only one Morgan missed.

Betting on elections became fairly common practice for Johnson. He got his sister involved in the action when she bet John Jacquemine "a ten Dollar pr of Boots Vs. a ten Dollar Bonet that Mr Polk would be Elected President of the United States."[65] Between presidential elections, Johnson expanded to placing bets on local contests. In 1847, Johnson met Mr. Woods at his shop, who had asked the barber to come up with a list of voters who lived in the "Swamp," the area a few miles outside of Natchez where Johnson had begun farming. The following day, Johnson wrote: "Gen. Stanton and Mr S. Wood went to the Swamp to day to see the Swampers. I Sent Down a Bottle of Good Brandy and a Bottle of Clarret wine and Something to Eat in the way of Beef &c."[66] Had Johnson been white, this might not have been that usual, but a free man of color hosting an event for a white man running for office appealing to his white neighbors might be a unique occurrence in the antebellum South. A few days later, he followed up with several bets favoring Wood in the election: "I made the Following Bets to Night, 1st I bet that Mr Wood would beat both of his opponents, with Mr. Odell, 5.00, Then $25 that he would, same way, 25.00, I then bet $10 with Winston, same way, 10.00"[67] Odell was a white man, but Winston was one of Johnson's apprentices. Just as he had brought Winston along in the trade of barbering and other manly pursuits, he demonstrated that politics was something that free men of color could engage in, even if not in the same way that white men did.

Johnson continued betting on these local elections in 1847 and brought more of his apprentices into the activity. At the beginning of November, he wrote: "Plenty of Excitement to day on the Election &c. I have made

Several Bets on the Election to day and to night and some of them pretty wild ones, I do think—I have made so many Bets on this Election that I cannot now Recollect them all." These bets were particular, representing Johnson's compulsive gambling issues. He recalled: "Mr Darling paid me the stake that we won from Mr Odell of Franklin County. We bet it in this way—1st that $5 that Cs majority would be under 50 & $5 that it would be nearle 40 than 50 & $5 that it would be nearer 44 than 50." Another of his apprentices, Jeff Hoggatt, also bet Darling five dollars that he would lose one of these bets. While Johnson might have simply used elections as another way to satisfy his need to gamble, he was interested in the outcomes of most of the results beyond just the satisfaction of betting or winning. The day after recording these bets, he expressed: "We have news to day that Judge Sharkey will be Elected by a Large Majority of Jud[g]e Wilkerson, Good Good Certain" and "Judge Sharkey is Elected Shure—Now I am Glad of that. Honesty is the best Policy."[68]

Johnson continued supporting the Democrats in 1848 and resumed betting anyone who agreed to the terms. In October, he mentioned meeting Baylor Winn in the Swamp, and after some discussion with him, the two men made a bet on the election: "we bet a Hat on the Election He bet me that Cass would Get a Majority of 2000 over Gen Taylor in the State of Mississippi." This was not a bet that Taylor, the Whig, would win; instead, it was over how large a victory Cass would have. Winn was one of his neighbors and was sometimes listed as a white man and other times as a free man of color in various records. Johnson had provided Wood with Winn's name as one of the voters in the Swamp in 1847. Winn later claimed that he had voted in several elections while on trial for Johnson's murder. Over the next several days, Johnson bet with several other men, including Mr. Stump, a white man who worked on Johnson's farm, and other men in town. On October 21, he made another bet with precise terms, noting, "I Drew a bet this Evening with Mr Lacock where I had bet him that Gen Cass would get a majority of 1000 votes by Giving him 2.50 cts credit on his acct."[69] The same day, he gave Winston fifteen dollars to bet on the election, making it clear that his favorite apprentice had taken on another of the craftsman's traits.

William Johnson was acutely aware that he could not directly participate in elections by voting, but that did not stop him from participating in the process to the degree that he could. His interests in politics did not stem from copying the sentiments of whites with whom he associated. Adam Bing-aman, his closest planter associate, ran for office several times as a Whig. Instead, Johnson selected the party and individuals he thought most closely represented his interests as a free man of color. Though Democrats were not any more racially progressive than their opponents, Johnson found individuals within the party who appeared open to the ideas of expanding the ability of free Black men to participate in society.

Political Dissent: Colonization and the "Inquisition"

Although Johnson stood with his white neighbors and fellow Democrats on many issues, he diverged on others. One of these differences was over the colonization of freed people to Liberia. As was the case across the South, the proslavery reaction in Natchez against the abolitionist movement of the 1830s grew after the Nat Turner revolt. Free people of color became the favorite target of proslavery activists. One local editor stated: "If the free coloured people were removed, the slaves could be treated with more indulgence. Less fear would be entertained, and greater latitude of course allowed. . . . [I]n a word, it would make better masters and better slaves." At the same time, though, the author wrote, "From the same cause also results another evil: the check, or rather stop, which has been given to the emancipation of slaves, no matter how meritorious their conduct."[70] In other words, though the editor favored the removal of free Blacks from Natchez, he also lamented that enslaved people who deserved freedom for service or character would not have a chance at emancipation.

The idea of removing Natchez's small free Black population had been floated before in town. As early as 1824, one local newspaper ran a series of ads over twenty issues suggesting that free people of color should move to Haiti.[71] The ads did not convince free Blacks to leave, but they might have induced whites to look into the American Colonization Society (ACS), both as a means to solve what they believed to be a problem and also as a way to improve their reputations as benevolent philanthropists within the white community. Mississippians began contributing to the ACS in the late 1820s, but the founding of a state branch did not occur until June 1831; the first attempt failed as enslaved people in the Natchez area had the impression that the Society signaled their imminent emancipation. As a clergyman from Mississippi wrote, "This, in the opinion of the friends of

Colonization, rendered it necessary to suspend any effort of the kind until public opinion should be rectified, and until slaves should see that they had been imposed upon."[72]

The creation of the Mississippi Colonization Society (MCS) stemmed at least partly from a desire to remove "dangerous" free people of color to prevent the re-creation of the Nat Turner revolt near Natchez. Being an officer or contributor to the Mississippi Colonization Society became a signifier of elite status in Natchez. Stephen Duncan, the state's largest planter, a physician, and the president of the Bank of Mississippi, served as the president of the Society from 1831 to 1840. Duncan personally contributed fifty thousand dollars to the MCS by the end of that period. Other prominent contributors included Dr. John Ker (who, along with Duncan, served as vice president of the ACS), David Hunt, and James Green, each a well-established planter. Other officers included governors of the territory and state, a Speaker of the State House, and many of Mississippi's religious leaders.[73] Contrary to what some modern observers might think, joining the ACS or MCS represented a commitment to the institution of slavery, not an attack upon it. These societies did not liberate enslaved people: they removed free people of color from the United States based on the same kinds of racist ideas that allowed slavery to continue and thrive; that is, the belief that men and women of African heritage either could not compete with whites, that they were a threat to whites, or that their very presence was a threat to slavery. Additionally, the commitment of the ACS to spreading Christianity in Africa appealed to many whites.[74]

In order to succeed, the Society needed free Blacks' willingness to travel to Liberia. The majority of free people of color in the state lived in Natchez. The numbers throughout the antebellum period remained small, partly due to another addition to the legal code in 1831 requiring all newly freed Blacks to leave Mississippi unless they secured legal permission to stay. Furthermore, it became increasingly difficult for enslavers to emancipate slaves. The law required that the enslaved only be granted their freedom as a reward for meritorious actions if the person in question would not become a public charge.[75] These restrictions placed checks on the growth of the free Black population eligible participate in the MCS. There were no checks on white participation, however. The Society's 1832 report noted: "The Society is increasing in numbers, some subscriptions have been attained. . . . [T]his has had a happy effect; the free people of color in this neighborhood have become awakened to the subject. . . . They have called a meeting among themselves, appointed two of their own color to visit Liberia, to examine the country, and, make a report of the state and condition of the colony."[76]

The two selected for this trip were Gloster Simpson and Archy Moore, who visited the colony and reported back to the Methodist church at Natchez. Simpson and Moore encountered a warm welcome in Monrovia. After the local Methodist meeting, Simpson declared, "I seem to be born a second time, the heavens appear to open over our heads—everything looks kindly around us—this is indeed the home of the colored man!" After touring the town, their hosts showed the visitors the graves of white missionaries, which moved Simpson to ask, "Shall there not come from our *own* ranks, men to take their places and preach to our benighted brethren the gospel of Christ?" Answering his own question, Simpson vowed, "For one I am willing and determined to come." After a three-week stay, the visitor published the following:

> During a residence of nearly three weeks at Liberia, we visited the four principal settlements, in all which we found the settlers healthy, well pleased with their situation, and improving their circumstances very rapidly. A uniform expression of gratification, that they had found a place of freedom and comfort in Africa, was uttered without exception. Such was the impression made on our minds, of the advantages of emigration to this Colony, that we are determined to report favorably of the object, to those who sent us—and as the best testimony of our full persuasion of its great advantages, have determined to settle our business and remove thence, the first opportunity. We see our brethren there, *freemen,* and advanced to the full privilege of unrestrained enterprise and Christian liberty.[77]

Simpson kept this vow, returning to Monrovia with his wife, Abigail, and their two daughters in April 1835. Archy Moore's family made the trip as well.[78]

Simpson's endorsement might have convinced several free people of color in Mississippi to journey to Liberia, and 571 people eventually made their way to the colony. Nevertheless, Mississippi's free Black population never appreciably changed in size from the 1820s through 1840, while the MCS and ACS sponsored emigrants from the state. The reason for this is twofold: many free Blacks had formed family and community ties that they did not wish to leave, and owners began striking deals with the men and women they enslaved that would send these newly freed people to Liberia. John Ker observed that this was more likely as "laws will probably be made in the slaveholding states to prevent emancipation, except on condition of immediate emigration to Liberia." Though no law stating that freed people must immediately remove to Africa passed in Mississippi, the state required that free people leave upon release from bondage. Colonization offered one option. Ker asked rhetorically, "Will not the hands of slavery be strengthened as to those who shall remain, except from the only ground of hope to the slave, the voluntary act of his master?" Ker felt that colonization would shift from the repatriation of free people to the emancipation of enslaved people to strengthen slavery by removing the example of free Blacks, who he believed "created many evils," and offering an incentive for slaves to behave well to secure passage to Liberia.[79]

Though many of Natchez's whites and some free people of color supported the ACS and MCS, William Johnson did not, but not for the same reasons northern free Blacks opposed colonization. For men like David Walker, among the most famous opponents of the ACS, rejecting colonization was rooted in attacking slavery, and Johnson was decidedly proslavery. Walker's direct call for Black men to resist slavery represented a form of masculine self-assertion recognized by many Black abolitionists in the nineteenth century: to be a man, Black men had to stand up for themselves against white oppression. Johnson rejected this form of manliness, and though his biographers and generations of historians have contended that this was because he aspired to white values, this ignores the sentiments he wrote in his diary.[80] If Johnson, or any free man of color in Natchez, publicly declared his belief in the equality of whites and Blacks in the antebellum era, he would have been jailed, removed from the state, or killed based on the state's laws and the sentiments of whites in the town. Still, Johnson privately opposed measures restricting free people of color and did what he could to improve conditions for his community when they were under attack. In 1838, he wrote: "to day was the day the Collinizationest had a Large meeting and here is the names of some of the Leading Parties or Head Dogs in the Bone Yard—Tis a pitty that they [are] not doing something Else better for there Country."[81] Johnson's opposition to colonization stemmed from how these societies viewed free people of color. Ker's support for colonization is best illustrated in a letter he wrote to a friend in Louisiana in 1831 stating, "The free colored people are more injurious to society than the same number of slaves, and their removal must therefore confer a greater benefit."[82] For Johnson and other free Blacks in Natchez, the idea that freedom could only be obtained by leaving the country was unthinkable and an insult to all he worked for in terms of his business and establishing his reputation. By calling these men "Head Dogs in the Bone Yard" Johnson intentionally did not refer to them as gentlemen or men of good character, though he did express admiration for them in other instances.

In another case, Johnson supported Ker's efforts in securing the freedom of hundreds of men and women whom Isaac Ross had enslaved, but these people were in a very different situation than his community of free people of color. Ker, a member of the ACS and a Mississippi state senator, wrote a letter in the *Natchez Weekly Courier* detailing Ross's will and the legislature's attempts to prevent its execution. Johnson remarked that Ker's letter and actions were "a Splendid thing."[83] At the time of his death in 1836, Ross owned between 160 and 170 enslaved people. Upon the death of his daughter Margaret Reed, his will offered all of them the option to become free and move to Liberia. Ross placed the following codicil in his will:

And it is my will and desire then and in that event [that those enslaved would choose to go to Liberia], that the entire balance of my estate, both real, personal and mixed, excepting always Grace and her children, Hannibal, Daphne, Dinah, Rebecca, Enoch and Merrilla and her children, be exposed to sale at public auction, one month's public notice being first given thereof in the papers printed at Port Gibson and Natchez, and the same sold on the following terms, to wit: one half of the purchase money to be paid in cash and the other half in twelve months from the day of sale, bond and unexceptionable security to be required of the purchasers, and to be judged of by my executors. It is further my will and desire that the proceeds of the sale, together with any money that may be on hand at the time of my decease, and any that may be owing to me, after deducting the amounts necessary for the payment of the legacies herein bequeathed, and all necessary expenses that may be incurred, be paid over to the American Colonization Society, provided they will agree to appropriate it in the following manner, to wit: First, to pay the expense of transporting my slaves to Africa; and, secondly, to expend the remainder for the support and maintenance of said slaves when there, the same to be done in such manner as the Society in their discretion may deem most to the interest and welfare of said slaves.[84]

The will did not require all of the people Ross enslaved to go to Liberia; instead, it offered them this opportunity for freedom or the option of remaining unfree and being sold to support the transportation and upkeep of the rest on their trip to the American colony in Africa.[85]

In keeping with the State of Mississippi's interpretation of wills during the 1830s, Ross had no reason to suspect that any legal issue would interfere with the execution of his will. Had the will not been explicit in granting these people the choice to go to Liberia only after Reed's death, there may have been no problem. Several of Ross's executors were displeased with the will but took no legal action until after Margaret Reed died in 1838. Before her death, and likely understanding the conflict concerning the will, Reed bequeathed her father's estate to Zebulon Butler and Stephen Duncan, two men committed to colonization. Jane Ross and Isaac Ross Wade, the surviving heirs, filed suit against Duncan and Butler, who intended to fulfill the wishes of those enslaved by Ross to emigrate to Liberia. Isaac Ross Wade and Jane Ross's attorneys claimed that Isaac Ross attempted to circumvent state law by freeing his slaves without the legislature's permission. In addition, Jane Ross's attorneys argued that Ross had willed the slaves to the American Colonization Society, which they declared was illegal since the ACS, by charter, only existed to transport free Blacks to Liberia, not to own or emancipate enslaved people. Finally, they insisted that while Margaret Reed could have sent the enslaved people to Liberia while she was living, she did not do so. Thus she had left them enslaved within Mississippi, where they had to remain enslaved since the legislature had not granted permission to emancipate them.[86]

In 1840, the Mississippi High Court of Errors and Appeals ruled against the Ross heirs, maintaining that the will did not intend to free the Ross slaves in Mississippi. Justice Trotter ruled that this case was not about "the character" of the enslaved people involved in the case but a matter of resolving whether colonizing and freeing slaves was in accordance with the state's laws and the maintenance of slavery. The ruling did not dissuade some from resisting Ross's right to send these men and women to Liberia. The following year, the state legislature declared that allowing the people Ross enslaved to leave the state set a dangerous precedent. By 1842, this sentiment had grown such that the state passed a law forbidding the manumission of slaves by will. Isaac Ross Wade also continued to fight, claiming that he had five hundred armed men willing to use force to stop these people's departure. Opinion in Natchez had shifted so strongly against colonization by the end of this case that Stephen Duncan allegedly directed the enslaved people Reed had granted him to run away and hide along the Mississippi River until he could arrange a boat to transport them across to Louisiana. He planned to find a ship from Louisiana to transfer the former Ross slaves to Africa.[87]

Duncan never had to enact the plan because of the ruling, yet the Ross/Reed slaves did not leave the United States until 1848. The litigation cost contributed to the delay as most of the money left to secure transport to Liberia was used for the court battle. Once the ACS had raised enough money to send the emigrants to Africa, they went on two ships. The first, the *Nehemiah Rich,* set sail from New Orleans on January 7, 1848, with thirty-five formerly enslaved people aboard. The majority (141) released from bondage by the settlement had to wait another year to leave and suffered a cholera outbreak in New Orleans, killing many on the long journey to Liberia.[88]

Johnson's support of Ker's efforts was not an endorsement of colonization but instead was based on granting the freedom promised to these people. Unlike himself, his family, and the rest of his community of free people of color, the people that Ross enslaved would not have the opportunity to live outside of bondage based on the will and state law. By the 1840s, even manumitting slaves in a will to colonize Africa conflicted with the institution of slavery, at least in many white southerners' minds. The proslavery argument that slavery was a "positive good" for all involved echoed throughout Mississippi, even among those who had viewed slavery as a "necessary evil" in prior decades. John Quitman, a prominent lawyer and politician who had once said that slavery was inhumane, had changed his mind by the late 1830s, declaring that the people of Mississippi had chosen "to retain, the institution of domestic slavery" and that "the morality, the expediency, and the duration of the institution of slavery, are questions which belong exclusively to ourselves."[89] Johnson lived through these changes and lamented how much they restricted the lives of free people of color.

The most disturbing of these restrictions began in Natchez in 1841 as town authorities threatened the freedom of all Black men and women in the town, which Johnson called "the Inquisition." This attack on free Blacks' rights came to a head in 1841 after several whites were killed in St. Louis by a group of free Black men. Four free men of color conspired to rob a store and a bank near the Mississippi River and, in the course, killed several whites and set fire to the properties. The *Missouri Republican* reported that "every one was shocked at the enormity and boldness of the deed, and felt, that whilst such crimes could be committed in our midst and the guilty escape detection, there was no security to any one." When the news of the crime reached Natchez, whites attempted to instill a sense of security in the town by lashing out at the entire free Black community. Public meetings demanded that authorities ban Black rivermen from landing in the town. Working-class whites complained that enslavers allowed enslaved people to live in virtual freedom by hiring out their own time, and the practice hurt the ability of white men to earn a living. A letter submitted to the *Mississippi Free Trader* complained that local courts had been disregarding the law and defeating the purpose of "the non-accumulation of free negroes in the State" and that "in this condition we believe are at least fifty negroes and mulattoes now in Adams County, who affect to be free." The author of the letter, who signed his name as "Civis," complained, "It is a matter of notoriety, that within the last five years a large number of slaves in this county have been thus *illegally* manumitted; and after having gone up the river, and set their foot upon the soil of Ohio or some other free or abolition State, received from them certain certificates which are called "free papers"; forthwith they return to Mississippi, to reside as "free people of color."[90] The *Natchez Courier* directly addressed free people of color and the enslaved, informing them that a "general meeting of the citizens of Adams County" would be held to enforce laws against slaves hiring their own time and "the propriety of . . . enforcing the 80th section of this same code [the revised code of the laws of Mississippi], requiring free persons of color to remove from the State."[91]

These newspaper articles were correct that enslavers transported men and women they enslaved to other states to emancipate them and that people were living in town as free who had not legally acquired their freedom, a practice so common that it was known as the "Natchez method."[92] For free people of color with trades and established reputations, maintaining connections within the community allowed them to remain in town even if their claims of freedom might not have held up in court. For men like Johnson, who had proof of his legal freedom and deep connections with both the Black and white communities, leaving town and starting over, even in a northern town, made little sense. Families like the Johnsons or McCarys had little to worry about, even when public opinion toward free Blacks became especially hostile. This was not the case for everyone. In 1834, Fanny Leiper became free though her owner took no action to ensure this was legal. In the same year, Fanny purchased a lot in Natchez for $150; by 1836, she had built a house on the lot valued at $1,500. Understanding the precarious nature of her status, Leiper had the deed of ownership written such that Joseph Winscott, a white steamboat engineer, was also listed as an owner to protect her property should it be discovered that she was not legally free. Wisely, Leiper never informed Winscott that his name appeared on the deed.[93]

Fanny Leiper lived in Natchez, apparently with her status unquestioned, until 1845, when she moved to Cincinnati. As an unmarried woman, Leiper could not form the connections within the community that Johnson could through shared masculine pursuits. Rather than selling her home, Fanny contracted Samuel R. Hammitt to rent the house. Shortly after leaving for Ohio, Leiper's neighbor, Malvina Hoffman, a free woman of color with whom Fanny had a close relationship, leaked the news to Winscott that he legally co-owned the property. Hoffman and Winscott then obtained the keys to the home and began renting it out and splitting the profits. When Leiper discovered the betrayal, she returned to Natchez and filed suit against Hoffman and Winscott to regain her property. The defendants did not deny committing this act and even acknowledged that Winscott had never lived in Natchez and did not act as a part-owner before Leiper's move. Instead, they argued that Leiper was not legally free and thus could not own property. The chancery court of Natchez ruled against Leiper. On appeal, however, the state supreme court reversed the ruling, noting: "If she had gone to Ohio merely for the purpose of establishing her freedom, with the intention of returning here to act as a free person, there would have been force in this objection. But it is not shown that she left this State with the intention of returning." The act of moving to Ohio made Leiper free and capable of holding property, so the court ruled that the property and all profits made from renting the house were returned to her. Had she remained in Natchez or attempted to return permanently, she would have had no recourse, and the home would have reverted to Winscott.[94]

Mississippi's laws worked against enslavers who wanted to release people from bondage and people like Fanny Leiper to prevent anyone from being Black and free in the state. Despite experiencing the same shifts in imperial control as Louisiana, Mississippi did not follow its neighbor's more permissive laws toward free people of color. The first code of laws for the Mississippi Territory, written in 1789, did not differ substantially from those of other territories controlled by the United States. It declared that all people of African heritage were presumed enslaved unless proven otherwise. The burden of proving freedom in Mississippi rested with the free Blacks in question, and as such, a lack of documentation could force free people of color into a state of servitude.[95]

Consequently, legal barriers made founding and maintaining a free Black community on the eastern side of the Mississippi more difficult than in Louisiana. In Louisiana, a "mulatto" was any person with one-fourth or more "negro blood," but under Mississippi law, mixed parentage was legally the same as being born to two parents of African ancestry. At least under the law, what mattered in Natchez and the rest of the Mississippi was whether a person had legal documentation certifying freedom, not the appearance of mixed ancestry. Free people of color were required to present themselves to the local court and prove their freedom to receive a certified document. Without the certificate proving freedom, they could be seized and sold as a slave, as it was the duty of citizens to apprehend runaways.[96]

A law passed in 1822 settled the question of legal emancipation. Under this law, enslaved people could be emancipated via a will or a legal action requiring documentation and witnesses and a special act of the state legislature. William Johnson became legally free via one of these acts, but after 1822, such cases became rarer. In 1823, only three people gained their freedom through the legislature; in 1826, there were twelve petitions for emancipation, and none was successful. Jacques Andres's attempt to free an enslaved girl illustrates the difficulties created by these circumstances. Andres issued a petition in 1822 seeking to emancipate "a female 'mulatto' slave who is the daughter of Ema, a slave owned by the petitioner." The girl, Maria Louisa, born in 1820, "was regularly baptized according to the Holy ordinances of the Roman Catholic Church." Appealing to a mixed ancestry and religious devotion might have earned Maria Louisa her freedom in Louisiana, but Mississippi rejected the petition.[97]

When "Civis" complained of people freed in other states returning to Natchez, he meant people like the Brazealle family, who did not find Mississippi a forgiving environment. In 1826, Elisha Brazealle left Mississippi and moved to Ohio, where he emancipated an enslaved woman and her son.

Brazealle acknowledged that he was the father of John Monroe Brazealle and willed all of his property to this child. Later, the family moved back to Mississippi, and the mother and child's freedom fell into dispute. This case, brought before the Supreme Court of Mississippi, posed two questions: was the manumission of John Monroe Brazealle and his mother in Ohio legal in Mississippi, and could he legally inherit his father's estate? The answer to the first question determined the second; if John Monroe Brazealle was not free, he could not own property. The court ruled that the act of emancipation might have been legitimate, but only if John Monroe and his mother had remained in Ohio. Since Elisha Brazealle had not secured the Mississippi legislature's permission, the two remained enslaved, and as such, John Monroe could not inherit his father's estate.[98]

Although the law had always favored limiting the number of free Blacks in Mississippi, the state legislature responded to Nat Turner's revolt by labeling free Blacks dangerous and undesirable. Along with restricting movement and employment for free people of color, lawmakers also sought to diminish their numbers by limiting manumissions and requiring freed people to leave the state, effectively strengthening provisions against free Blacks enacted in 1822. Free Blacks could petition local boards of police to remain within the state if they could find a reputable white citizen to attest to their worthy characters.[99]

The killings in St. Louis in 1841 intensified whites' distrust toward free Blacks and led them to look for threats within Natchez's free Black community. For several weeks during the summer, free people of color were brought before the police board to prove that they were legally permitted to live within the town. Johnson noted that on August 17, 1841, there were "all sorts of Tryals [sic] going on. The different offices has been full all day and they Continue to arrest Still—The Lord Knows how these things will terminate for I have no Conception myself." Johnson had no reason to fear being arrested as the legislature manumitted him. He was among the best-established free men of color, socially and economically, in the town; however, many of those he associated with were at risk. On August 18, 1841, Johnson reported that "the Harrows [horrors] of the Inquisition" were "still going on in this city" but that he was thankful that rumors of the arrest of "Harriet Cullen or Harriet Johnson" were not true. Like William Johnson, Harriet Johnson (not related and the same person as Harriet Cullen) had been legally emancipated and was a property holder.[100]

Several of Johnson's close associates were put on trial in the coming days, with some ordered to leave the city within thirty or sixty days. Johnson appeared unworried but confessed to his diary that there was "Something about this Law" he did not understand, "for the Report Seys [*sic*] that a Bond is required After the Lycences [*sic*] is obtained. I cannot understand the matter fully." To secure their positions as free, Johnson observed, "lotts of F.P.C. are running around Town with Petitions to have the Priveledge [*sic*] of [remaining] in the state, tis Laug[h]able almost." Among those "running around" was Wellington West, Johnson's friend who sometimes worked in his barbershop. West secured several signatures from leading planters to enable him to stay in Natchez. Johnson remarked that "those names are enough to make any Common man Proud—Those Names are an Ornament to Any Paper—Those are Gentlemen of the 1st Order of Talents and Standing."[101] White men of similar standing offered their support to Johnson and his family. Major J. Shields, whom Johnson described as "One of Our Noble, Generous and Gentlemanly young men," visited Johnson during the height of the Inquisition and offered his protection. However, Johnson told Shields that he would let him know if he needed assistance and added, "such men as he is, is an ornament to Society."[102] Shields's description and the compliments he paid to those who supported West were probably genuine expressions, but Johnson never worried about being forced from his home. For so many free people of color, leaving their homes, even for the North, represented a change they were unwilling to make, and some even took drastic steps to remain. As Emily West has observed, some free Blacks took the drastic step of petitioning to become enslaved to stay close to family and remain in their communities.[103] Undoubtedly, Johnson's confidence resulted from his understanding of his legal status and the support he could have gotten from men in town had he needed it, but it more subtly represents an attack on the Inquisition. If so many of the town's leading men were willing to step forward and support free people of color, then the reasoning behind the Inquisition itself was problematic.

Other free Blacks who had lived in Natchez without incident for most of their lives found themselves under attack. On September 9, Johnson reported that "poor Andrew Leeper was, I understand, ordered off today, and so was Dembo and Maryan Gibson. They are as far as I Know innocent and Harmless People And Have never done a Crime since they have been in this state that I have heard of." Mary Ann Gibson was likely the daughter of Samuel Gibson and a woman named Esther, both of whom were free people of color. When Samuel Gibson died in 1823, he willed his estate to "the issue of my Body begotten on free woman of color named Esther." Dembo worked for the Gibsons after gaining his freedom in Ohio. The Leipers were a large free Black family in Natchez. Some of this family gained their freedom from Charles Lynch, former governor of Mississippi, who freed Robert Leiper Sr., along with his wife and daughter, in 1826. Lynch then entered agreements that allowed the Leipers to purchase other family members from his estate. According to Johnson, Andrew Leiper had nothing more than a bill of sale between Mary Leiper (Andrew's mother) and Lynch to prove his freedom. Lynch had agreed to allow Mary to purchase Andrew for two hundred dollars, of which Mary paid all but fifty cents. Of the situation, Johnson observed, "I see very plainly that Lynch Can do as he pleases in the affair—Oh what a country we live in."[104] The town's most prosperous free people of color realized they could not maintain their relative privilege and speak out against the Inquisition. Still, at least privately, Johnson was angry over the increasingly harsh treatment afforded to members of his community.

Amid the Inquisition, news reached Natchez of another episode of racial violence in Cincinnati. Johnson wrote: "Old Peetor Boiso arrived from Cincinnatti Bringing news of a Cincinnattii mob that had taken Place Just has [as] he Left He Says that 2 Darkies and 1 white man was quarrelling and the 2 Darkies Killed the white man." Afterward, the two assailants fled to a Methodist church and had a shoot-out with a group of citizens, resulting in "them Killing 14 or 15 white Citizens." Like the event in St. Louis that precipitated the Inquisition, the rumored Cincinnati violence could lead to even more legal and perhaps extralegal actions against people of color in town. The following day, Johnson noted, "Every body is inquiring about the Cincinanatti news—we have nothing very authentic from thare yet."[105] The *Free Trader* reported details of several men wounded in a riot that seems to have happened after the initial shoot-out that Johnson heard about and declared, "a member of Capt. Rehfus' German Company, was way-laid and attacked on his road home, by a party of blacks who beat him very severely." Johnson, however, had become increasingly skeptical of the whole event, writing in his diary, "Every acct. we have Lessens the number and I would not be Great Surprised to find it all a Lie."[106] The next day, the newspaper reported: "The violence of the populace was restrained by the military. . . .

About 300 negroes had taken refuge in the jail and jail-yard where they were protected by a guard."[107] Johnson was correct that the story of what happened in Cincinnati was unclear, and perhaps for that reason, this did not lead to further actions against free people of color or at least efforts beyond what they could already expect.

The Inquisition appears to have run its course by the end of September 1841, but Johnson noted the consequences for free people of color. In 1844, Johnson wrote: "Grafton Baker another individual who Flourished here in the way of the Inquisition a few years ago is now in the work house in New Orleans for vagrancy. He was bare footed when I herd from him Last."[108] Baker, who had done well in Natchez, had been forced out of town by the Inquisition and wound up destitute. As Johnson observed, the move against his community had destroyed lives. He also wrote of a trial between "a Mr Gibson" and "the Daughter of Poor Old Sam Gibson, who the world knows to be free." This was Mary Ann Gibson, whom Johnson mentioned as having been "sent off" during the Inquisition. As Johnson expressed, Mary Ann Gibson had lived as a free woman in Natchez for years before the Inquisition.[109] When forced to leave Natchez, Mary Ann and her mother "went Out to stay with this Gibson and now he puts up a Claim to her, by Saying that Sam G. her father belonged to his Father and that he had went out of the State and was set free and returned to it again." This confusing account implies that Mary Ann Gibson and her mother moved in with a white family, also named Gibson, as a result of the Inquisition and that this white family had, at one point, owned Samuel Gibson. Samuel Gibson's return to Mississippi after being freed elsewhere was commonplace before the 1830s for free people of color. It replicated the means by which so many people became manumitted in Natchez, including Johnson's mother and sister. In the court case, the white Gibson claimed that Mary Ann Gibson's father had belonged to his family and that, in returning to Mississippi, "he became the Property of the Said Gibson," which resulted, in Johnson's understanding, because of "Some old Law passed so seys Potter in 1807." The court found in favor of the white man, and thus Mary Ann Gibson, who had been a free woman, became his slave. Johnson, exasperated that the court had taken her freedom, remarked, "Greate God, what a Country."[110] Though Johnson never expressed any fears that the Inquisition would target him or his family, he noted those who suffered life-changing consequences due to the event.

Even after the Inquisition, white inhabitants frequently made public statements against the activities of the town's free Black population. The *Natchez Courier* ran an article in 1849 directed at "Public Interest" that stated: "We have been requested by several gentlemen to publish the fourth and fifth sections of a law to be found on page 948 of Hutchinson's Digest, the existence of which they incline to believe has been entirely forgotten by those who should have in it most frequent remembrance. We cheerfully publish it for the satisfaction of our friends in particular and the information of the community in general." The laws that the paper printed dealt with free people of color and enslaved people: the fourth stated it was "Not lawful for slaves or Free Persons of Color to keep House of Entertainment ... or to vend any goods, wares, merchandise, or spiritous liquors ... on conviction thereof ... [the offender] shall be liable to, and receive not less than twenty or more than fifty lashes" for each offense. The fifth made it clear that "it shall be the duty of each and every constable and Justice of the Peace, in this state ... [to] prosecute every violation of this act" and failure to do so would result in a fine "not exceeding fifty dollars."[111] While the article might have satisfied those who complained about people of color operating these establishments or selling merchandise, the fact that they still were doing this, even if they might have been outside of the law, illustrates two things: first, that the town's whites were willing to ignore the law and trade with people of color if it suited their interests, and, second, that the Inquisition, though disruptive to the free community of color, did not destroy it.

Via his barbershop, Johnson helped young men develop into responsible members of this community. When political attacks like the Inquisition or even the racist underpinnings of colonization threatened that community, he resisted as much as possible. In 1850, Johnson wrote, "It was to day that I paid Mr Newman Hester Cummings tax which was four dollars and fifty cents."[112] The sum was small, but actions like this demonstrate that Johnson did not hold himself separate from other less fortunate people in Natchez. Instead, he sympathized with them and took action when he was able. After the Inquisition's intensity had died down, Johnson wrote of another instance of charity he performed. In 1844, he wrote: "Lawyer Baker this day has Gotten two dimes from me and as good [as] begged me for them; he is nearly in rags and is gone from the paths that he Once moved in How the mighty has fallen, but a short time ago and he was a sword persecutor of the Poor Friendless Colord."[113] Johnson's entry shows not just a

THE BARBER OF NATCHEZ RECONSIDERED

measure of satisfaction that Baker was now in the same kind of pitiful shape that many people of color were in as a result of the inquisition, but also it clearly shows which side of this conflict he was on and whom he viewed as members of his community.

Conclusion

Besides his discussion of the annexation of Texas and the Mexican War, Johnson only dealt with international politics in one brief entry on Haiti. In 1849 he wrote: "Nothing very new more than The Republic of St. Domingo has changed her Destinnys very much for the worse by Proclaiming Her President Emperor, So Seys the report, but I hope tis not true, Soluke is a very Dark man, a Black Man and has a wife and one Daughter to this date."[114] Johnson referred to Faustin Élie Soulouque, who declared himself emperor for life and took the name Faustin I, and, as Johnson feared, he ruled with brutality.[115] Johnson's attention to international topics stemmed from his self-interest. Generally, he opposed all three things he mentioned: he was against the annexation of Texas, the Mexican War, and Soulouque's overthrow of the Haitian Republic. His opposition to expansion partly came from the sense that locals in Natchez went to fight and that these conflicts hurt his business. His opposition to Soulouque's actions is more complicated than the others. On the one hand, he lamented the fall of a republic, especially a republic founded and operated by men of African heritage (Soulouque was born in Africa, brought to Saint-Domingue via the transatlantic slave trade, and fought in the Revolution). On the other, though, Johnson mentioned that Soulouque was "a very Dark man, a Black Man," indicating a sense of racial difference from himself. While Johnson does not elaborate beyond "I hope tis not true," given his other political feelings on matters of race, it is entirely possible that Johnson was more concerned about the former than the latter; that is, he was more worried that the second republic in the Western Hemisphere operated by free men of color like himself had fallen.

William Johnson was acutely aware that he was prevented by Mississippi's racist laws from voting, holding office, or serving on juries. However, he still asserted his will and participated in Natchez's politics. Though white men used full citizenship to create the fiction that all white men were created equal, this was also a conscious choice to keep all women and all nonwhite men excluded. As Johnson's life clarifies, there are multiple ways to assert belonging in the body politic. Johnson was politically conscious and participated to the extent that he could, relied on the law, performed his civic duties, attended speeches, held a political event in the country, bet on elections, harbored anticolonization thoughts, and did his best to resist and keep track of the Inquisition. None of this activity suggests that he meekly stood by and watched as whites determined what was possible for himself, his family, and his community. Moreover, Johnson expressed his views via betting with whites or holding the election event for whites at his farm. In other cases, he articulated his anger during the Inquisition and kept track of the men and women who suffered. There is no doubt that Johnson had white friends and respected several others, but this does not mean that he always agreed with them and feared repercussions if he differed from them. Even at the height of the Inquisition, Johnson expressed no worry about his position. His security resulted from his respectable reputation as a businessman and his relationships with white men in manly competitions. He was a careful and shrewd observer of local politics and understood how to position himself within that system. His neighbors knew that Johnson was on board with them in their civic duties to one another because he participated in them. He conformed to the law and used it when he needed to, even when he had to go to court against whites. As with other aspects of his life, Johnson found a way to assert himself in Natchez's political life.

CHAPTER FOUR

Protecting and Providing for a Family

MOST OF THE LIFE Johnson wrote about was male-dominated—his business, hunting, fishing, gambling, other competitions, and even politics—but he also had multiple roles as the head of a growing family. He was a husband, father, son, brother, uncle, and surrogate father to his apprentices. As with his other roles, Johnson took his responsibilities with his family seriously and centered this around protecting his free Black family within a slave society. Across the United States, but most especially in the South, denying Black men traditional masculine functions associated with being a husband and father, particularly as the family's breadwinner, public voice, and protector, became a way to perpetuate slavery and enforce white supremacy. Though enslaved males could be fathers and husbands, their children and wives were legally the owner's property. Families only remained together at the whim of the enslaver; market conditions, the enslaver's death, or simple vindictiveness could split a family. Slavery, then, necessarily limited several of the behaviors that marked men in the minds of southern whites.[1]

Johnson's roles in his family necessarily differed from that of enslaved men because of his freedom, but protecting his family's freedom required constant effort. Though Johnson's diary deals far more with his business and social interests than with his family, when he did write about his children, wife, mother, and sister, it usually had to do with protecting them in the present or setting up his children for future success. Johnson's position as a husband and father closely resembles what Libra R. Hilde calls "paternal honor," an expression of manhood that relies on taking care of others rather than dominating them. In her study of enslaved fathers, Hilde found that, while all admired "heroic resistance" to slavery, "formerly enslaved people recognized the diverse ways in which men provided for and protected their children," and that they "praised caretaking men who invested in their children not just materially, but emotionally."[2] Johnson's family roles reveal how Black men asserted their masculinity and that individuals found multiple ways of performing their manliness.

Johnson's parents did not always offer a positive model to follow. His father had some relationship with the family, but despite freeing his children and their mother, he did not provide any kind of defense for his free Black family in a town and state that often detested their very existence. References to his father are infrequent compared to other family members and indicate that the two did not have an especially close relationship. His mother, Amy, however, was a different story. She lived in Natchez her entire life, and she and her son frequently interacted, though often those dealings were tense or even hostile. Amy Johnson had a license "to retail in Natchez," and like her son, she enslaved people, some of whom worked within her house, but she hired others out in town for profit.[3] William Johnson frequently assisted his mother in financial matters, loaning her money or helping her with other issues, but he mostly worried about her volatile temper. Her outbursts, often public, could threaten her freedom. His concern for limiting her exposure to legal or social punishment defined most of their relationship in William's adulthood.

William and his wife, Ann Battles Johnson, had ten children during their marriage. Though surely rooted in love, Johnson's choice of a marriage partner also held additional significance: marriages between free people of color were recognized by law, unlike those of the enslaved. By marrying, the couple distanced themselves from enslaved men and women and guaranteed that any children they had would be born free, something imperative for two people born into slavery. Biracial children like Ann Battles and William Johnson legally had no father when they were born, a condition their children did not experience. Even though their town, state, and increasingly the entire South viewed free Black people with suspicion and often outright hostility, the Johnsons managed to raise and protect a large family.[4]

William's success as a barber eventually allowed the couple to build and live in a three-story brick house in downtown Natchez. Primarily using the labor of men they enslaved, Johnson constructed a two-story brick structure containing a kitchen and place for the people they owned to live behind the family's residence. The home still stands in Natchez today and is a museum dedicated to the barber's life. Though not as elaborate as the many surviving antebellum homes of the wealthiest families in Natchez, it is an impressive structure. Like those mansions, it contains period furnishing and personal items. Even if the house was not as large or well-appointed as Natchez's many mansions, it remains a testament to Johnson's considerable wealth for a man of color in the South. In addition to the material comforts that Johnson provided his family, he also offered cultural opportunities for his children that many whites in town could not afford or might not have valued as much as Johnson did. He taught his children to read and sent them to private tutors and schools. Books, newspapers, and magazines surrounded them. They attended art lessons and received instruction using the family's several musical instruments. Natchez was a stop for several traveling shows, including a circus, which the children, and their parents, attended.[5]

Like most wives in the era, Ann Johnson operated the household, but William was involved in his children's education and socialization. He noted several times in his diary giving lessons directly to the children, and as his sons aged, he began taking them with him on hunting and fishing trips with their extended family and friends. Bringing his sons along on these trips integrated them into the community of men their father valued. They could see his example, those of their uncle and other free men of color, and the various white men who were often present. Johnson was also responsible for disciplining his children when they acted out, fought with others, or did not conform to his rules. Johnson's sons William, Richard, and Byron all learned the barber's trade and practiced it as adults.[6] He focused on his role as a protector of his children, teaching the boys how to behave in a masculine world that equated their racial background with slavery.

Amy Johnson and Her Long-Suffering Son

William Johnson spent a fair amount of space in his diary complaining about people who did not live up to his expectations, but no one exasperated him more than his mother. The white William Johnson freed her in Louisiana in 1814, and she, Adelia, and William lived in a separate household from the children's father in Natchez. White William Johnson's interactions with Amy are unclear.[7] Amy traded small items, bought, hired out, and sold enslaved men and women. Johnson's biographers described her as "illiterate" and claimed that "she seemed to possess few attributes that would move her son to compassion or love."[8] Of course, bonds between parents and children are more complicated than this, and it is not usually the case that they have to earn the love of one another. William loved his mother, but he also felt responsible for maintaining her lifestyle, especially her freedom. Though Amy was independent, her status as a single woman of color could put her at disadvantages unknown to her son; regardless of race, William's reputation as a respectable man conferred benefits that she never had.

Amy did not make it easy for her son to help on her behalf. She maintained her separate household but frequently overextended herself financially, and William had to step in to help. In 1836, he wrote, "Loaned Mother $100 to Pay Mr Murcheson for the woman Mary & her child Moses." She purchased the woman and her child for eight hundred dollars on installments. A few months later, he complained, "Mother mislaid or Lost A Receipt for $400 that she paid Mr Murcherson for Mary." His concern over the loss of the receipt might have been out of a fear of losing the money he had loaned her, but more likely was out of concern that she might not be able to confirm ownership of the two enslaved people and could lose them if challenged. The transaction was more complicated because Amy did not buy Mary to keep in her household but instead hired out her time. Just before hiring Mary out and again in 1836, Johnson recorded loaning his mother another one hundred dollars, in both instances toward the agreement to buy Mary and Moses. Still, even afterward, he found, "This Leaves a Balance Due Mr Murcherson of $70."[9] Out of the purchase price of eight hundred dollars, William loaned his mother three hundred dollars. She might have paid back some of this money during the year, but he does not mention that, perhaps indicating that she would pay him back when Mary began earning money or that he never expected to be paid back. Johnson noted that his mother had paid him fifty dollars on a loan he had made her, but that may or may not have been the same one.

Regardless of the decision on this particular purchase, William frequently had to settle his mother's debts. A few days after buying Mary, Johnson also "Loaned Mother $20 to pay Selser the Butcher," and then a few months after that: "I paid Mr Mitchell to day $100 for Mother, it was a note that she owed to Mr Merritt Williams for Dinah. I was the Indorser on the Note."[10] In both cases, the men came to William rather than Amy for payment. It is possible that they approached Amy first, and she either referred them to her son or could not pay, and these men turned to William as a result. Businesspeople reaching out to Johnson to pay his mother's debts was not uncommon. In 1843, the firm of "Patterson & Wiswall" came to him "to Know if they Could by any way Collect $40 that Mothers owed them for goods," and two days later, John G. Taylor approached him to collect on a debt that was seven years old. It might have been the case that Johnson knew his mother was not especially good at keeping track of her debts, especially if she was illiterate. Though he did not make any remarks expressing his anger toward her for these debts, there is little doubt that he found it annoying. It is also likely that these men looked to William for repayment because they preferred to deal with a man. William still helped her regardless of these issues, especially when purchasing human beings. In 1837, Johnson recorded, "To day Mother paid me Sixty Dollars and now she owes me $600 dollars towards the Girl Sharlot."[11] Johnson might have viewed these debts as investments rather than liabilities and might have been willing to help.

Johnson did not hold back his displeasure over her temper, whatever his exasperation level at his mother's financial dealings. As Jeff Forret and others have made clear, women, and Black women in particular, were less violent than men but did assault and kill others. Enslaved women had various reasons to resort to violence against others, sometimes to defend themselves and their families and, in other instances, to resist the dehumanization of slavery. Amy experienced slavery both as someone who was enslaved and as an enslaver. She was a victim and perpetrator of violence. Like her son, Amy grew angry when others did not conform to her will, but she showed less restraint than William and unleashed her temper against others with little regard for consequences.[12] William first mentioned Amy's tendency to give in to rage in 1836. Johnson, after a particularly trying few days in which he lost a horse and felt that he had been scammed on another by a butcher whom he called "a most infernal Rascal," wrote: "To day I was as mad as the very Old Harry. . . . Mother and old French had some Difference. French he Left and Ranaway. . . . Oh the Deel could not be in more passion than I was."[13] "Old French" was "French William Johnson," the mixed-race man who was most likely William Johnson's half brother. French William worked for Johnson, so his fight with his mother was bound to disrupt his business.

Amy's temper flared up several more times, in some cases publicly, which could bring about legal trouble for a free woman of color. Public nuisances, especially fights, were common in antebellum Natchez, but given the frequent hostility that free Blacks had to deal with in town, drawing negative attention could result in arrest and possible removal from the state or, in some cases, a potential revoking of freedom.[14] In June 1837, Johnson recalled: "This morning M[other] Commenced as usual to quarrel with Everything and Every body, I, Knowing perfectly well what it Grew Out of, I thought I would take the quickest way to stop it, and I accordingly took a whip and gave her a few cuts." Perhaps Johnson thought brandishing the whip would lead his mother to stand down because that usually worked with enslaved people or his apprentices, but in this case, it seemed to make the confrontation worse. On first reading, it appears that "by gave her a few cuts," he meant using the whip on her, but he did not. He must have simply snapped the whip in her direction a few times. He continued: "As soon as that was done M. commenced to quarrel and abuse me Saying that I done it to oblige Sarah and advancing on me at the same time Dareing me to strike, which I would not do for anything in the world. I shoved her back from me three times."[15] The fight grew out of her argument with the enslaved woman Sarah, and Johnson's threat with the whip, rather than putting an end to the disagreement, obviously made it worse as she pushed the barber three times, daring him to use the whip on her. As with his apprentices, Johnson no doubt worried that his mother would continue her rash behavior in public and probably believed that the threat of physical violence would deter her in the same way it did with the boys in his household. Still, he miscalculated severely, damaging his relationship with his mother, at least in the short term.

In fact, after the incident, the two did not speak for several weeks. About five weeks after threatening Amy with the whip, her temper flared up again. Johnson wrote she "threw Salt all on the floor of the door, Quarrells and makes all maner of fuss for nothing at all, I made Sharlot her Girl go and scour it up but would not Say a word to the Old Lady about it."[16] The same evening, he described another event: "the old woman Commences and makes a Terrible Quarrelling and abuses me a good deal for giving Moses a Small flaking for runing and hallowing in the Street before the Door, I whiped Bill too as he was One of the Party."[17] Whatever the initial cause, Amy took exception to William punishing the enslaved boy Moses, perhaps because she took this as an assault on her authority, but just as likely because she and her son had been on bad terms for over a month since he threatened her with the whip.

The two reconciled five days after this incident through the intervention of William's brother-in-law, James Miller. Johnson wrote in his diary, "To day Mother and myself Spoke together and it is the first time Since the first of July Last This was done throug[h] the interfereance of Mr Miller."[18] Miller was in Natchez on a visit and used his influence with the two to help them set aside their differences, at least publicly, for the time. Despite the reunion, Johnson felt the same about his mother's temper. As he wrote to his sister later in the fall of 1837: "tell Mr Miller that mother does a great deal better than I expected she would—She has quit running out in th streets to complete her quarrels—now she does pretty well—about 3 quarrells or three fusses a week will satisfy her very well—and before he came up here she used to have the bigest Kind of a fuss Every morning."[19] Even if the two had reached this temporary truce, Johnson still expressed frustration with his mother, noting a few weeks after they began speaking again: "This evening Mother was Seting on the Porch asleep and tumbled right over, and fell Clear down to the bottom of the steps—She hurt her Eye very much and Bruised her face a good deal."[20]

While James Miller might have been able to help the mother and son bury the hatchet, this did not result in Amy calming down or treating those around her differently; instead, it seemed to bring William back into his mother's disagreements. By November 1837, he wrote: "The old woman is on a regular spree for quarrelling to day all day—oh Lord, was any One on this Earth So perpetually tormented as I am."[21] What is notable about this entry is not that she began her "quarreling" with others again, but the degree it bothered him. Johnson only rarely expressed this kind of emotion in his diary. He mentioned times when he was angry at the men who worked for him, free and enslaved, and talked about being disgusted or enraged at things around him, but he only mentioned regret, despair, or feeling sorry for himself when discussing his family members. Johnson's role with his mother was complicated. Though she was his parent, he frequently intervened in her affairs to settle her disputes with other community members or the enslaved people within her household. Johnson probably felt his relationship with his mother had flipped, and he had to behave more like a parent instead of a child.

Johnson only mentioned one more incident where he had to intercede in his mother's dealings. This is probably not because she settled down or became better at keeping up with her business dealings; instead, he might have given up devoting space in his diary to keep up with such things. In December 1837, Johnson wrote: "Old Esdra came down and had a Small fuss with the old woman about her Girl Sharlot. The woman took her way two days or three before her month was Out, and the old fellow Came Down and showed his Receipt and the old Fellow wer perfectly right in his Calculations[.]"[22] When Sharlott's time with Esdra ended, the dispute could have led to severe repercussions had William not intervened. Still, he solved the problem and chalked it up to a mistake in the date rather than an irrational move by his mother.

It does not appear that the two had another falling out, but Johnson's attention seemed to turn away from his mother after 1837 though she lived for another nine years. It might have been the case that Johnson's growing family and the responsibilities they required and his more complicated business dealings shifted his focus away from her, but her death took a toll on him. On January 6, 1849, the enslaved man Jim brought news to Johnson from his mother's home that she was very sick and a doctor was with her. When he found out, he ran to her house, where he "found Her in Bed and oh my God How changed She Seemed. She fainted from weakness but She felt Better." He discovered that she had not slept well the night before and "Had taken Sick . . . and was up and down often in the Course of the night and that She had Got very weak." After Johnson arrived, he noted: "The Doctor, Blackburn, came in a few Minutes and Gave Medicine and we commencd to treat for cholera . . . but her Stomache would not bear the medicine." When the medicine did not work, he witnessed that she "Continued to Sink until twenty minutes of 3 oclock when we Lost Her for Ever—oh My poor Dear Mother is no more."[23]

Johnson made several entries detailing the sense of loss he experienced when his mother died. He wrote the day after she died: "To day has been a [day] of Great trouble to me and all of my Family. The Remains of My Poor Mother was Burried, oh my God. My Loss is too greate. Oh my Poor Belovd Mother is Losst to me forever in this world." A few days later, he wrote two letters informing James Miller and his niece of her death and noted, "oh my God it Seems even now that it is a Dream but alas My Lord it is too true."[24] Johnson paid for an elaborate funeral and hired seven or eight carriages from Robert Smith for the procession and buried her in the "town's leading cemetery."[25] Her interment is in the white section of that cemetery, but how segregated that cemetery was is unclear. Perhaps no one other than William

Johnson had ever attempted to have a person of color buried in that section. There was no outcry or resistance to her burial here. Moreover, William also was buried in this "whites only" section. It is reasonable to assume that the cemetery was segregated, as was common across the South. It might have been seen as a posthumous civic honor to bury William Johnson in the white section to recognize his life and tragic murder, but Amy Johnson never held the same kind of position in town that her son did.

Extended Family, Children, New Orleans Connections

William Johnson's closest contacts outside of Natchez were his sister, Adelia, and her husband, James, and their children, who lived in New Orleans. The two parts of the family frequently exchanged letters, gifts, and items for sale and visited each other on multiple occasions. The Millers left Natchez for New Orleans in 1830, searching for new financial opportunities in the much larger city with a sizeable community of free people of color. During their visits to Natchez, the Millers usually brought their children and sometimes enslaved men and women, probably to help transport their luggage. James Miller joined Johnson in hunting, fishing, and gambling when in town. As their sons grew older, the boys increasingly joined them and learned to participate in their fathers' masculine behaviors. Adelia spent time with Ann Johnson and her mother. These visits also served larger purposes; they helped maintain connections between the two parts of this extended family and the communities of free people of color in their respective cities. As Johnson and Roark point out, with the community of free Blacks in Charleston, maintaining these business and kinship connections allowed for autonomy from whites, enabling them to depend on each other. These bonds became especially important for their children, who moved between the two towns frequently as adults, and, in at least two cases, led to marriages linking these communities of color together.[26]

Adelia had at least some of her mother's temper. In 1847, the *New Orleans Daily Delta* reported an event between Adelia and one of her white neighbors, the kind of conflict that Johnson worried his mother would start. The paper described Adelia as "Mrs. Miller, f.w.c [free woman of color], the wife of old Miller the wealthy colored barber in Common Street," and the man that she argued with as "Mr. Hannekar, by birth a Dutchman—by profession a dyer." The two had already had a dispute over a dog, resulting in a lawsuit, but this conflict involved a woman the Millers enslaved and Hannekar's daughter. The article stated: "A little girl ran to him with the intelligence that some slaves belonging to Mrs. Miller were beating his daughter. Arming himself with a stick, he rushed up to her premises with the intention of terribly chastising, if not killing some one of the inmates of Madame Miller's house." When Adelia answered the door, Hannekar contended that she said, "dat he vos a shdinking Dutch devil and knowed nothing about the matter" to which he replied, "dat she had petter as been to work in de field, dan insulting one of de American bobulation." The article, which intentionally mocked Hannekar's accent, continued, "Some other equally complimentary remarks took place between the parties, when Mrs. Miller committed an assault by shaking her fist in his face." Though other neighbors testified to her "orderly deportment," she had to pay a bond of five hundred dollars for her appearance at trial for the assault.[27] Despite the lighthearted reporting of the newspaper, even in the relatively more accepting environment of New Orleans, it was no small matter for a woman of color to be accused of assaulting a white man. Adelia seems to have never appeared in court for the charge.

Sometimes Adelia wrote letters complaining about Johnson's apprentices or men he enslaved, but mostly the siblings exchanged family news and gossip. In one letter, she wrote to him about her sons and their educations: "In contemplation to send my two boys away with young Yebreska to school in Kingston and Mr Miller talks of going with them and wants you to accompany him, but whether he does or not I think I shall take and send them there. They will get a trade."[28] The letter speaks to both siblings' concern for their male children, namely, how they would make their livings within a slave society. Learning the barbers' trade had allowed James and William to establish themselves as free men of color, and they expected their sons to need the same type of trade to maintain their freedom and support their own families. Her son, William Miller, named for his uncle, eventually moved to Natchez to live with her brother for a time; William Johnson Jr. was sent to New Orleans for school after his father's death.[29]

The Millers' trips to Natchez allowed the young boys in the family to integrate into their fathers' masculine behaviors. For the enslaved, learning to hunt and fish could be essential to help provide food for dependents, but for these free men of color who could earn money via their trade, these trips were more for leisure and manly competition. While they were in town in

1843, Johnson wrote: "I wrode Out in the afternoon and took William and James Miller and my Little Wm. . . . Wm M got behind the saddle and Like to have fallen off."[30] William Johnson Jr. was seven years old and his cousins a bit older, but the boys from New Orleans, especially William Miller, seemed to have less experience in riding horses, which the elder Johnson found amusing. The Mississippi trip allowed the Miller boys to engage in mischief (Johnson noted that William Miller hit one of his apprentices with a brickbat) and other family bonding activities like picking blackberries. This trip in 1843 marked the first time Johnson took the younger boys in the family out for hunting and fishing trips. On August 3, Johnson went out to "the Swamp . . . and took my William and Little James Miller" for a fishing trip. As with virtually every venture of this kind, Johnson kept score: "We fished for an Hour & ½, I Suppose So—James Caught 4, my Wm 8 and myself 12." Though he did not mention letting the boys shoot, he also hunted while on the trip and noted that he "Killed 1 Large Rabit, 8 Black Birds and 6 Jack Snipe or Plover, and I Killed One of the Largest Kind of Snakes—Swamp Mockoson."[31] On the same trip, he recalled: "I wrode Out this Evening in my Buggy and took Wm Miller, Little Robt McCary & Richard & Byron all with me and Wm McCary, William Johnson & James Miller wrode on Horse back—We went Out as far as Mrs Paines fence and then Came back and Stopd, played ball a while & c."[32] This ride included his two younger sons and two of Robert McCary's sons, with the younger boys riding with him in the buggy and the older ones riding their own horses. The ride included seven of the next generation of free men of color in the region, all learning the masculine socialization that Johnson believed was crucial for success.

Johnson took the boys out several more times during the visit. Most of these excursions were either after or before working in his shop. It is clear that he found spending time with these boys both entertaining and worthwhile, and while the Millers were in town, he seemed to have spent almost all of his time with the boys rather than out at the race track or competing with his adult friends. On another buggy ride, he mentioned: "The time was agreeable to us all, only Wm & James had a fight Out in the Butchers House William got the better of the fight He struck James in the Eye, made it Blood Shot."[33] This was a fight between James and William Johnson Jr. rather than his younger brother because Johnson does not mention that it was either William Miller or William McCary, another namesake and his best friend's son. Johnson does not mention punishment or chastisement for either boy after the fight, indicating that he thought it was a fair one, that it was a part of what it meant to grow up with other boys, or that he was somewhat proud that his son, younger than his nephew, had fought and had the upper hand. Two days later, the boys went fishing with Johnson and Robert McCary. Whether they understood it was a competition or not, Johnson dominated the field, reporting that he "Caught 63 Fish, Mc 26, Wm Mc, 32, my Wm 25, James 17, Robt 7, Wm Miller 3."[34] Perhaps because of this trip and his experiences with the boys, Johnson began bringing William Jr. with him on his outings and spending more time with his other sons. In October 1843, Johnson took William Jr. with him on a squirrel hunt, and though he still did not allow the boy to shoot, William Jr. did ride his own horse. The following month, he bought a white pony especially for William Jr., and the boy rode it to the fair with his father. By early 1844, Johnson began including his younger sons Richard and Byron on some rides.[35]

Johnson was also involved in his children's education. Just as he taught his apprentices to read and write, he devoted time to helping his children learn these skills. Given that his ability to keep up with his finances, business, and understanding the world around him was rooted in his literacy, his work toward imparting these skills to his children is not surprising. Though other states along the Mississippi River banned education for all African Americans, enslaved or free people of color found ways to teach their children. John Meachum, pastor of the African Baptist Church in St. Louis, taught free Black children until Missouri passed a law banning all instruction for Blacks. In response, he moved the school to a riverboat to avoid the law. Born into slavery in Virginia, Meachum trained in carpentry and used his money to purchase freedom for himself and his wife. In his book entitled *An Address to All the Colored Citizens of the United States,* Meachum explained the importance of education:

Many of the colored people are free, and have neither master nor owner. Then surely you can train up your children in the way they should go, and when they grow old they will not depart from it. If you fail to do what is in your power to do with these children how can you look for a blessing. In time past, your fathers were deprived of this blessing, and of course they could not be charged with not raising their children in the right manner; that is, if they did all they could according to their situation. But as you are free, (thanks be to God for it,) the guilt comes on your own head. Industry and education should be your concern about this young race. Look over the whole world, and see the nations all endeavoring to advance to a higher state of life. Industry and good education is the principal way of advancing in life.[36]

There were no schools for free children of color in Natchez, but all of Johnson's children became literate and received more formal education than their father. The Catholic Church offered schools for free Black children in New Orleans, and at least two of the Johnson children, Anna and William Jr., went to school there. William studied arithmetic, geography, and grammar. In Natchez, Catherine, Byron, and Richard were all tutored by James McCary, son of Robert McCary. Three of Johnson's daughters became teachers as adults.[37] Johnson recorded with pride in 1849: "Richard and William wrote their first Letter to day that they Ever wrote. William wrote to Lavinia Miller and Richard wrote to his Sister Anna Johnson." He wrote in 1850, "The Letter from N. Orleans to day states that my Little Anna did not make her Speech at the Examination as was Expected She would, Thus I am Disappointed."[38]

In addition to introducing his sons to masculine performance and education, Johnson disciplined his children, usually reserving punishment for when they stepped out of line in public. As with his mother's behavior, Johnson worried about his children getting into confrontations with others that might put their status in jeopardy. Raising Black children in an environment like antebellum Natchez undoubtedly represented a daunting task. As Hilde has made clear, to protect them, parents had to teach their offspring "to adopt and present an outward demeanor that mollified the white power structure."[39] In December 1841, Johnson reported: "I Gave my Little William a very serviere whiping to day up at the Shop for his bad Conduct, Throwing Brick and so forth, and sent Him Down Home—oh I gave him what I thought was right in the Case."[40] Johnson does not detail who or what William Jr. threw the brick at, but damage to property or injury to a passerby could have resulted in serious consequences for the young boy, and the severe whipping he gave him certainly was designed to prevent him from doing this again.

In May 1845, Johnson wrote that he was "very Mad nearly all Day Tis about my Son William It appears that he went out to Drive a calf to the Commons and it farther appears that 2 of Dr Jones children Got in a fuss with Him and what Ever name that Called Him he returned it." Johnson certainly did not go after the white children William argued with, and his anger with his son seemed focused on the fact that he had returned the insults to the white kids rather than the insults themselves. This instance contrasts with William's earlier encounter with an enslaved boy. Johnson wrote: "I had a Little run in to day after a Black Boy that Slapd my Little William. I got near Enough to give him a very seviere Kick on his but—I don't think He will attemp[t] to runaway from me Soon—the Little rascal belongs to Mr Racy Parker." In another incident, he recalled: "R. Parkers Daughter both told some Lies on my Children this Evening and has Caused me to whip them. It was wrong in me to do it tho I whipt them."[41] Johnson knew that these girls had told lies about his children but punished them regardless, perhaps because the Parker girls were white, and he felt that he needed to dole out the whipping either to impart the lesson to his kids that they should not argue with whites or to keep up the appearance to whites that he believed the lies and took steps to correct his children's behavior.

Johnson also spent a lot of time worrying about his children's health. Richard was sick in 1841 for over three weeks, and Johnson tracked his condition in his diary every day, noting when he was feeling better or worse, detailing his symptoms, visits from doctors, and in several instances, remaining in the house to take care of him rather than going to his shop. During his illness, several other free Black community members came to help the Johnsons, including Robert McCary and Hester Cummings, who stayed with the boy all night to give his parents a chance to sleep. Though this was the only long-term illness that any of his children had, Johnson frequently had several doctors in town come to the house to treat them when they were sick. He kept close track of cholera and yellow fever outbreaks in Natchez and other nearby towns to keep his family safe.[42]

When Johnson arranged for Ann and four of their children to travel via steamboat to New Orleans, protecting his children was paramount. Negotiating the passage was challenging because ship captains limited free Blacks who traveled onboard. William met an agent in Natchez to arrange for a stateroom rather than have his family stay in the "ladies room" on the ship. William found the negotiation difficult because the ship's captain told him "he could not spare one and that it was against the rules of his boat" to charter staterooms to free people of color. Johnson, however, did not relent and convinced the captain to let him have a stateroom "on Conditions which I told him would answer."[43] These conditions are unclear but essential to Johnson, given the degrading behavior that his family might experience on the trip. J. S. Buckingham, a traveler throughout the South, noted that while on board a steamship, one group of mulatto women had to sleep on the floor, despite their fine dress and jewelry indicating that they could afford better accommodations. During the day, Buckingham observed, these women could interact with whites on board the ship, but the social differences were reasserted at mealtime. At these meals, free women of color "had to retire to the pantry, where they took their meals standing; in contrast of their finery in dress and ornament." What disturbed the traveler most was that even if he or anyone else had chosen to speak against this practice, "any such sentiment would undoubtedly injure the very parties for whom his sympathy might be excited, or on whose behalf it might be expressed."[44] To prevent his family from experiencing similar degradation, Johnson met the captain's terms on the stateroom.

The trip represented the Johnson family's attempt to forge another connection with the much larger community of free people of color in New Orleans. No doubt Ann and the children, William Jr., Byron, Richard, and Anna, stayed with Adelia and James Miller in the city, but visiting was not the goal of this trip. Instead, Ann had the children baptized at the St. Louis Cathedral. Though it seems that most free Blacks in Natchez were Presbyterian, and there was a Catholic church in town where the children could have received baptism, having the children baptized at St. Louis Cathedral created a separate record that the children were, in fact, free. The St. Louis Cathedral had long served the African and African American communities of New Orleans and Louisiana. Baptizing the Johnson children in New Orleans created a new and vital connection between them and the town's free Black community that might prove critical should something happen to Ann and William or if conditions changed drastically for free Blacks in Natchez. The children's baptism record allowed them to fit into this new community, and several of his children spent at least portions of their lives in New Orleans after their father's death. Interestingly, Ann lied to the priest doing the baptism, claiming the children were born in New Orleans

Parish to make them eligible to have the rite performed. She took her other children for baptism in 1856 and told the priests that they had all been born in Concordia Parish, across the river from Natchez.[45]

Johnson's associates' frequent movement between the two towns is how he learned that his sister had become very ill. One of his apprentices, Jeff Hoggatt, was bound for New Orleans, perhaps serving as a body servant for someone in Natchez, and Johnson asked him to check in on his sister. Hoggatt, who returned on the ship the same day, reported to Johnson, "Mrs Miller is very Low indeed and that I aught to go down and see her as soon as Possible." Johnson left for New Orleans the next day and recorded: "I did arrive this Evening about 4 or 5 Oclock and Started to the Residence of Mr Miller where I Expected to find my Poor Dear Sister alive, but on getting near the House Patsy told me that she was Dead. Oh, Mercifull Father. Have Mercy on me—Oh my Greate God."[46] Adelia's death was torturous for Johnson as he wrote: "Oh how sad, how very sad I feel to night. The future seems all dark. No ray of light illumins its dark unpenetrable gloom. . . . Would that I could blot out from memory the past week, which has indeed been one of Unhappiness to me."[47] In the wake of Adelia's death, Johnson arranged to sell the enslaved woman Sharlott, owned by his mother, to James Miller, presumably to help him operate the household. Tragically, only about a month later, James Miller Jr. died. Johnson mourned the loss of his nephew, writing: "Poor Poor James, he was a good young man and Promised to be a very smart and usefull one. Oh how soon it is that he has Follwd his Poor Mother, my only sister."[48] Following Adelia's death, William Miller, the couple's second-oldest son, spent much of his time living with the Johnsons in Natchez, probably as a way to lessen the burden on his father.

Lavinia Miller, one of Adelia and James's daughters, remained close to the Johnson family and established another connection between the two towns' free Black communities by marrying William McCary, the son of Robert McCary. In November 1850, Johnson was surprised to learn that "Mc Received a Letter from his William and the Contents of it was that he had got the Consent of Mr Miller to Marry his Daughter Lavinia and that he Mr Miller was going to Set him up in Buisness." The prospect of his best friend's son, named for him, marrying his niece might have appeared as welcome news given the work he put in to help set up the next generation of free people of color in Natchez. Instead, he wrote: "So Mout [must?] it be, I am affriad that both of the young Ones are Small Potatoes, I feel So, Cant help it."[49] Johnson often called young people, Black and white, who he believed did not have much promise "small potatoes." It was one of his most common insults, though not as severe as "rascal," which he reserved for men he thought had character flaws. It might be the case that he thought of Lavinia in this way only because she had agreed to marry William McCary. His niece was close with the Johnsons and made several trips to Natchez during her childhood, probably when she first met her future husband. Lavinia frequently exchanged letters with his wife and sons.[50] Why he did not think much of William McCary is another mystery, but it might have something to do with the nickname that he gave him: "The Gum Sucker," probably derived from a noise he made with his mouth. Maybe Johnson found this annoying or offensive, but he never mentioned any problems with the young man before the proposal to his niece. On the other hand, he also does not mention him very often at all; presumably, McCary did not bring his sons out with him often in the kinds of manly pursuits that Johnson had included his oldest son in since he was seven, though he does note his presence on some fishing trips.

Johnson does not appear to have told his friend or brother-in-law about his opposition to the marriage. Johnson wrote about a month after finding out about the engagement: "William McCary, The Gum Sucker, went Down this Evening on the Natchez [a steamboat that operated between the town and New Orleans]. Oh what a green Creature he must be. I loaned him $14 To day He told me that his father told him to Come to me and ask the favor, I told him that I had a Large amount of money to pay this month and Could not Spare any more."[51] Given that his father told him to come and ask for the loan, it must be the case that he had not related his opposition to the marriage to his friend. His excuse for not loaning more money to the younger man was probably contrived, though whatever dislike he had for him, he still loaned him some money. The couple married on January 6, 1851. Johnson noted that Robert McCary Jr. and another free man of color named Bill Burns returned from New Orleans after the wedding, but he did not go, nor did he mention anyone in his family attending the wedding. He was wrong about William McCary being a "small potato," though; in 1874, William McCary became sheriff of Adams County, Mississippi, an office that a free man of color could not have possibly held in the South during Johnson's life.[52]

Conclusion

Though Johnson wrote about other peoples' relationships, he rarely mentioned his wife, Ann, or daughters. There is a handful of entries on each. Other than the discussion of Anna not giving her speech in New Orleans, the only other instances when he brings up his daughters are their births, and in several of those, he does not use their names. This omission should not indicate that Johnson did not care or value them, nor is it evidence that they did not think highly of their father. The few mentions of Ann Johnson might be because he wanted to keep his relationship with her private from later generations who might read his diary. It is doubtful that Johnson ever expected to have his diary or correspondence read by anyone outside his family. He may have never wanted his children or grandchildren to read about those intimate details. That he does not write about his daughters is probably a reflection of how masculine-centered his life was. All the people who worked in his shop were men, and only rarely did he have a woman or girl as a customer. Most of his activities beyond work were male-dominated, as was the norm in nineteenth-century America. Had he lived longer, he might have written more about them. All of his daughters were still very young when he died. Anna, the oldest daughter, was ten. William Jr., Richard, and Byron were fifteen, fourteen, and twelve, respectively, and each of them had begun spending time with their father in social activities and working on their farm. His youngest child, Clarence, was less than a month old when Johnson died. He rarely discussed his three oldest sons until they became old enough to join him at work or on regional trips. This was probably more of a result of what he thought the purpose of the diary was (recording meaningful events daily) than the neglect of his younger children.

A closer reading of his diary reveals that, despite the cruelty he imposed on those he enslaved and sometimes on his apprentices, he also showed kindness to those less fortunate and was especially sensitive to children. In one such instance in 1842, Johnson wrote: "Beky Fraizer, a poor woman, Died yesterday or to day. I Am told that the Poor woman has Left Six poor Helpless Children to Suffer in this wide world, Poor Children. I am Sory for the woman I hope it will be in my power to render them some assistance." Johnson does not mention the woman's or children's race, indicating that they were white (he usually noted if they were Black or free people of color).

The same week he mentioned the death of a "Colord Child" and expressed sorrow, though he did not know them. He also moved an enslaved woman named Peggy to his mother's home "for mother to attend to her" after she had injured her foot. During this week, several people in Natchez died unexpectedly, and he expressed, "I feel Gratefull this Evening of Our Lord that I and my Family are well at present."[53] In other words, even though historians have suggested that Johnson offered no insight into how he viewed the world beyond the most materialistic of details, he saw the misfortune and anguish of others. He expressed relief that his family had been spared from such suffering.

Johnson offered family-like assistance to others on rare occasions. In 1845, Marie Brustee visited Johnson and wanted him "to go get her passage on the Princess to New Orleans—I saw her afterwards that she had better remain at my house, that I would see Mr. Brustee and things would turn Out right."[54] The Brustees were a free Black couple in Natchez who were close enough to the Johnsons to serve as godparents to some of their children. In this situation, it seems as though Marie was considering leaving her husband, and Johnson offered her to stay at his house instead so that she could work things out with him. In another case, he entered into a unique agreement: "I paid Mrs Mix Sixty five Dollars for her Little Boy John. He only has One Eye, poor Little Fellow She made warranted the title to be a good One &c. and the old man She made me a present of, which I accepted and will try and take Care of Him if I can." While this was not the kind of nominal slavery that many free Blacks practiced across the South as a way to protect family members who were not free, it was a similar relationship as Johnson did not take on John or "the old man" with the idea of profiting from either of them. He does not mention what kind of situation Mrs. Mix was in to release these two enslaved people to Johnson for such a low price, but the implication both from his description of the two and his vow to "take care of him" strongly implies that Johnson took these two into his household more out of a sense of generosity than out of greed.[55] Finally, a few days before his murder, Johnson wrote of "Our Poor Little Ellen . . . the Daughter of Phillip & Sylvia," who perished from "Something Like Consumption." Ellen and her parents were all enslaved by Johnson, who expressed what appeared to be a real sadness and regret at her passing: "She will be better off in another world No doubt."[56] Johnson recorded several deaths in his diary, but outside of his mother and sister, he rarely mentioned more than just the fact that these people died. He thought Ellen's death was a tragedy, but as with all the other people he enslaved, he did not express any regret that she had never lived as a free person.

These examples of children and other people of color who experienced fortunes much worse than his family indicate how seriously Johnson took his role as protector of his family. These were the hardships that Johnson tried to prevent for those who relied upon him. He tried to limit his mother's exposure to legal action due to her poor bookkeeping and temper. He maintained a close relationship with his sister and brother-in-law and their children to protect their futures and set them up for adulthood success. Nobody in antebellum Natchez took more action to set up the next generation of free people of color on the path to success. Along with training his apprentices, he educated his children and helped socialize his young sons, nephews, and his friends' children into masculine behaviors. Even though Johnson was an avid follower of politics, he had no way of knowing how much life for the next generation of free people of color would change by the 1860s. Johnson had every reason to suspect that the lessons he taught this next generation would work for them just as they had for him.

CHAPTER FIVE

Contrasting Masculinities

POOR WHITES, FREE BLACKS,
AND SUBVERTING THE RACIAL ORDER

JOHNSON'S SUCCESS in connecting to his community based on a shared sense of masculine identities led him to seek an occasion to assume another marker of American freedom and masculinity in the nineteenth century: becoming a landowner. Owning a farm created another form of revenue for Johnson and another outlet for his seemingly boundless energy. His purchase of land in the area just outside of Natchez that he called "the Swamp" also led him to deal with a new set of neighbors who were even less tolerant of a free man of color and were not interested in the reputation that he had created in town. Johnson found that his neighbors in the Swamp did not have the same morality or sense of civic duty to one another as those living in Natchez. Most of the other Swamp residents were poor whites: small farmers and laborers, along with a few free people of color, virtually none of whom had the level of education or wealth that Johnson had. These men had different ideas about masculinity and were more concerned with establishing dominance and answering perceived slights with violence. His neighbors, some of whom lived on the margins of southern society, shared with the planter class a sense that submission to others was unmanly, but their economic circumstances required them to work for others. Many men who lived in the Swamp resisted deference and asserted their masculinity through violence (or at least threats of violence), heavy drinking, and neglecting work at virtually every opportunity. Johnson often found himself out of his element in dealing with men much more willing to use threats and whiteness's legal or cultural power against him.

Johnson's farm shared a property boundary with Baylor Winn. Shortly after the purchase, Johnson learned that Winn cared little about his reputation or neighbors' rights and treated his own children with nothing less than sadism. While Winn might have been economically similar to Johnson, he did not share Johnson's sense of masculinity; instead, like some of the men who were his neighbors, he chose to use every advantage he had to dominate others around him. Winn was also a man with a malleable racial status, often living as a free man of color but sometimes claiming to be white. Johnson seemed unclear on Winn's racial status, and Winn used his undefined status to his benefit. Eventually, the two entered into a dispute over timber rights and property lines. Unfortunately for Johnson and his family, his experience in Natchez did not prepare him to deal with a man like Baylor Winn. Even when Winn had proven himself dishonest and dangerous, Johnson determined to rely on the legal system and compromise to settle their differences. Winn did not accept the generous terms Johnson offered him in their dispute and instead murdered him, then used the murder to establish himself as white and thus outside of any punishment for the crime.

Johnson and "the Swamp"

Like almost all Americans in the nineteenth century, William Johnson understood that owning land was one of the markers of men's status. In the South, enslaving people was also critically important to demonstrate that a man belonged in society. Ownership of both had been essential since the Spanish controlled the region. In 1792, the governor of Spanish Louisiana wrote to Manuel Gayoso, governor of the Natchez District, "I have resolved to tell you not to admit, in the future, any vagabond, or any Americans other than those who are landholders or who present themselves with negroes or who are recognized by men of integrity."[1] In other words, the Spanish authorities had decided that owning land and enslaving people was equivalent to having someone testify that new entries to the region were people of integrity and that only these people should be allowed to settle in the area. The ownership of enslaved people had come to mark men in Natchez as worthy members of society even before the cotton boom or an abolitionist movement had led southerners to suspect other whites of disloyalty.

Johnson understood this was a source of power for the leading men in Natchez. Unsurprisingly, he believed that acquiring land, in addition to the people he had already enslaved, would enhance his status even in a community that equated his race with slavery. Johnson's first entry in his diary from October 12, 1835, recorded his first land purchase: "Bought at

Auction 162 acres of Land at $4.12 ½ per acre Belonging to the Estate of Mr Lewis." As important as he believed land ownership was, he could not resist selling the plot he purchased to Adolph Flecheux for eight dollars an acre, almost doubling what he had paid for it.[2] Johnson was still interested in acquiring land and tracked farmland's cost but did not consider another purchase until the early 1840s. His interest in the area that he called the Swamp, around six to eight miles outside of town, probably stemmed from the amount of time he spent hunting and fishing there and the relatively low land prices. He considered buying the "Collier Place" but determined that the land did not lend itself to farming because it was too swampy. In 1842, he ran into "Judge Dubison" and asked him "what he would take for the Natchez Island, and he told me that he Could not tell wat the Owner of it would take for it but would write to him and Let him send On the In-structions, titles, &c and would Let me Know."[3] Natchez Island was down the Mississippi River from the town, and Johnson did not come to terms with its owner to purchase it.

In 1845, Johnson purchased 120 acres called "Hardscrabble" from Winslow Winn, a free man of color whom Johnson and McCary associated with, for six hundred dollars. Hardscrabble bordered another tract of land owned by William Mosbey, who had fallen on hard times financially. In fact, he had approached Johnson for a loan a few years earlier. Baylor Winn, who was no relation to Winslow Winn's family, ran into Johnson in May 1845. As Johnson remembered, "he was partly persuading me to take Mosbey's Property, I told him that I did not Like to distress a man in his situation &c." Johnson had also expressed that he had "been in a terrible way" about wanting to buy land in the Swamp, however. Ultimately his desire got the best of his conscience.[4] Baylor Winn's urging probably helped move him to the conclusion that he should purchase the land, but it probably should have been a red flag that Winn considered Mosbey's financial struggles an opportunity rather than a problem.

Ultimately, Johnson approached Mosbey to purchase his land, but the white farmer was less willing to part with it than Johnson expected. At the end of 1845, the two met in Natchez, and Johnson believed that they had an agreement, but Mosbey, despite his hardships, still held out on the sale. The two continued to haggle, and eventually Johnson heard that "Mr Gregory Bot the Mosbey Property Last Monday. So I herd to day tho I dont know how true it is—he is to pay three Thousand Dollars for it. So I don't know.

... I hope he will not raise the money. No harm ment." Apparently, Johnson heard this directly from Mosbey but later learned from a white laborer in the Swamp "that Mr Mosbey told me a Lye. . . . [T]is very strange how man will act at times."[5] Whatever he had heard about the sale did not turn out to be true. On September 15, 1846, Johnson wrote: "To Day I was in the Swamp very near all day, And I had a talk with Mr Mosbey about his Land, And after a Long Confab about it He offered it to me for $3000." It appears that Mosbey floated the price out to Johnson as a negotiation tactic. It worked. Johnson purchased 242 acres at this price, and then for another one hundred dollars he bought "his Corn & stock of Hogs & Cattle, farming utensils and Everything that He had about the Primises."[6] Two months later, he purchased an additional 403 acres at auction that he called "the School land." This land was far from the other holdings bought from Mosbey and Winn. It was too swampy to farm and had a large lake. He likely obtained the land simply because it was so cheap, about $1.25 an acre, and probably thought he could turn a profit on it at some point.

After purchasing the Mosbey land to go along with Hardscrabble, Johnson began turning a considerable amount of his attention to clearing the land and farming, requiring expansion and reallocation of his workforce. Several men and women he enslaved and had set to work in his home, barbershops, or as hired-out laborers found themselves clearing and planting fields. Since he was not a full-time farmer, he was determined to hire someone to supervise his farm and workers while he was in town. In 1847, Johnson struck a deal with a white man named W. H. Stump to work the land for a third of "what is made on the ground" and a third of the profit made from timber sales from the wood cut by "Billy, Phill and Peggy." Stump worked on another farm in the Swamp the prior year, and Johnson had met him while negotiating the purchase from Mosbey. Next year, Johnson paid Stump fifteen dollars monthly and provided housing for him and his wife. Johnson paid considerably less for an overseer than large planters in the area. William Minor usually paid his overseers between eight hundred and one thousand dollars per year, whereas Murden Harrison of Lowndes County paid five hundred to six hundred dollars.[7] Of course, there were significant differences between Johnson's farm and the plantations of these men, not the least of which was that Johnson never committed to growing cotton, no doubt because there was no way he could produce it at a scale that would be profitable. Johnson also never was as wealthy as the region's planters.

On Stump's side, he did not seem to have any better options than John-son's offer. Interestingly, fifteen dollars per month was also the base pay that he offered to his apprentices. Perhaps Johnson believed that tying Stump's compensation to the farm's productivity would lead to better results from his overseer, but he surely was disappointed if this was the case. His skin color did not prevent Johnson from criticizing his white tenant, at least in his diary, or from having high expectations of his labor. In August 1847, Johnson noted that Stump was "on the Gallery as usual and the hands at work cutting wood, They have made very Little Head way indeed at wood cutting." However, he did not mention publicly confronting Stump about his poor job performance.[8] Stump attempted to negotiate with the barber over his wages but was disadvantaged. In late December 1847, Johnson trav-eled to the Swamp to make Stump an offer to keep him on for the following year. Johnson wrote: "I offerd him fifteen Dollars per month and he Said that he Could not think of staying for Less than twenty Dollars per month. So I told hem that I could not give it, and remarked at the same time that if he Could get more he was doing very wrong to stay."[9] Though it appeared that Stump would not stay at Hardscrabble, he had reconsidered by January 4 and agreed to work for another year for fifteen dollars per month. Why Stump changed his mind is unclear. Perhaps, as Johnson said, finding em-ployment that paid better was difficult.

Johnson's relationship with Stump and the other white men who worked on his farm was complicated by more than just their racial difference. Men like Stump, who lived and worked in Mississippi's backwoods, had different conceptions of masculinity than the planter class. While all white men in the antebellum South seemed to adhere to the idea that submission was a sign of unmanliness, yeomen or poor whites who were not slaveholders did not have the experience of dominance over enslaved people but still found ways to show they were not submissive. On the one hand, some historians have argued that nonelite men did share a sense of domination over women and children within their households and could unite in a belief in white male equality in politics.[10] But on the other, it is clear that the economic and cul-tural milieu of the Old South placed men like Stump on the outside of power. Some of these backwoodsmen who lived, as Elliott Gorn has argued, "with families emotionally or physically distant and civil institutions weak," found that a man's role "was less defined by his ability as a breadwinner than by his ferocity." As a result, these men fought in a no-holds-barred fashion, gam-

bled, drank heavily, and favored violent sports like cockfighting. One traveler to the South remarked, "The lower class in this gouging, biting, kicking
country, are the most abject that, perhaps, ever peopled a Christian land."[11]

For these same men who found themselves financially on the fringes
of the economy, working for others certainly appeared to be submission;
however, Stump and those like him could offset this sense of dependency
or submission by applying another trait held by southerners of the era: la-
ziness. C. Vann Woodward called the South's propensity for valuing free
time the "Southern ethic." Unlike in the North, where industriousness was
a source of pride, southerners did not think of hard work as a virtue because,
after all, how virtuous could labor be if it was performed by the enslaved?[12]
William Johnson valued his leisure time, but he could engage in it because
of how hard he worked, a critical factor for maintaining his status as a respectable free man of color in Natchez. Whiteness meant that workers
like Stump did not have to work so hard to achieve status or protect their
freedom. By shirking work and concentrating on time off, Johnson's white
workers could deny they were submissive and claim a level of control over
the relationship that belied their economic realities.

Perhaps to establish a connection based on a shared sense of masculine
performance, Johnson frequently went on hunting and fishing outings with
Stump just as he had with men in Natchez. Stump's experience living and
working in the Swamp probably helped Johnson meet others who lived
there as well, and by sharing these typical male bonding events, he hoped
to become closer to the men in his rural neighborhood.[13] One morning in
December 1847, Johnson went on a hunt and listed the party as "B. Winn,
2 Gregorys, C Wolcot, Calvin Winn, Stump & Myself, William & Gim."
This hunt included white men, at least one enslaved man in Jim, free men
of color, and two Winn family members whose racial status was intentionally unclear. The group hunted for two days, and during it, they killed two
of Johnson's sows.[14] The hunt's results indicated that these men were less
discerning of the animals they shot at than were Johnson's regular companions, killing hogs regardless of whether they were wild or someone else's
property, offering a sense of the more reckless nature of these men.

Stump also served as a source of information for news in the swamp. In
December 1847, Johnson traveled to his farm and found Stump talking with
a "Mr C" and James Gregory. He recalled: "The talk turnd on the Murder
that was Committed down at the Creek by Jacob Marks—Stump Said that

he was told that Johnson was Severely beaten by Marks on Saturday Last a week ago." This "Johnson" was not a member of William Johnson's family and later was referred to as "Indian Johnson." Marks attacked this Johnson with a "cotton wood stick until it had worn out" and a "Large stick or hoe Handle." C. Gregory claimed that the beating "done Johnson some good." This beating, though, was not what killed him. These men believed that the fatal attack was committed by "John Williams, Tate, A[lex] Johnson, & this Mark." Stump, the Gregorys, and Johnson all agreed "that it was a greate outrage and that it aught to be taken notice of and that it was the Business of any Person to take Notice of it."[15] Six days later, Johnson heard that authorities had arrested Jacob Marks for the murder. Alex Johnson, one of the alleged coconspirators, had been renting a house on William Johnson's land and was employed to take care of his "stock, &c." After learning about Alex Johnson's possible role in the murder, William Johnson told his tenant that "I wanted to get some wood choppers as Soon as I Could and that I would like to have the House that he Lived in for them to Live in as I did not want them Among my people and that I would Like to have it about the 1st of January—he said he would."[16] Since he never actually hired this group of woodcutters, it is reasonable to assume that he had decided to end his arrangement with Alex Johnson over the rumor that he had murdered someone. While Johnson had witnessed and even associated with men of dubious morality who acted with extreme violence on occasion, having a possible murderer living on his land was probably a bridge too far for a man who was very conscious of his reputation.

For his part, Alex Johnson did not accept the arrangement with the kind of equanimity that his landlord initially assumed. A few days later, William Johnson learned from Winslow Winn "that he had herd Alx Johnson say that I was cutting a greate many shines in Coming by his House Calling my Hogs and Gim was in the habit of doing the same and that he intended to [give] me a real niger Beating and that he would Beat me to death and that he would whip Gim the 1st time he came along calling of my Hogs."[17] Despite all of his interest in fighting, this was the first time that Johnson mentioned receiving such a threat. Alex Johnson was white, but he also was in a lower position than William Johnson in that he was a tenant on his farm and thus had been earning his livelihood from the free man of color. Alex Johnson's expression of anger toward William and Jim looking for hogs near "his" house was likely due to his impending eviction. The barber did not react to the threat, as he recorded in his diary, "I Listen to his remarks and did not say anything in reply." On the same day, he found unrest in the Swamp over the earlier discussion with the Gregorys over the murder and Alex Johnson's involvement.[18] Given the tension, William Johnson's views about masculinity, and the need to assert oneself, it might be surprising that he did not attempt to physically respond to his tenant's threats, particularly from one named in a serious crime. Regardless of the differences between these two men in financial terms, Alex Johnson was still a white man. To take any action beyond not renewing his agreement with him could have subjected the barber to punishment under Mississippi's laws.

William Johnson's encounter with Alex Johnson probably should have indicated that men in the Swamp differed from those he had dealt with in town. Men like Alex Johnson did not care about William Johnson's reputation or association with white men of wealth and power in Natchez. Most of these men lived on southern society's fringes, belonging to the group usually referred to by historians as "poor whites" and colloquially as "poor white trash." Overall, these were people, perhaps a sizable part of the population of the antebellum South, who were, as Keri Leigh Merritt describes, "truly, cyclically, poor" and marginalized within the slave economy because of their lack of education, skills, and their inability to compete with the adaptability of enslaved labor.[19] Johnson encountered poor white men throughout his life in Natchez's streets, but his relationships with them became much more permanent as a farmer in the Swamp, and he dealt with them in much more personal ways. Free Blacks or slaves working with poor whites was not uncommon, nor were interpersonal and sexual relationships. The Swamp was a site where the complexities of these interactions are especially evident. As many historians have pointed out, persistent poverty in a culture that was already permissive toward violence and not well-policed led to assaults and murders within groups of poor whites and between poor whites, enslaved people, and free Blacks.[20]

Johnson was either unable or unwilling to change his approach to these new surroundings with men who did not operate in the same ways as he did. Hunting, fishing, and gambling did not allow Johnson to establish the same relationships with his neighbors in the Swamp as those in town. Johnson had rented space to whites throughout his life and had disputes with tenants but never recorded being threatened or hearing a threat like Alex Johnson had made. Stump approached Johnson with a plan from his neighbors to capture

Jacob Marks, the man who most agreed had a direct role in "Indian" Johnson's death. His overseer said "that he would go in if the rest of the people in the swamp was willing to raise money, to pay an officer to go after him and take him." Johnson took a more cautious approach. He replied, "I did not want to have anything to do with them at all, but for the sake of getting those men out and of getting the right one, I would be willing to throw in something."[21] Johnson was reluctant to get involved in this, likely because of the potential for vigilante justice and the chance that something would go wrong or they might apprehend the wrong person. Johnson preferred to allow the law to take its course in this situation. Still, he reluctantly agreed with Stump that he would go along with the plan to get those men, and he almost certainly included Alex Johnson among them, out of the Swamp. Just as he had in Natchez, Johnson recognized that it might be his civic duty to contribute to the effort to police the neighborhood in this way, but unlike in town, he had reservations about how his neighbors would receive his participation. Johnson's reluctance in the whole affair turned out to be well-warranted. A week after he spoke to Stump about a community intervention, he wrote, "The trial of Tate, Alx johnson & Williams Came to day and they made a short Buisness of it for there was no witness against them and they were discharged, and this is the way that they were Punished for the murder of Poor Johnson."[22]

William Johnson did not seem to take Alex Johnson's promise of violence very seriously, but he was not the last neighbor to threaten the free Black farmer. Nearly a year after the incident with Alex Johnson, Stump told his boss, "Mr Ford had Said that he would give me a Damned thrashing on first Sight."[23] Unlike Alex Johnson, who lived on the margins of society, Washington Ford was a landowner whose property abutted Johnson's, and as such, dismissing the threat was not as easy nor was it understandable: he had evicted Alex Johnson but could not imagine what he had done to offend Ford. As he told Stump: "I was Greatly astonished to hear Anything of that Kind for I Know very well that I had never Said anything disrespectfull of Mr Ford and I thought it very Strange indeed that he should have made such th[r]eats." Moreover, he told the overseer: "I have nothing in the world against Mr Ford and I have never Said anything about [him] that Could Lead to Such talk on his part, and I told him that I thought may be he was Just talking for to be a talking for I did not think it Possible that he would do it for Nothing."[24] Johnson did not consider this simply an expression of Ford's racist displeasure at having a Black landowner as a neighbor.[25]

Neither Alex Johnson nor Washington Ford issued challenges to fight and certainly not invitations to duel since none involved held the kind of planter status where such behavior was expected. Instead, they issued threats of whippings and beatings, placing the free man of color on the level of an enslaved man rather than an equal. William Johnson had few options to respond to these threats: he certainly could not confront these men physically as win or lose, he would be subject to severe punishment from the law, and his sense of manliness would not allow him to simply back down and give up the farm. Perhaps because of his frustration with his neighbors and Stump, but certainly to earn a faster profit, Johnson attempted to partner with a white man on his farming enterprise. In early 1848, Johnson wrote that he rode down to the farm with Mr. Wren, and "his object was to Look and See for himself and to crop it with me this year if we could agree on the terms. The Proposition I made him was that he should put on an Eaqual Quantity of Hands with me and divide the Profit by an Eaqual and fair Division of the Crop." He also suggested that the two could split the profits from woodcutting equally. Along with providing half of the labor, Wren would pay half of their expenses and half of Stump's salary as the farm's overseer. The deal fell through, and though Johnson did not explain why, it could have been because of Stump's unwillingness to work. As Johnson noted, he was "Down in the Swamp all day and did not see Stump the whole time I was thare" because rather than working, he was "out on a Hunt with Mr Winn & others."[26] It is possible that Wren was not impressed with Johnson and Stump's ability to manage the farm since the overseer was not even present.

Johnson and Stump continued to have problems with their working relationship. In January 1849, Johnson complained: "I find that there is Scarcly anything down thare done when I am not thare, I found Mr Stump and Little Winn going down the Road when I Came down this mor[n]ing."[27] Shortly after, Johnson wrote, "Mr Stump was up from the Swamp this morning And Came for a Settlement I think and Said that he thought of Quiting Down there." Five days later, the two met again, and Johnson tried to make a deal to keep him on, but Stump declined the terms. Even though Johnson often complained about Stump's work habits, he seemed to respect the man. After severing their working relationship, the two spoke to one another, socialized on hunts, and placed bets together. It is unclear what Stump did for work immediately after he left Johnson's employ, but he remained in the Swamp. Johnson loaned him money and also helped the illiterate white worker with correspondence. In 1849, Johnson wrote that he "got a Letter today from Indiana from Mrs Rachal Johnson, It was directed to me tho intended for Mr Stump, In the Letter she requested me to read it to Mr Stump." A few days later, he helped Stump with the reply: "I wrote a Letter to day to Rachel Johnson for Mr Stump."[28]

Like many white men in the Swamp, Stump's whiteness did not give him an advantage in material terms over the free man of color, but his refusal to do the work indicates an attempt to resist submission to Johnson despite the relatively close bond they had formed. In a system in which planters at the top of society forced the enslaved to work for them while they lived lives of leisure, work to provide for one's self or family became less important to asserting masculinity than other behaviors that demonstrated a lack of submission. For Stump, working when he wanted and leaving to hunt or fish when Johnson was not around allowed him some opportunity to prove to others that he was not dependent like a woman, a child, or a slave, despite his reliance on a Black man for his livelihood.[29] Stump worked on Johnson's terms and left we he could no longer abide by them. Though it might not have been financially satisfying for either, the relationship between the two men was Johnson's most successful personal relationship in the Swamp.

Johnson probably intended to keep Stump working for him even though he was not an ideal overseer because he felt his other options were no better. That turned out to be the case. It took Johnson a month and a half to find someone to replace Stump. On March 1, 1849, Johnson recorded that he had "made a Bargain to hire Mr Saml Clark to work by the month for me at $12 per month, Farming work of all kinds."[30] The month-to-month employment did not lock either man into the relationship, and Clark was willing to work for less than Stump had, which was a bargain. Still, as with most of the poor white men Johnson dealt with in the Swamp, he found his new employee unsatisfactory. In June, Johnson wrote that he "Paid Mr Clark ninety Eight Dollars to day in cash He has Cut according to what Little Winn Seys 109 Cords of wood, and Said that our agreement was that I was to Pay him 1 Dollar per Corde for all the wood that he cut for me in Gum and 7 bits for the other Kinds of wood." Johnson, however, found the deal suspicious, writing: "I paid him but at the Same time I have no Idea that we had any such a bargain, I am Certain that he is a [a] prety Smart Rascal."[31] Given that "Rascal" was the biggest insult that Johnson mustered for anyone he encountered, it is clear that he believed that Clark had cheated him, and though he does not record it, it appears that the two parted ways after this incident.

After dealing with Clark, Johnson employed another white man named Langford on his farm, and if anything, he was an even worse employee. Johnson was no teetotaler, but he was disdainful of those whose drinking interfered with their work or other aspects of life. At the same time, he was willing to give problem drinkers a chance to reform their ways. The best example was his treatment of the enslaved man Steven, whom Johnson reluctantly sold away because of his drinking problem. When his apprentices or enslaved people drank, he often punished them physically, but he certainly could not do that with his white farmworkers. Langford had a drinking problem. His first diary entry on Langford recorded that he was drunk and had shown up to work on the farm late because he had gone to watch a horse race the day before. A few weeks later, Johnson was at the farm to work and worked alongside Langford for most of the day, but noted: "We worked at it until Dinner then Mr Langford Got Drunk and did no more work, This was his Last Job." The next day, Johnson ended his employment and took Langford and his son to Natchez in his buggy. By the next week, though, Johnson agreed to allow him to return, but "He goes down to work on Conditions, that is, he is to take no more Sprees If he does we are to Settle forthwith."[32] Langford lasted on the job for about another six weeks, when he confessed to Johnson "that he had been Sick Ever Since he had been Down or nearly so and that he had not Done but 14 ½ days work Since he Came Down &c." A month later, Johnson went to the farm and informed Langford that he "had no farther use for Him and that I wanted to Settle with Him." Johnson paid Langford for a month and fifteen days' work, though the overseer pointed out that he had worked one fewer day, Johnson told him he did not "Care for a Day or two."[33] As with Stump, Clark and Langford resisted submission to Johnson by cheating him or not working.

Johnson's final full-time white overseer was H. Burke, and like most of the other poor whites that Johnson employed, Burke came with baggage. Johnson's first mention of Burke in his diary was not about work but his relationship with Emeline Winn, his neighbor and the daughter of Baylor Winn. In May 1847, Johnson wrote: "B. Winn's Daughter came down to H. Scrabble [the farm] without Shoes She had Just Escaped from Irons that her father had chained her in to Keep her from Getting Married to a

Mr Burk the wood chopper, and the young One tried also to Escape but she did not. So stands the affair."[34] Burke must have met Emeline Winn during his work as a woodchopper, and Baylor Winn decided to confine her with chains rather than have her marry the poor white man. Winn was a cruel and immoral man, and along with Emeline, he had also chained up his younger daughter to keep her from leaving. Johnson did not record any kind of surprise or shock that Winn treated his daughters in this manner, but it appears that Emeline Winn stayed at his farm overnight and then left to hide out with the Tate family before crossing the river and marrying Burke in Louisiana the next day.[35]

Johnson hired Burke two years later and cultivated a relationship with his white overseer as he had with Stump by hunting and betting with him. Unlike with Stump, though, Johnson's bets with Burke were based on his performance and perhaps used as an incentive to work harder. In February 1850, he wrote: "I made a Bet to day of $10 with Mr Burke that we did not have all 185 Cords of wood. This I won."[36] Johnson was probably pleased to win the bet, but his employee had not done the work he claimed. Unfortunately for Johnson, Burke's work habits continued to be problematic. A few weeks after winning the bet against him, Johnson noted, "I found Burke up at the Point Fishing, him and little Winn, and when he Saw me he started down from the Point and went to the house and Got the hoe and went to work on the Levy before the Door Oh what Rascally Conduct for a man that pretends to do Buisness."[37] Shortly after that, he recalled: "Mr Burk was up to day and brot $27 for 12 Cord of wood that the S. B. Griffin Yaterman took. This I Recollect was 13 Cords that I Left thare and he reported Only 12. This is strange I think and I dont Like it."[38] Later, Burke, his wife, and three enslaved people who worked under Burke's direction visited Johnson at his home in Natchez. The group of them "Brot up 8 Sacks of Wool in the Skift, This was of the Last cutting from the Sheep—Now I was fully of the opinion that the work that I Left them to do in Lower cut would have been Done in a single day after I Left, ie on Friday and now it is Saturday night and They have not done it yet."[39] So, in addition to not doing his work to Johnson's satisfaction, Burke did not have those under his authority performing the work that he left them.

Johnson's biggest complaint about Burke was his drinking. In February 1850, Johnson observed: "Burke is, I think, beginning to Drink a Little too much for my Interest, It wont do at all, no Sir."[40] By the time he hired

Burke, Johnson had learned that this was a problem he would not be able to solve. He could not impose physical punishments on white men as he had on his apprentices or the people he enslaved and could not convince these workers to live up to his model of respectability and dedication to the job. Since Johnson was not on his farm daily, his overseers worked and drank on their own schedules. The only real option Johnson had with these men, other than providing financial incentives to work harder or longer, or at least better, was to fire them. It did not seem to occur to Johnson to offer them money to improve their work habits, and if he fired Burke, whoever replaced him would almost certainly have the same problem as the rest of the poor white men in the Swamp who might have been willing to work hard on their own behalf but could not see doing this for someone else as a viable option. This limited labor pool must have been on his mind, as nearly every time he asked his workers about Burke's conduct or encountered the man himself, Johnson found that Burke was drunk. On another trip to the farm, Johnson "found Burke a Ploughing in the Potatoe Patch, and I recollect That he told me yesterday that he had Done The Ploughing in the Potatoe Patch on Saturday—I found him Drunk." After working on the potato patch, he shifted to the cornfield, doing work that Burke told him he had completed already. Rather than admonish the man, Johnson took up working himself and seemed pleased the next day that "Burke was again to day tolerably Drunk" but "still he was able to work some."[41]

By the fall of 1850, the working relationship between Burke and Johnson had run its course. Johnson's sons and nephew had visited the farm and reported that "Burk Does not do any work at all, but always Hunting."[42] Two days later, Burke came to Natchez and told Johnson "that he was offered Good Wages by Mr Winn to work in the swamp and that he was agoing to work for him. I told him that was all right, I had no objection at all." Over the next four days, the two men settled their business, Burke went to work for his father-in-law, and Johnson replaced him for the next month with B. Wolcott. After they concluded their working relationship, Johnson wrote: "Major Winn Came up out of the Swamp yesterday Reports that Burke was drunk the night before he left and had abused him very much and for no Cause, Tis Strange what a Man he is, tis indeed." "Major Winn" was Baylor Winn, Burke's father-in-law and employer. Johnson bought Winn "a Hat, a Vest, a pair of Pants, and 2 undershirts."[43] Baylor Winn had become openly hostile to Johnson by this point, and poaching Burke's service away might have been an expression of that, so Johnson's willingness to help him, given their increasingly antagonistic relationship, was a remarkable expression of sympathy and generosity. Surprisingly, Burke continued to work for his father-in-law after this event.

Johnson's relationships with his neighbors in the Swamp and the white men who worked for him presented challenges he did not experience in Natchez. This resulted from his different position in the Swamp as a farmer rather than a barber. Whereas in Natchez, his shop provided a service for white men, a central place for news and gossip, and a site where he had to defer to them to maintain his business, none of that was true in the swamp. His reputation was neither well-known nor as important to the men who lived in the area. These men had a different conception of manliness than Johnson, which manifested in resistance to the work Johnson paid his overseers to complete and threats of violence from his neighbors that put him on the level of an enslaved man. The poor white men who worked on Johnson's farm also presented a different challenge from his apprentices and enslaved men. He could not impose his sense of masculine work habits or behaviors on them through violence or other forms of control. Like his urban workers, Johnson complained about his overseers' performances, but in contrast with the men and boys who worked for him in Natchez, he did not have power over his white employees beyond keeping them employed. Unlike his relationships with his enslaved or free Black workers, Johnson rarely confronted his white workers, and even then, usually only when he was ready to fire them. The lack of reliable workers in the Swamp led Johnson to continue working relationships with men who drank too much, were unreliable, and sometimes seemed to cheat him. His conflicts in the Swamp resulted from these different ideas about masculinity with these men as much as race, but his final disagreement in the Swamp placed race and Mississippi's racist legal system at the center of a moral controversy.

Baylor Winn and the Performance of Race in Mississippi

Johnson first mentioned Baylor Winn in 1831, when he bought turkeys from the man, and the two had several interactions, usually involving selling livestock or brief meetings in town or on hunts. The two were well-acquainted enough that Winn tried to convince Johnson to purchase Mosbey's farm and become his neighbor, but as mentioned above, Johnson was hesitant to take advantage of the farmer who had fallen upon hard times.[44] Before buying the land in the Swamp, Johnson knew Winn but did not know the kind of man he was until he purchased the land and began seeing him and his family more frequently. In many ways, Winn appears to have had an opposite idea of how to be a man than Johnson did; rather than cultivating a reputation of respectability, Winn seemed interested in simply dominating others. Edward Baptist and others have written about this style of masculinity shared, on some level, between planters and poorer whites, concentrated on "unflinching toughness" toward everyone around them, to render any perceived opponents impotent, and the sense that to do anything less was a form of unmanly submission.[45] Even if Johnson had subscribed to this type of masculinity, his openly acknowledged heritage as a free man of color prevented him from doing so. Winn kept his racial status shrouded in mystery. Sometimes Winn was known to be a free Black man, but he was considered white in other situations. Even Johnson appeared confused by Winn's status at various points in their relationship. Moreover, Winn's actions toward his family and Johnson demonstrated that he was a sadist as a father and was willing to threaten and even commit murder to serve his selfish ends.

When Johnson first purchased Mosbey's farm, Winn and Johnson established a friendly relationship. Johnson had dinner with Winn and several of his other new neighbors only a few days after purchasing the land. However, Johnson began writing about Winn's strange behavior in the first few months of operating the farm. Johnson bought the Mosbey plot in September 1846 and the additional acreage that he called "the school land" in November. By January 1847, Johnson noted: "B Winn was Cutting near my school section" and "In going along by the Cypress Byou, I found that the Flat Road that B. Winn had cut was on a part of My School Land, He has got a Lot of men in thare Cutting Timber." By the end of the month, Johnson wrote: "Bailor Winn is at this time Got a Large force in the Swamp at work Cutting Out wood and Cypress timber, to run it to Orleans."[46] Within the first four months of sharing a boundary with Winn, Johnson noticed that his neighbor ignored property boundaries and simply cut wood wherever he wished.

Perhaps he did not immediately confront his neighbor because he believed this was a mistake rather than an intentional violation of his property rights. Evidence suggests that Johnson felt Winn and his family lacked his level of sophistication. In April 1847, Johnson noticed: "Jasper Winn was up from the Swamp, Tate, B. Winns wife and Tates wife &c. Very Green

Locked arm Came up to see the Show of Animals and they were a Show themselves for Sure."[47] Jasper Winn was one of Baylor Winn's sons, and Tate was another of his neighbors in the swamp with a dubious reputation. Johnson found them "Green" and "a Show themselves" because they did not know how to behave in the city. Interestingly, Baylor Winn's wife, Elizabeth Becktell, was a white woman, and the two had only been married about five months. Jasper Winn was not her son; his mother was named Gregory and was Baylor Winn's first wife. None of her children appear in any records as free people of color, which probably means she was also a white woman.[48] The Tates were also white, so this was not a "show" because they were an interracial group parading within linked arms through the town, but instead because they drew attention to themselves with their behavior. In 1847, Johnson's writing recorded his belief that all of the Winns were white. When local politician S. Woods asked for a list of voters in the swamp, Johnson included "B. Winn" and "Jasp Winn."[49]

Even with his suspicions that Winn was cutting wood on his property and his dim view of most people in the Swamp, Johnson still engaged with Winn in the same kinds of masculine recreation he did with his acquaintances and friends in town. In October 1847, the two men went for a horse ride, similar to Johnson's rides with Robert McCary. He recalled: "On my way Home to day I found B. Winn out on Black Hog Lake and we wrode together as far as the back part of his Field or Dwelling House. He Spoke of having the Swampers up for Living in Adultry Down there, that it was a Shame &c."[50] A few weeks later, the two, along with "2 Gregorys, C Wolcot, Calvin Winn, Stump . . . William & Gim" went on a hunt together over two days. Calvin Winn was his youngest son; William might have been either William Johnson Jr. or his nephew William Miller. This group demonstrated the kinds of masculine camaraderie engaged in between whites, free men of color, and enslaved men and was the same type of bonding activity that Johnson participated in and led with men of various statuses in Natchez. This same outing, though, is the one that resulted in Baylor Winn shooting several of Johnson's hogs. Johnson appears to have shrugged this off as just the kind of disorderly behavior he expected from men in the Swamp, especially since Stump shot one of Winn's boars.[51]

Winn's disapproval of "Swampers" living in adultery might have been why he kept his two daughters in chains. Unlike Johnson, who was deeply involved in setting his children up for future success, Baylor Winn treated his children with cruelty. Before learning that Winn had bound his two daughters in irons, Johnson observed one of them and Jasper around the Swamp, socializing and flirting with other young people. In one instance, on a trip to Winn's to pick up some corn that he had bought and had shipped down the river to his neighbor's farm, he noted, "Mr Gay passed us this Evening with Mr Winns daughter under His arm," and he also saw that "Jasper had a Tennessee gal and all Hands were marching along up the Road." He wrote two weeks later, "I Saw Mr Gay away up by the paupaw Patch Locked arm with B Winns Eldest Daughter."[52] His eldest daughter was Emeline Winn, the same one who later ran away to marry Burke. Winn's complaint about adultery in the Swamp implies that he thought they had influenced Emeline and perhaps his younger daughter, Mary, toward unsavory behavior. He felt the only way to protect their virtue was to put them in chains. Johnson's only comment on Winn's behavior toward his daughters was, "so stands the affair."[53] There is no mention of how long Mary was kept in irons to keep her away from men, but Mary married a white man as her sister did. In 1848, Johnson recorded, "Mr Jordan gets married to Mr Bailor Winns Daughter Mary to night."[54] Winn did not seem to object to these marriages after the fact and eventually hired his son-in-law Burke away from Johnson, indicating that he had come around to the pairing. Johnson does not mention any sense of racial differences between Winn's daughters and their husbands, and he does not record others in the Swamp reacting to these interracial marriages.

This relationship is also evidence of the malleability of the Winn family's racial status since Mississippi banned interracial marriage. Interracial sexual relationships, especially between white men and Black women, were not scandalous during the antebellum period since slavery kept virtually all power in white men's hands. However, marriage between whites and Blacks could be more problematic as they could elevate the Black partner's relative power.[55] Emeline's marriage to Burke in Louisiana might have been an attempt to find a place where the law was more forgiving of interracial pairings, but it also could have been the case that they went to the neighboring state where no one knew the couple and thus could not contest her racial status.

Winn expected obedience from his sons, but like his daughters, they resisted their father's will. Johnson tried to model behavior for his sons: he brought them along with him to the Swamp to work, on hunting and fishing trips to experience the kinds of masculine performance necessary to fit into a slave society, and provided them with education to allow them to succeed in the same ways that he had. Winn appears to have treated his children as property, and like enslaved people who resisted their owners, his children pushed back against their father's treatment. Johnson noted that Jasper Winn "has left his father and came to town—He wants an overseers Birth" in May 1848, about two weeks after his sister Mary left the household to marry Jordan.[56] After Mary left, Calvin Winn, the younger son, remained the only child left in the Winn household. By October 1848, Calvin managed to leave as well. On the way down to his farm, Johnson encountered Baylor Winn, "and he told me about his Son Calvin having Left him the night before or Last night and that if should meet him he intended to cowhide him and would do it where Ever and when Ever he Could find Him."[57] Calvin must have returned to his father at some point, and it is not clear if he received the promised beating, but that he ran away from him, just as all of his other siblings already had, speaks to the hostility between them.

The relationship between Baylor and Jasper Winn remained tense after the younger man left his father's household. Apparently, like Calvin, Jasper left his father only to return later and then got kicked out of the house. In November 1849, Johnson noticed that "Jasper Winn Came up with fish and has been Drunk all day in Town and was here to night Dancing at M. Johnson." His father must not have sanctioned Jasper's carousing because a few days later, Johnson noted: "Jasper Winn is in town, His Father has driven him off—This was the Effect of a Spree." While in town, Jasper tried to buy a horse from Johnson, maybe with the notion of leaving the area, but he declined to make the sale either because he did not think that the younger Winn could afford the horse or to refrain from interfering in his neighbor's family disputes.[58] It is not clear what Jasper did to support himself in the interim, but in 1850 he became the overseer for Washington Ford, another landowner in the swamp whose land was on the opposite side of Johnson's farm from Winn.[59]

Even though Johnson had listed Jasper Winn as a "voter" in 1847, others in the area believed the Winns to be free people of color regardless of the legal confusion over their status. At some point, Jasper married a white woman, and like his sisters' marriages, this union did not seem to be challenged by the state's racist laws; unlike other members of his family, though, he did receive some opposition from locals. In 1850, Johnson heard from "Mr Michael Johnson," (no relation) that he had nearly gotten "into a Difficulty with two of the Brothers in Law of Jasper Winns wife He said that the one of them said that any man that would take the part of a Colord Man Marying a white woman was a Damed Rascal. At that Johnson Call him a Lyar," and the two got into a fight that only stopped short of a fatality because neither could find a suitable weapon.[60] Johnson does not thoroughly explain the conflict, probably because he did not think it needed explaining, but it remains confusing. It is unclear why Michael Johnson called Jasper Winn's brother-in-law a liar. There might have been more between the two men that resulted in the fight, but it could have been that Michael Johnson believed Jasper was white and thought he was defending his honor.

The Winns were not the only family to move between white and Black in antebellum Mississippi via participation in activities legally reserved for whites. As Ariela Gross and others have argued, white manhood in the South required a civic and legal performance. By interacting with society in ways that were supposed to be reserved for white men, such as voting or serving on a jury, men (and sometimes women) could claim the privileges of whiteness in court.[61] Several men in Mississippi attempted to use the court and the state legislature to formally change their racial categorizations or remove the restrictions on free people of color. Many of them did so with the support of whites. Some of Natchez's most prominent citizens petitioned the legislature to elevate the status of Johnson's brother-in-law and mentor James Miller, not precisely to equal that of white men, but to such a degree that he would be immune from being removed from the state by later laws.[62] The petition never claimed that Miller was white or should be considered white, but other men did make these claims within the state and throughout the South.[63] In Mississippi, the earliest of these challenges was made in the 1820s by Malachi Hagins, known as a free man of color and a resident of Jefferson County, who asked the county court to remain in the state and for additional rights. In his petition, Hagins contended that he was "descended from several generations of free ancestors," including his grandmother, whom he maintained was a white woman. Establishing his freedom would not have been an issue if this were the case, but petitioning for the additional rights he sought required further evidence. To this end, Hagins reported that his father "died in the American Revolution fighting on behalf of the 'Revolted Colonies,'" that he had lived in Mississippi for more than twenty years and had "married a white woman, fathered nine children, and acquired land cattle and nine slaves." He did not prove that he was white but did show that he had behaved in ways usually reserved for white men, especially when marrying a white woman. Hagins only asked that he receive "security & protection, such rights and liberties, as the legislature might deem 'humane, politick, and right.'"[64]

Twelve white residents of Jefferson County were more specific in the rights they wanted for Hagins. These dozen residents filed a petition confirming that Hagins had married a white woman and had ten children with her, and following the status of their mother, they would be free but still legally Black. They maintained that Hagins had "conducted himself with great propriety" and as "an honest and upright man." These residents asked the legislature to allow the family to remain in Mississippi and "to extend to Hagins and his children the right to sue and be sued and 'all the rights, privileges, and immunities of a free white person of this state.'" Malachi Hagins and his children were allowed to remain in the state, but the legislature did not grant legal whiteness, which could only be held by those with less than one-eighth African heritage.[65] Still, Hagins's situation demonstrates that some residents in nineteenth-century Mississippi believed that some aspects of racial identity required public performance. If Hagins behaved in the ways white men did, then changing his classification to white made sense culturally, even if the law did not agree.

A similar case occurred concerning the children of William Barland. Barland, a wealthy resident of Adams County, secured permission from the state legislature to set free a woman he enslaved, named Elizabeth, along with the twelve children he "had begotten on her." He told the legislature he had freed her and the couple's first three children from bondage in 1789, but a fire destroyed the records. In 1814, as he neared death, Barland petitioned the legislature to free his family "in consideration of the general good conduct of the said Elizabeth as a friend and companion during thirty years, and the love and affection your Petitioner bears for these his children." The legislature granted the petition, and Barland stipulated that his children receive at least two thousand dollars from his estate. Each child would be "schooled and brought up in the principles of virtue and morality."[66] Upon reaching adulthood, Barland's children, some collectively, some individually, petitioned the Mississippi legislature to remove the status of "free Negro."

The petition of William Barland's son Andrew Barland offers the most explicit commentary on what made a person "white" in antebellum Mississippi. The petition acknowledges that he was the son of a white man and a mixed-race woman and that his father had given him "a decent education and property enough to be independent." Moreover, Barland, like Hagins, claimed that he had "intermarried with a respectable white family" and had "enjoyed all the privileges of a free white citizen," including serving as a juror, giving testimony in court, and voting. As a result, Barland asserted that he had been "treated and received as well as tho he had been [a] white man of fair character." Barland may never have troubled the legislature but for an altercation with a white man named Joseph Hawk, who questioned Barland's whiteness to prevent Barland from testifying in court. Barland sought to convince the legislature that though he was not legally white, he had participated in the community in ways only white men could. In effect, he had performed whiteness in a way that his audience—white Natchez—had found convincing. If his white community accepted him, then in a sense, he argued, he already was white in every way except under the law.[67]

Beyond participating in the community as a white man, Andrew Barland insisted that he held the same interests as whites. The petition included references to "his education, habits, and principles," which he maintained were in line with whites serving in the legislature. Furthermore, Barland reminded the legislature that he enslaved people, which, he argued, meant that he could "know no other interest than that which is common among the white population." As further evidence that he held the same interest as whites, he mentioned that his sisters had all married white men and had "always rec[eived] the same respect shown to white women of the same station in society," and thus, his extended family shared his position.[68] As in the Hagins case, several whites concurred that Barland should be considered white. Their close day-to-day interactions with Barland and Hagins convinced them to put their names and reputations on the line to help the cause. However, the white men in the legislature were less willing to make the color line so porous. They had no qualms with Barland remaining within the state, testifying in court, serving on juries, or voting, but paradoxically, they did not agree to classify him as white. Andrew Barland's siblings, who also filed petitions seeking to become white, found the same result as their brother.[69] Perhaps by publicly classifying the Barland family as Black, the legislature hoped to end the anomaly created by their performance of whiteness.

If the successful public performance of whiteness did not make one white, sometimes the failure to engage in that performance could result in someone considered white being recategorized as Black. In 1830, Antoine

Krebs inherited land from his father. A few years later, he died, leaving a son named Augustine, a daughter Eugenie, and a dispute over who owned the land. Augustine's racial status soon became the subject of a lawsuit. Augustine sold the title to his father's land shortly after Antoine Krebs's death. Eugenie's husband, Jacob Batiste, challenged the sale, claiming that Eugenie, not Augustine, was the rightful heir to the land because, though the two siblings shared a mother, they had different fathers. Batiste claimed Augustine's father was a Black man. To prove this, Batiste demonstrated that Augustine had married an enslaved woman, had never exercised the right to vote, and had never testified against whites in court. In deciding the case, the judge ruled that, "though several witnesses testify that he was considered to be a white man," the evidence contradicted this, and as such, "the subsequent recognition of him by Antoine as his son, and the marriage of Antoine to his mother, could not render him his legal heir." The court ruled that Augustine had committed fraud. It returned the land to Eugenie, and Augustine lost the commonly accepted whiteness he had held before the case.[70]

These cases offer rare glimpses into the overt challenges that some free people of color posed to the South's racial order, but none successfully changed their legal status, even if they might have enjoyed a social recognition of whiteness. Baylor Winn never petitioned to be classified as white, but he often performed whiteness similarly to Hagins and Barland. Rather than attempting to change his status through the legislature, he used his performance of whiteness as a defense in the murder of William Johnson.

A Conflicting Style of Masculinity

The argument that ended Johnson's life began over Baylor Winn's refusal to acknowledge property boundaries when cutting timber. As he had with all of his dealings, Johnson attempted to resolve his dispute with Winn through reason and the law, but his neighbor used threats and an escalating intimidation level to get him to back down over the timber rights. What Johnson encountered with Winn was another man who did not subscribe to the brand of masculinity that he practiced. Like his white workers or other men living in the Swamp, Johnson found that his usual modes of honest exchanges and expecting others to do the right thing simply did not work. Though Johnson had experience with men who had alternative notions of masculinity, he did not have an answer for Winn, who viewed murder as an acceptable way to resolve a disagreement and a method to erase any sense of loss or submission to a rival.

Residents in the Swamp frequently argued over property boundaries. Some of these arguments resulted from men double-dealing as they tried to take advantage of others, some from a lack of established landmarks and the wild condition of some of the land, and still others were simply misunderstandings. Johnson's first conflict over property lines was with Winslow Winn, a younger free man of color whom he considered a friend if not an equal. In November 1846, he was "Surprised to find that Mr W. Winn had sold his Land to Mr Gregory ie he told me that he had promised to do it and the ten Acres which he supposed he had in the tract that he sold me." In response, Johnson found a surveyor and went to the probate office to locate a map of the Swamp. Within five days of finding out that Winn had tried to sell the same plot of land twice, he had arranged for a fair way of settling the disagreement over the boundaries that also conformed to the law. However, when they completed the survey, they "found some opposition in the Survey by Disenterested men as they Called themselves, that was the two Mr Gregorys and Mr Ford." Of course, one of the "Gregorys" present was "Mr Jas Gregory," who was interested in the survey as he had "Conditionally purchased W. Winns Land." Along with the others, he wanted to stop the survey, at least for the portion of the land he claimed. Finally, he consented to have the entire plot surveyed, and, as Johnson was disappointed to find, "it turns out to have only a fraction over Eighty acres in it instead of 130. . . . [T]is strange very strange." After discovering that Winn had sold the land twice, Johnson learned the plot was smaller than he believed.[71] In response, four days after the survey, Johnson "got out a Garneshee vs. Mr. Gregory for the money that Winslow Winn owed me," which he claimed was "76 Dollars including the Interest on the Money Loaned &c and 75 Dollars on acct of the Deficiency of the Land, that he Sold me, So Mr Gregory paid me or the officers $146—So our dispute is over and done with I hope."[72] Johnson did not record any further problems with Gregory but later discussed "Little Winn with trecherous ways" with Ford, indicating that he thought Winslow Winn had tried to cheat him.[73]

In this case, Johnson, Winslow Winn, and Gregory all acquiesced to the survey and the law and agreed to settle with one another, perhaps with some hard feelings, but not all conflicts in the Swamp ended with such little animosity. In 1850, Johnson's neighbor Washington Ford had an altercation with another man named Mr. Tyson. Ford had built some houses on his land, and Tyson tore them down. Johnson wrote: "Mr Ford Came home yesterday and To day he Came in. . . . He told me that he would Take his hands and go Out and put up the Houses that Tyson pulld Down, and said that if Mr Tyson Came about Thare he would shoot him full of shot." Apparently, Tyson had viewed the houses that Ford constructed as an encroachment on his property rights. Ford utterly rejected the assertion, telling Johnson: "he had got advice on the Subject and That he would Killed [*sic*] him if he Came to interupt him. . . . He would Show them how it was to Take forcible possission, He Said old Mrs Tyson, a Damed old Rip, had Came out thare with a Gun and she being a woman he Left, but Said she had not Better Come out thare again This Evening."[74] It is not clear who had given Ford the advice to threaten the Tysons' lives in this case, but two days later, he noted that "Mr Ford has imployed Mr Martin in the Case between Mr Tyson and himself, Harah for the Swamp and its inhabitants, Some of them will be ashamed of there Proceedings before the Court is over, We Shall See, what we shall see."[75] Rather than employing violence, Ford hired a lawyer, William T. Martin, to settle the problem. Johnson's discussion of this dispute demonstrates the contempt that he held, at least privately, for many of the people who lived in the Swamp. He thought Ford's threats to kill the Tysons were the wrong course of action, but Ford's willingness to do so was illustrative of how many in the Swamp resolved to settle disputes and was in keeping with the type of masculinity observed by other men living in backwoods areas in other parts of the South.[76] Perhaps Ford's failure to follow through on his threats led Johnson to believe that Baylor Winn was similarly inclined to speak about violence but not engage in it.

It turned out that Winn was far less reasonable than Johnson's other neighbor. Johnson suspected that Winn had been crossing their property line to cut wood and clear a road, but he first identified Winn cutting wood "to Float out," that is, to sell for profit down the river in January 1848. The only response in his diary was, "So goes the world," but that did not mean he intended to let the trespass go.[77] Johnson met with Winn several times after this but did not confront Winn's woodchoppers until January 1849, when he noticed that "Mr Winns chopers are Cutting wood over my Land and I requested the Little Irishman not to cut any more, He Promised not to do so tho he Said Mr Winn had told him that was the Line."[78] The "little

Irishman" indicated that Winn had shown him a different property line than what Johnson pointed out. A few months later, he and Winn met in the woods, and the two divided the wood cut by the men his neighbor enslaved. However, a few days later, Winn violated whatever agreement Johnson thought they had made: "Mr Winn Started the other Day to New Orleans with a Raft of timber that was Cut up the creek—I am under the belief that he is Cutting timber in Every Direction without any regard to Lines or anything Else[.] So Any man that will do that Kind of Buisness is not an Honorable Man."[79]

Johnson had disputes with others in Natchez and always resolved them by appealing to his adversaries to do the right thing or bringing the law to bear. In these other dealings, even when he expected to lose, Johnson turned to the law for recourse rather than trying to resolve his problems through intimidation, violence, or other kinds of behavior that were dishonorable or placed him in peril because of his racial status. In Baylor Winn, though, he encountered an opponent who was unconcerned with these considerations. Despite his sense that Winn was "not an Honorable man," Johnson believed the only way to settle their disagreement was to establish their property boundaries. To that end, Johnson wrote to the surveyor general, "To Get the Old Field Notes of The Swamp Lands." In his letter, he conveyed that the survey notes he was asking for were more than forty years old and, he presumed, "the Only Survey Ever made" of the area. He expressed that "It is a matter of the Greatest Importance to me to Get the Information asked with as Little Delay as Possible."[80]

A few weeks later, Johnson began visiting the property line with others and discussing securing a survey to clarify the boundaries. He met with Winn in September 1849 and told him he was "Ready to have the Land Surveyed that we were in dispute about, he thought it was not quite Dry Enough in the Swamp yet." Winn's response seemed like a reasonable reason to wait, and Johnson did not record any sense of suspicion. He received the field notes and took them to the surveyor, "Mr Kenny," to look at them. Before the survey could begin, he had to give notice, and when Johnson next saw Winn, he "askd him if he was willing to wave the 10 days notice and have Our Lines resurveyd—He to my Greate Surprise refuse to agree to have the Lines run Out after having told me to write to Jackson and get the old Field Notes." Perhaps Winn had told Johnson to get the old field notes because he thought they would be difficult to obtain, that Johnson would not bother, or he hoped they were lost. Winn's partner on his farm, Benjamin Wade, had no problems with the survey, but Johnson noted he could not reach a similar agreement with Winn: "After a Long talk I could Come to no terms, and so the matter Stands." He spoke with a lawyer named Mr. North, who told him he would talk to Winn and Wade and noted that both Winn and Mr. Gay had come to his house in Natchez to see the old field notes. After looking at Johnson's deeds, North expressed "that he Could See no Reason why I should not Survey and Seemed to think it Strange that Mr Wade and Winn Should object to the Survey."[81] Of course, Winn's opposition to the survey stemmed from his illegally cutting timber on Johnson's property and attempting to delay having this exposed.

Johnson determined to rely on the law to settle his problems with Winn, but his neighbor, who knew he had been cutting wood that was not his, began to escalate hostilities with the notion of bullying Johnson into backing down. Winn started acting aggressively, telling Johnson's sons "that he intended if he Caught Any of those mules out Side of my Field, that he would run them out of the Swamp." As he had with other threats like this, Johnson's only response he recorded in his diary was, "Very well, we will See what we Shall See."[82] This warning was just the beginning of Winn's attempts to bully his neighbor into backing down from continuing the survey or proceeding with a legal case. While threatening his livestock, Winn continued to cut timber on Johnson's side of the property line, and he learned from Billy Wolcott that "a Large Sow of mine . . . [had been] shot through the head by Some One and he give me to understand that She was Killed by Bailor Winn."[83]

With his growing concern over Winn's aggression and his need to prove that he was right about the property lines, Johnson reached out to William Mosbey, the man that he purchased the land from in the first place. Unfortunately for Johnson, Mosbey's reply did not help settle the matter but confirmed what he experienced with his neighbor. Mosbey wrote, "In regard to the Dispute about the Survey and Lines, all I have to say is this I never was Satisfied with Forsheys Survey but I Knew well that if I got into a Contention with B. Winn about it he would by false witness prove" that the lines that he knew to be wrong were accurate. He concluded the letter by writing, "Every honest man Knows B. Winn to be a Black Hearted wretch & those in Co with him to be no better."[84] Johnson probably would have preferred to know this before purchasing the land, but he might have discounted Mosbey's relationship with Winn in favor of his own. By this time, Mosbey's assertion tracked well with his experience of the man, especially since he suggested the survey. Winn, someone who was brutal to his children, had no respect for property lines and killed livestock to intimidate, represented a potentially more dangerous adversary than Johnson had encountered up to this point.

Still, Johnson's diary clarifies that his sense of masculinity prevented him from backing down from his certainty about the property lines. Johnson did not achieve his success by cowering. In November 1849, Johnson learned from his overseer (and Winn's son-in-law) that Winn had cut wood and was preparing to haul it away for sale, "and he Knows that he do not own a foot of it." Johnson went to the surveyor, who told him the only way to stop Winn and get recourse was to sue him, but also "that it would be better to have a talk with Mr Wade about it before Suing him" as it seemed that Wade was the more reasonable of the two partners.[85] Instead, Johnson wrote a letter to Winn requesting that he stop cutting the wood until he could complete the survey. He showed the letter to a "Mr Inge" and then had Burke take it to Winn. He remained confused over the way that Winn and Wade behaved over the whole event but expressed in his diary, though probably not in his letter, "Now the truth of the Buisness is that old man Winn is an overbearing old Colord Gentleman, and it will be found out So before Long if he fools much with me, for I know him too well."[86] This critical line makes it apparent that Winn had been presenting himself as a white man. It is unclear how or when Johnson determined that Winn was a free man of color, but he intended to make that known in this disagreement. The only other time Johnson obliquely references Winn's race was when he listed Baylor and Jasper among the voters in the Swamp.[87] Winn might have attempted to use his racial ambiguity to get Johnson to back down from their conflict, but Johnson would not fail to contest the issue regardless of his opponent's race. Even if most of his neighbors knew that he was a free man of color, the State of Mississippi understood Winn to be white, which offered him full citizenship and far more power than Johnson or any other free person of color. Winn's status was central to how this conflict eventually concluded.

Two months after requesting that Winn stop the cutting, Johnson directly confronted him about the wood he had taken. According to Johnson's diary, Winn maintained that "he would not have Commenced to haul any of it if [Johnson's] teams had not to have Commenced on it first"; in other words, he claimed that he only cut and collected the wood in the disputed area because Johnson's workers had done so first. Johnson told his neighbor he had not ordered his workers to cut wood and that he would get the survey "as soon as we Could do it Lawfully."[88] This standoff represented the last semipleasant exchange between the two.

Eight days after this meeting, Winn moved from threatening livestock to threatening Johnson's life. A neighbor visited Johnson and told him that "Mr Bailor Winn had Said in his Presence and in the Presence of Mr Jno Olive That if I Came in the Swamp to Survey or attempt to run the Lines On Land, that we are now in Dispute about that he would Shoot me." Johnson replied, "I thought it his way of Talking and that I did not think he would do it." His dismissal of Winn's threat was not just an attempt to appear tough before his neighbor. He went out to the property line that day and invited his visitor to come with him to help put up the chains to mark the boundary.[89] The surveyor, "Mr Konchee," told Johnson that he was doing the right thing by resurveying the land, but Mr. Ford, who owned the land on the opposite side from Winn, told him "that he thought that I was wrong for Contending for more than was in the Survey made by Mr Forshey which was done I think wrong."[90] Ford, who was frequently critical of Johnson, might have been worried that he would look to his other property lines next.

Winn continued to menace Johnson and worked to prevent the survey. On the day the survey was scheduled to begin, Winn showed up to argue against it. Johnson recalled: "He Just told Khonke that he had no right to make the Survey and that I had no right to order the Survey to be made, and talked and Humbuged the mater over untill it Grew So Late that Khonke postponed the Survey until Tuesday next." Winn did not stop the survey with his arguments. It was instead the overt threats of violence that led the surveyor to reschedule. Several men from the Swamp had come out to witness, help with, or try to prevent the survey, but only those with Winn brandished guns. Johnson recalled: "Here was Calvin Winn with a Double Barrell Gun & the old man with his revolver, and he talked very Large. Spoke of what he would do if I made a mark on his Land, he would put a mark on me & I never Said anything but Just Told him that no man would put a mark on me I was not afraid of it at all."[91]

As far as Johnson's papers indicate, Winn's words represented the first time anyone had directly threatened him in person. His defiant response fits in with the masculinity he admired in the men he witnessed and heard about fighting and dueling when he was younger. Given the number of men present, behaving otherwise would have ruined his reputation in the Swamp, but his lack of fear appears genuine. After the threat "to put a mark on him," Johnson wrote: "I was Siting on the fence at the time and I thought from his maner of wriding up to me, that he intended to Strike me but if he had—Enough Said—Shure as you were born—Well on Tuesday next the Survey will Commence again—It was Outrageous Conduct on the Part of old man Winn."[92] Most men who showed up to the survey expected a violent confrontation between the two men as Winn had not been shy about making his threats in front of witnesses. Just as Johnson had expressed interest in fights and went to duel sites in the hope of glimpsing some excitement, there is little doubt that these men were expecting a similar form of entertainment. That Winn did not act on his promise of violence made Johnson the winner in this case. As he noted in his diary, "To day I was Discoursing pretty sharply On the Conduct of B. Winn and Our atempt to Survey, Public Opinion very much against him."[93] Winn had embarrassed himself by making the threats but not carrying them out. Though he temporarily stopped the survey, he had wounded his reputation in the Swamp and likely elevated Johnson's. Winn surely carried this humiliation with him as their conflict continued.

After Winn's behavior, Johnson spoke with his lawyer, William T. Martin, about proceeding with the survey. Martin told him that he "had better Take an officer Down with me if I apprehended any interfearance from Mr. Winn so as to take Charge of him." Johnson responded, "I thought that he would Think better of it and would not attempt to act as badly as he had done before," and decided not to take an officer with him. Johnson must have felt that in standing up to Winn, the older man would not try to intimidate him any further but also decided that he would "not attempt to do anything that will Cause a Difficulty." To prevent additional conflict, he declined the suggestion of having an officer present and taking out an injunction to prevent Winn and Wade from cutting timber in the area. Once again, Johnson expected to win the dispute by modeling the correct behavior and trusting the law, and Winn would consent to the decision. After discussing the event with his lawyer and taking a few days to calm down, Johnson even wrote: "Now I am in hopes that I will be able to proceed with Out any further Interruption from Mr Winn. . . . Peace to the old Gentleman I have no ill will vs. him."[94]

Unfortunately for Johnson, Winn did not share his ideas about how men should behave in a civil society. Winn only concerned himself with his interests and continued to resist Johnson's efforts to establish a fair deal. The survey began on January 29, 1850. The day before, Winn told the surveyor he should "take Depositions &c. and Observe old Land marks &c." He also said that Johnson "Cannot go beyond The marks of Land that I Purchased to." Winn still appeared desperate to control as much of the survey as possible, and once it started, "Mr Winn Cursed and tore around at a wonderfull rate, Cursing me at times and then the Boys that was to help clear the way, [through] all this I done nothing Nor did I say anything but Suffered him to go on untill he got tired or ashamed I dont Know which."[95] Winn certainly knew that the survey would prove his guilt, but rather than admit this or allow the survey to take place, he continued to disrupt the proceedings or to try get Johnson to engage in a fight to shift the nature of the conflict and get away with his trespass. The surveyor completed his work, and Johnson gave his notes to his lawyer, who assured him, "He thought that there Could be No Difficulty about the Land for it appears to all be right, and the Court would Set it all right."[96]

The issue subsided for a few months as they waited for the court to weigh in on the dispute, but Johnson and Winn continued pursuing their interests. Johnson spoke with Ford and secured his land certificates to William Mosbey and George Winn (Winslow's father). Both established that Johnson had legally purchased the land and provided another confirmation of his land's boundaries. Johnson learned in May 1850 that the court had decided to commission their survey, but in the meantime, Winn continued his program of intimidation and efforts to marginalize Johnson: he stole and rebranded one of his cows, and he might have influenced the cutting of a road that required more work than Johnson wanted, and he had a fish fry and invited several people from Natchez, but not his neighbor.[97] Winn continued to try to disrupt any attempt to complete a definitive survey. When Johnson rode out to his land with the surveyor, he reported: "Soon after we past Mr Winns we herd him Shoot off his revolver. Six Barrels was shot." It is hard to believe that Winn just happened to be firing his revolver shortly after the two men rode by, and the act was no doubt meant as further intimidation. After firing the shots, Winn rode down to the survey site with his son Jasper, and the two carried "a Large Stick" and "an Overseers whip" with them. Again, as with the shooting, there is no other explanation for the two to be armed except to give the impression that violence was imminent. When the survey began, several Swamp residents helped with the measurements, served as "chain bearers," and gave their assessments of the survey's boundaries. Johnson noted that they agreed on where they should begin, except "The old man Winn was not Convinced of the Same or he pretended that he was not." After Winn's continued resistance, Johnson expressed to one of the lawyers: "I am now in this mood at present. I [am] not very willing to Come to a Compromise at all—but Let it Rip."[98]

As the court case between Johnson and Winn (along with his partner, Wade) began, the two men's relationship continued to take weird detours. Johnson started investigating Wade and Winn's partnership, Winn continued to threaten to take Johnson's cattle, and Winn convinced Johnson's overseer to come to work for him instead. In the midst of all of this and the beginning of the court case, which included summons for everyone involved, Burke, Johnson's former overseer (and Winn's son-in-law), seems to have given Winn a beating. Despite all of the arguments over the land, woodcutting, and the survey, Johnson still displayed kindness to Winn, took him in after Burke's attack, and purchased new clothes for him.[99] Johnson's diary entries on taking care of Winn betray no sense that it was unusual to help this man who had threatened his life on several occasions. Neither man suggested that this changed their relationship. For both, this bizarre event illustrated the ways that each viewed masculinity. On Johnson's side, he could not refuse to help out a neighbor in distress who had taken what appeared to have been a savage beating. On Winn's, he took advantage of Johnson's kindness with no indication that he would reverse his course in their disagreement because of Johnson's help. By this point, it does not seem that Johnson expected Winn to change his ways, but he nevertheless extended support.

As their day in court neared, Johnson became increasingly nervous about the proceedings. He spoke with a white man in Under-the-Hill who knew about his case, who told him he would get "100 hands to cut wood" and remove all of the timber in the disputed area between the neighbors. The man told Johnson he doubted "wether I Could make him pay for the trespass, as he would plead Ignorance of the Line &c."[100] Johnson expressed his anxiety by paying close attention to the courthouse and tracking the movements of anyone who might be involved. He followed his neighbors Ford, Gregory, Stump, Burke, and others from the Swamp called into court to testify. He discovered that "Old man Winn was in town to day and he was making a greate deal to do in the way of Talking." Once his case finally came up, Winn and Wade's lawyer secured a delay of the case until the next term. Johnson was displeased and wrote, "I would have been Glad to have had the Case Gone off."[101]

The delay pushed the case back until May 1851, and except for a few minor problems involving livestock, the two parties remained peaceful and reached a compromise before the court could offer a ruling. In the settlement, requested by Benjamin Wade and written by Johnson in May 1851, he proposed "that Sectional lines between Our respective lands as retraced by Mr Kenny & Certified to the Circuit Court Shall hereafter be taken and regarded as out true Boundaries, and that any & all Lands at Survey are included in lands belonging to me, Shall be abandoned by you, as Justly belonging to me." In return, Johnson agreed to "release my Claim To [damages] against you and Dismiss by Suite." Each side paid its respective share of the court costs. Johnson also requested that they pay him for the twelve or fifteen cords of wood his workers had cut, but Winn had sold. Wade came to him the next day and told him that he and Winn had agreed to the compromise.[102] The agreement was extraordinarily generous to Winn; if he had lost the case, he would have been responsible for all of the wood cut on Johnson's land as established by the survey, which had been going on for at least three to four years. The case had taken up a lot of Johnson's time and much of this thought for several years, so having it settled surely felt like a relief. He paid his lawyers, North and Martin, seventy dollars for their representation in the case, then began to turn his attention to other matters, including buying more land and another son's birth.[103] It appeared that Winn's harassment had stopped and that he expected life to return to normal, but less than two months later, his neighbor ambushed and killed him.

Murder and the Consequences of Legal Racism

Whereas Johnson had been willing to rely on the law and compromise to settle his boundary problems, Baylor Winn subscribed to a different type of masculinity that rejected civil authorities' imposition and agreements between men. As his behavior through June 1851 had shown, Winn did not share Johnson's ideas about how a man should relate to others. Johnson prided himself on respectability, honest dealing, and engaging in civic duty.

Winn focused only on his interests and had a record of cheating, stealing, and oppressing his family. Johnson, his apprentice Edward Hoggatt, one of his sons (probably William Jr.), and one of the men he enslaved were attacked while traveling back to town on June 16, 1851. Johnson and Hoggatt both died from gunshot wounds. The first newspaper article on the incident did not mention race, reporting that Johnson was "an esteemed Citizen and long known as the proprietor of the Fashionable Barbers' Shop on Main Street." They described Winn, the probable assailant, as a "planter living some seven miles below Natchez." The article noted both men were wealthy and, as a result, claimed, "the best Lawyers in Natchez have been arrayed for the prosecution or defense." Authorities arrested Winn about an hour after the double murder.[104] Winn never claimed to be innocent of the charges; doing so would have been difficult as there were two witnesses to the attack, and he had made several threats against Johnson in the presence of others. Instead, he claimed that he was white, meaning the evidence against him—Johnson's son's testimony and that of an enslaved man—was not admissible. In making his defense based on race, Winn, like others who had appealed to the Mississippi legislature to change their status from Black to white, claimed that he had participated in society in ways that only white men could, thus leaving an all-white jury with the task of not only deciding if he was guilty of murder but also if obvious guilt was more important than maintaining white supremacy.

Four days after the murder, one of the city's newspapers explained the circumstances leading to the crime, the victim, and the accused murderer. The paper described Johnson as "a free man of color, born and raised in Natchez, and holding a respected position on account of his character, intelligence and deportment." Without a doubt, Johnson would have been pleased with that description as it confirmed his hard work to earn this reputation. Basing its portrayal of events on "testimony elicited from the Coroner's Jury," the article noted that Johnson and his group had stopped near Winn's house on the way back to town for him to "light a segar." The paper reported that Johnson and Winn "had had a legal dispute relative to the boundary of their plantations, which adjoined each other. The dispute had been decided in favor of Johnson, who for the sake of peace had dismissed the suit, settling it at less than his legal rights." Winn followed the group down the road and, at some point, must have gotten ahead of the group and hid behind some bushes and then opened fire when they approached. Johnson took three bullets, "one entering his lungs and going through him, one passing through him along the lower part of his back, and one point through his arm." The assailant also shot Edward Hoggatt in the back. The paper reported, "Johnson died at two o'clock that night. His dying declarations were taken in form, charging upon Baylor Wynn the commission of the crime."[105]

The newspaper also reported Winn's likely guilt. The article pointed out that "Very strong circumstantial testimony points to him as guilty of the deed," including horse tracks from the site of the shooting back to his house, declarations from several of the people Winn enslaved that he had been out on the horse that night, and that "he had previously been repeatedly heard to threaten Johnson's life" along with the testimony from Johnson and others that Winn had been the shooter. The article also noted: "Wynn, we understand, claims to be a white man and has voted and given testimony in court as such. On this point will depend the admissibility of much of the testimony against him."[106] That Winn did not offer a defense for the act but rather a claim that he had behaved like a white man makes it clear that he had planned the attack and trusted that the law was on his side.

After being arrested, Winn was held in jail while an investigation into the murder occurred, but he offered no defense against the charge. Though Johnson and much of Natchez had considered Winn to be a free man of color, he claimed that he was, in fact, white. In January 1852, a special session of the Adams County Circuit Court met to investigate the murder, and a grand jury returned a bill of indictment against Winn.[107] After determining that Winn had shot Johnson, the prosecution was careful to point out that the charges were against Baylor Winn, "a free man of color." These charges against him came from Johnson's companions' testimony and enslaved men owned by Winn. If Winn could prove that he was not Black, Mississippi law required that all of the testimony against him be ruled inadmissible as no one of African heritage could testify against a white man. As Kimberly Welch has made clear, for cases involving Black litigants in the Slave South, the story they crafted in court shaped the outcomes.[108] Winn began his defense by asserting that his skin color resulted from mixed ancestry, but it was a mix of white and Indian, not African, blood. To convince the jury that he had Native American rather than African heritage, two witnesses from Virginia who professed to know Winn's family testified that he descended from Indians.[109] In addition to denying that he was Black, Winn recognized that he needed to prove his acceptance as a white man in Natchez. He claimed to have participated in the community of Natchez as only a white man could: he had given testimony in a court of law, had voted, had married a white woman, had served as a road overseer, and the census listed him as white. Furthermore, the tax rolls of Adams County, which specifically recorded people of color within households, always listed Winn as white from 1834 through 1852.[110]

As earlier appeals to the legislature had demonstrated, it was easier to prove a cultural acceptance of being white than a *de jure* definition of whiteness. The prosecution carried the burden of proof, but Winn faced the problem of convincing whites that he was not Black. Winn's first hearing ended in a mistrial as the jury could not determine his race. In trying to discredit the defense witness's knowledge of Winn's ancestry, the prosecution created confusion among the jury. One of the witnesses claimed that Winn's Indian blood came from a tribe known as the "Pamunky," while the other swore it was "from the Mattapomi or some similar name."[111] The Johnson family and their lawyer contacted court officials in King William County, inquiring about the Winn family's racial status to counter the witness testimony that he was of Native American blood. The family received notice that the county listed the Winn family as "free negroes" beginning in 1802.[112]

Since the jury could not be sure of Winn's race and was unwilling to allow Black testimony against a potentially white defendant, the case was thrown out of court. Authorities scheduled a second trial in neighboring Jefferson County because of the perception that publicity had tainted Natchez's jury pool. Frank Alexander Montgomery, a member of the jury in the second case, recalled that the case made by the prosecutor William T. Martin "was one of the ablest I ever heard, and though it took, as I remember three or more hours in the delivery, the attention of the jury never wavered."[113] On April 26, the *Natchez Daily Courier* reported that the jury in the case "returned a verdict, at 7 o'clock last night, which establishes the fact of Winn being part Indian."[114] Notwithstanding Martin's speech, the prosecution could not convince the jury that Winn was Black, and thus none of the prosecutor's testimony could stand as evidence.[115]

Pressure from locals in Natchez led to a third trial held in Wilkerson County, but this time the charges were brought against Baylor Winn as a white man. This new trial signifies two critical things: Winn had convinced the court that he was legally white, and once established, he had become a new legal entity and, in effect, had become a different person, thereby allowing the state to try him again for the same crime. This trial, however, enabled Winn to go free as there was no admissible evidence. Interestingly, the leading newspaper of Wilkerson County, the *Woodville Republican,* seemed less concerned with the result of the case than with the disappointment of all present that they could not hear the lawyers' arguments.[116]

Baylor Winn turned Mississippi's restrictive laws to his advantage. By casting doubt on his racial categorization during the trial, he escaped a murder conviction and transformed himself from Black to white. Before the trial, Winn had lived alternately as white and Black, but afterward, he gained the full legal protection of a white man. Winn's acquittal took two years, during which time he was in and out of jail; by proving whiteness or casting doubt on his racial status, he gained the protection of Mississippi law. This protection was critical when the Johnson family attempted to reinstate the charges against Winn in 1853. Again, authorities arrested Winn, but he was held only for three days this time. While in school in New Orleans, William Johnson Jr. wrote to his mother "that the excitement was rising again about that trial," and "I hope the excitement ain't died away on our side and I trust to god he wont get clear." Unfortunately for the young man, "excitement" was not enough to convict a white man. The court decided that Winn could not be put on trial again as the Johnsons' race disqualified them from bringing the case to court or filing suit against a white Baylor Winn.[117]

Though Winn had effectively become white due to the trial, the community still recognized that he was a murderer. Baylor Winn disappears from the records of Adams County after his acquittal in 1853. Perhaps he feared retribution from Johnson's family or his white associates. There was a genuine possibility that the Natchez community could have subjected Winn to extralegal punishment, as Mississippians were no strangers to vigilante justice. Winn escaped this fate like many others searching for a new start in the nineteenth century: he and his family moved to Texas. By 1860, Baylor Winn, age sixty-one, of Virginia; his wife, Elizabeth, age twenty-nine, of Tennessee; and his adult sons, Jasper and Calvin, appear in the census of Atascosa County, Texas, where Winn died on February 9, 1864, a free white man. As a final act of cruelty toward his children, he left all his property to

Elizabeth. He explicitly noted, "it is my will and desire that my children namely *Jasper, Calvin, Mary,* and *Sarah,* have no part of my property, lands and effects which I may have at my death."[118]

Conclusion

All of the posthumous articles in the newspapers on Johnson establish that he achieved the kind of respectability he had worked toward his entire life. Still, his life experience had not adequately prepared him to deal with someone like Baylor Winn. Winn's life perfectly contrasts with Johnson's view of masculinity: he did not deal with others honestly, chose threats over negotiation, and was abusive to his family. Johnson relied on the law to settle their boundary dispute, and when it was clear that he would win his case, he compromised with his neighbor to try to restore some peace, but Winn must have viewed even the generous settlement as an attack and committed murder rather than go forward with what he must have perceived as a personal loss. Edward Baptist has argued that for men who subscribed to this kind of backwoods masculinity, murder was an expression of dominance that, in this case, was used to overwrite the apparent loss of face Winn experienced in their court case and their settlement.[119] Winn escaped murder charges against him via the verdict, but after leaving Mississippi, he could reestablish himself in Texas as a white man. He could use the trial to prove his whiteness if anyone challenged that status. Though his biographers frequently imply that Johnson felt frustrated that he could not fit into white society in life, they note that he, like his mother, was buried in the white section of the cemetery supported by the Natchez Cemetery Association.[120] As everything about his life indicated, he strived to be the best man he could be for his customers in the barbershop, his community, and his family. Even though Winn took him from his family, Johnson's model and example lived on well after his death.

Epilogue

HIS CONTEMPORARIES in Natchez considered Johnson "in good pecu-
niary circumstances" at the time of his death, which had kept his family
comfortable. Still, he had also been the source of that wealth and the head
of a household with nine children.[1] Despite his untimely death, the Johnson
family managed to weather his loss through his work creating deep connections to Natchez and New Orleans via his extended family network. The
training and education he provided his children and the relationships he
had established through his former apprentices and the men and women he
enslaved also helped the family survive the challenges they would face in the
decades to come. Ann Johnson proved more than capable of taking charge
of the family's finances in the years after his death, and his sons continued
their father's legacy at his barbershop and in farming with various degrees of
success. Interestingly, notwithstanding the profoundly masculine world that
Johnson lived in, three of his daughters most closely represented Johnson's
legacy of civic duty and responsibility to their broader community by using
their educations to teach the children of formerly enslaved people in the
years after the Civil War. Through their positions as teachers, Anna, Catherine, and Josephine offered their students the same kinds of opportunities
that their father had provided to his apprentices: the training to succeed
in a society still governed by racism. Though their father achieved a high
level of economic success, his children faced challenges brought about by
secession and the Civil War, the economic and social changes that followed,
and personal and family difficulties partly caused by their father's murder.

Challenges for Free People of Color in the 1850s

Even though her husband took care of most of the family's business affairs
during his life, Ann Johnson stepped into that role when he died. Ann did

not appear to have taken an active role in William's decisions during his lifetime regarding the barbershop, farming, or other enterprises to generate money. However, she managed the household, including housekeeping, raising the children, and supervising several men and women whom the couple enslaved. Ann and her daughters all were seamstresses, and before and after William's death, they marketed their products with the labor of enslaved people in Natchez. Ann also sold produce from her garden and dishes she prepared in her kitchen in town and down the Mississippi River to New Orleans.[2] Though she did not partner with her husband, she had her own experiences that enabled her to transition to becoming the head of her household without relying on men for assistance.

When William died, the Johnsons held considerable wealth, but Ann had to make some hard choices to maintain it. In 1860, the Johnsons' wealth placed them among the state's wealthiest free people of color. They held enslaved people valued at $6,000, land worth $8,000, and their two houses in Natchez valued at $7,500.[3] Shortly after William's death, Ann decided to sell all of the farmlands her husband had purchased with the notion that it made more financial sense to sell the land than to try to generate a profit from it. William Johnson never generated much income from the land, but it seems clear that his purchase was rooted at least as much in raising his status among men as it was in earning money. Ann rightly noted that the family would be better off making an immediate profit from the land, especially given her husband's struggles to find a capable overseer. Additionally, Ann continued many of the other ventures that William had pursued: she leased out space in the buildings they owned to tenants and expanded this business by constructing and purchasing additional buildings in town, she loaned out money, and she continued to operate the barbershop. William Jr., Richard, and Byron, the couple's sons, took up the barber's trade. The youngest son, Clarence, was only about a month old when William died and so had never had the opportunity to learn from his father and became a blacksmith instead. The barbershop remained a vital income source for the family even after Ann died in 1866.[4]

The Johnsons' efforts to maintain connections to the free Black community of New Orleans paid dividends for their children and their extended family. Ann supported her oldest son, William Jr., and oldest daughter, Anna, by sending them to New Orleans for school, while James McCary, the son of their father's best friend, tutored several of the other children.[5]

Their sons frequently traveled to New Orleans for business and social occasions made possible by their parents' close relationships. Though the barber could be cruel to his apprentices, several remained close with the Johnson family. Some of these men followed his example and married free women of color, thus continuing the community into what turned out to be the last generation of free Blacks in this slave society. Jeff Hoggatt married Emma Miller, James and Adelia Miller's daughter, and Byron Johnson attended the wedding.[6] Lavinia Miller married one of Robert McCary's sons. James Miller continued his relationship with the family as well, writing to Ann in 1853, "I Hope God will Bless us Boath to Live to see our Children a Comfort to us Boath," after complaining of being stuck with a houseful of small children and that his son William was "of no use to Me in this World."[7] The extended family traded, bought gifts, and exchanged news about other free people of color. Richard Johnson served as godfather to Jeff and Emma Hoggatt's first child.[8] The Johnsons also remained close with the Brustee (or Brustie) family, who had lived in Natchez and later moved to New Orleans.[9]

One of William Johnson's white acquaintances, Adam Bingaman, stayed in touch with the family after his friend's death. Bingaman, a wealthy planter and famous horse breeder in Natchez, moved to New Orleans in 1850. Before leaving Natchez, though, Bingaman entered into a relationship with Mary E. Williams, a free woman of color. The move to New Orleans probably stemmed from a desire to live where such a pairing was less likely to be condemned than in Mississippi. The couple had two daughters, Charlotte (who went by Tene or Teen) and Elenore. The women in the family wrote to the Johnsons with news and gossip. Adam Bingaman took it upon himself to keep up with William Jr., whom the family sent to live in a New Orleans mental institution in the 1860s.

The 1850s were far more complicated for other free people of color in Natchez who were less well-off than the Johnson family. As the argument over the Union's viability came to dominate politics in the South, free people of color faced a far more significant challenge to maintain their communities and identities than in prior years. By 1859 a new version of what Johnson called "the Inquisition" began, sparked by a new law that would "exclude from this state all the Free Negroes and mulattoes without any distinction, after the first of July A.D. 1860." The notion that free people of color would be forced out of the state "without any distinction" led many to seek extreme measures to remain with their families and communities. Some secured the signatures of white citizens, asking for exceptions to the law. Several citizens of Adams County wrote a letter of general protest to the legislature, acknowledging that though there were some "vicious and evil disposed" free people of color, there also were those "who have spent a life free from reproval, or even the suspicions of improper conduct." These citizens argued that laws that sought to expel free people of color should consider this second group and make exceptions, taking care to "discriminate between the loyal and disloyal, and remove only the unworthy."[10]

Like the surviving Johnson family, some did not seem overly concerned with this new law, having escaped the earlier Inquisition, but others took surprising actions to remain in Mississippi. Rather than leave the state, several free people of color petitioned the legislature for permission to become the property of trusted white associates. Typically, these petitions were similar to those of Joe Bird, who, though born free, asked the legislature to "elevate himself from his present condition into Slavery." The perception that becoming enslaved as a means of "elevating" his position fit closely with the proslavery rhetoric so pervasive in the late 1850s. Others, like Agnes Eahart, a free woman of color and resident of Natchez, asked the legislature for a special license to remain free and remain in the state. Eahart's petition listed her eleven children's names, all born free, perhaps to gain support. Furthermore, she stated she would post a five-thousand-dollar bond to guarantee her family's good behavior. Eahart's petition's success is unclear, but in her case, as had been true of others throughout the nineteenth century, free people of color recognized the limitations and possibilities afforded them within Mississippi law and custom. Petitioning for enslavement demonstrates the radical steps that free people of color were willing to take to stay within their communities.[11]

In spite of these growing attacks on the freedoms of free people of color in Mississippi, the Johnson family was able to maintain their status and retain their property. The work that William Johnson had put into raising his children, training his apprentices, and establishing a reputation worked to sustain the free Black community even in the midst of growing condemnation as politicians grew increasingly defensive about protecting slavery in the wake of the turbulent 1850s. However, the Civil War and its aftermath ended much of the legacy Johnson left behind.

The Civil War and Emancipation

The end of slavery represented a strange transition for free people of color. During Reconstruction, Black men were no longer banned from full citizenship as they had been, and it also opened up opportunities for Black men in employment and government service that had never been an option in the United States before. Nevertheless, the distinction of being free and of color no longer made them exceptions to the rule. For the Johnsons, who built their fortune from slavery, the collapse of that system eliminated much of their wealth. The 1860s marked the beginning of the end of their lives of privilege that William had built.

The enlistment of Black soldiers for the Confederacy is a topic that has engendered heated conflicts between scholars, amateur historians, and neo-Confederates. The idea that enslaved men would, or even could, choose to fight for their enslavers to preserve slavery presents either a commitment to illogical thinking or a severe and willing misunderstanding of the peculiar institution.[12] For free Black men, though, enlisting in the Confederate army was an option, perhaps to demonstrate loyalty to the South to maintain their positions within society. One of William Johnson's apprentices, William Hoggatt, enlisted in a regiment of free men of color.[13] Byron Johnson also joined the fight on the side of the Confederacy, but unlike Hoggatt, he had no choice in the matter as he was conscripted into the Black Mississippi Militia and joined in March 1864. The more common experience for the Johnson family and their acquaintances was not for people they knew leaving to fight in the war, but rather people they enslaved using the opportunities generated by the conflict to run away to freedom. Ann Johnson noted that one of the men they enslaved ran away in July 1863 by taking "himself off on a yankee boat," and "John left on the 27th of the same month. On Monday Cindy left. . . . On Thursday old Sylvia left on the 1st of August on Sat 1863."[14] In September 1864, Catherine Johnson recorded in her diary that "Jim came up with the news that Clifton had gone off with some recruiting Officer. We was in hopes that he would never leave us, but turned out like everything, to be all hopes. I suppose it is no use grieving after spilt milk." This was the same Jim whom William Johnson purchased in 1844. He remained with the family twenty years later, even as slavery was dissolving and others who had been enslaved almost as long, like Sylvia, had chosen to leave. The Union army occupied Natchez in July 1863, offering

Cindy, Sylvia, and the others the opportunity to leave. Clifton held on for another year and only escaped when enticed to join the fight against the Confederacy and, no doubt, earn money promised to recruits. While earlier historians have argued that free Blacks might have been more benevolent than whites as slaveholders, the men and women whom the Johnsons held in bondage chose to leave the exploitation of slavery when given a chance.[15]

Even after the Confederacy's defeat, the Johnsons retained some of the men and women they had owned though they were now free, but freedom gave them the option of leaving. In September 1865, Catherine Johnson wrote: "Some of Sicily's (our new servant) relations has sent for her. I hope that she will not leave us for though she is not very handy she seems willing and that goes a long ways to make one satisfied with a servant." This line seems to contradict the next, though, as she wrote: "And another thing, Sicily has grown very trifling and at time very insolent if it was not that Ma has had her so long she would soon set her a drift. I think it would come hard with us to part with Marian though." As the editor of Catherine's diary points out, describing Sicily as "a new servant" but also contending that "Ma has had her so long" is probably a reference to her transition from slavery to freedom, from enslaved person to "servant," as the family had long enslaved both her and Maria.[16] Catherine also seemed conflicted about their relationship; she thought Sicily was not a particularly good servant and that her family was doing her a favor by keeping her employed. However, she also did not want to see her leave. The mixed resentment and confusion Catherine expressed echoes the sentiments of other women slaveholders as the peculiar institution ended in the South.[17]

In her diary, Catherine deals with the transition from a family of privilege to one that struggled in the years that followed as their finances and health suffered. Like her father's, Catherine's diary provides an in-depth insight into the nature of life for the Johnson family. Unlike William's diary, which contained much of the day-to-day operations of life with little direct mention of how he felt, his daughter's is the opposite: the entries are sporadic and include much more emotion than simple descriptions of her quotidian existence. Catherine identifies the source of much of her family's suffering in her first diary entry in May 1864. Like many of her entries, this one is full of sadness, and most modern readers would probably conclude that she had some form of depressive disorder. She began the entry by describing a raging storm outside and wrote: "To me it sounds like the Cries of sorrow. Yet I love the sound for at present it becomes well my feelings which are like the day, gloomy and sad." While the rest of the family slept, she felt "restless and wakefull," and her thoughts retreated "back to the past with its Joys and sorrows. Back to the time when we were *happy thoughtless children* when the earth seemed to be one abode of happiness I grieve to think how quickly the scene changed. Our home was so happy until . . . No, I will not write of that dark time. Suffice it to say it fills my soul with a bitterness that will remain forever. I cannot *forget* & I cannot forgive."[18] When she wrote this entry, she was twenty-one years old; she had been eight at the time of her father's murder. In thinking back on her childhood and the time that had been pleasant and without care, it seems clear that she is referencing how things changed after her father's murder, the event that she could not forget or forgive. Throughout her short diary, Catherine details the unfortunate decline of the Johnson family. At the project's beginning, she places their father's untimely loss as the precipitating event. Of course, the massive changes brought on by the Civil War, Reconstruction, and the beginnings of Jim Crow America were things that even William Johnson would have struggled with, but from this document, it is apparent that many of the children's lives would have turned out differently had they had his presence in their lives.

Though most of William Johnson's world centered on things masculine and he worked hard throughout his life to set his sons and apprentices on the model that he had made for himself: respectability, competition, assertiveness, participation in his community, and protection of the family, two of his sons found themselves unable to live up to those ideals. Catherine Johnson describes the hardships her brothers, William Jr. and Richard, faced. The two had been operating the barbershop alongside their brother Byron, supporting the entire family. Byron's conscription into the Confederate army might have contributed to the hard times, but according to Catherine, William Jr. was the center of most of their problems. In May 1864, she wrote: "Everything goes on in the same hum drum stile. Only William seems to grow worse. I am afraid that he will lose his mind entirely. He sets talking to himself and laughing in a manner that is very annoying to us particularly when strangers are here." Catherine described her brother's worsening mental state that she blamed on his marriage: "I wish he could be more like he was before his marriage and the miserable time that succeeded it. Alas, I fear that happiness for him is over. He is a perfect wreck of his former self. So much for not heeding the advice of his family and friends."[19] The advice she mentions dealt with his marriage, which the rest of the Johnson family opposed. Catherine does not describe the problem with William's marriage at any point, but like her father, who admonished the young men in his employ about their relationships with women, she believed it had ruined his life. Their father almost certainly would have agreed with her analysis that making the wrong choice in a marriage partner could be disastrous.

Her descriptions of their family dynamics detail the various problems the Johnsons had to deal with in the 1860s. First, it seems clear that all, or at least most, of the Johnsons' children still lived together with their mother in Natchez, though only three of the nine children were under twenty years old. Their predicament might have resulted from the challenging economic times brought by the Civil War. William Jr. was in his late twenties when Catherine wrote these entries, and his wife and young son also lived with them, meaning that Ann Johnson's household held three generations of Johnsons. The second revelation that Catherine's diary makes plain is that Byron, not his two older brothers, had stepped up to stabilize their family. When Byron left for New Orleans because of his conscription, Catherine, who called him "Bebe," wrote that his departure immediately caused rifts within the family. The day after he left for New Orleans, she wrote: "How much I miss Bebe. He has only been gone one day and yet the house is as still and dull as though some member of the family had died. . . . Ma is so much grieved at Bebes departure she says it is like a breaking up of the family." She also expressed worry over how her youngest sibling, Clarence, was dealing with Byron's exit: "He will miss Bebe's influence and I fear grow worse for the loss of it."[20] Before he left, Byron had reached out to Robert McCary with the notion of renting out the barbershop to someone "if he could get a good rent for it." The barbershop represented the third problem for the Johnsons: not only was Byron in charge of the barbershop rather than his two older brothers, but he also approached McCary about finding someone to rent out the shop instead of turning to William or Richard to do so. He did not think that the two of them were capable of the task or, as Catherine speculated, "But I don't know that they will do with William for I think he will strenuously oppose any such measure."[21]

Catherine continued her lamentation at Byron's absence in her next entry, nearly a week later. While Byron was away, the family seems to have turned to Anna Johnson, the oldest daughter, to run the household, but

Catherine doubted her ability to make ends meet on her "slender income," much of which came from preparing food and selling it to people who came into town via the river. That week, Catherine's pies generated very little income because of customers with "a very reckless character." William Jr. remained her most significant concern, however, as she complained, "If it was not for William and his family, which he has brought here for us to provide for, our circumstances would be much better and the children might receive a chance at an education, which is their right."[22] The children she mentions are her younger siblings, Eugenia, Louis, Josephine, and Clarence. She blamed William for disrupting her life; he had hurt their chances of getting the education the older children had received. By referring to education as "their right," Catherine invoked their father, who had viewed learning as critically important to his children's success and had taken a direct hand in it for the older siblings. She continued: "My heart swells with indignation and a bitter, bitter feeling of resentment towards him when I look at them and think for his sake they are growing up in ignorance. Poor Bebe he has nobly done his part and I pray that God will bless him where ever his fate may take him."[23] The passage demonstrates that Byron took on their father's role, managing the family's business interests, serving as an example to others, and supervising the children's access to education.

By the beginning of May, Byron had still not returned to Natchez, though the Confederacy had surrendered weeks prior. Catherine received a letter from her brother but noted to her dismay that "it contained nothing much of a gratifying character," at least about the barbershop. Between her entries in March and May (there were only two in between), someone had approached Ann Battles Johnson about purchasing the shop. Byron was reluctant to advise his mother on the shop's sale since he had been away so long. Catherine agreed that it was "a complicated matter and one that gives Ma considerable trouble for iff she allows the man to have the shop, Bebe says he might retain William only untill he could gain possession and then discharge him to be a dead weight on Ma's hands." Catherine felt that "he could not be any more so that he is now," but also worried that if they did sell the shop, "Even iff he gives the promise to retain him, how could we hold him to that promise after he discovers that William is incompetent to fill any office however simple. Oh! it seems as if he will never regain his power of mind again."[24] While Byron was there, she noted that things were better because "his influence counteracted the evil effect of William's ways." Once again, Catherine mentions longing for the past and how full of despair she was for their current conditions, so much so that she wrote, "If my life's thread could end now, I would not repine."[25]

When Byron did return to Natchez, even his efforts were not enough to correct conditions at home. The Johnsons did not sell the barbershop, but to make ends meet for the family, Byron worked in the shop more, even on Sundays, about which Catherine explained, "It is a bad habit, but he quiets his conscious by saying that the spending of ones sabbeth in the persuit of gain is a general and not an individual sin." Their father almost always worked on Sunday and never gave any sense that he believed this was a sin. Perhaps the family had become more religious after his death, or it might be the case that he did not record such thoughts. As Catherine had contended, William Jr.'s condition deteriorated, "He has become periodically insane." She blamed his wife for both his mental issues and the family's woes: "each day her presence becomes more untolerable. I have grown to hate her, and when I think of her as the author of all our troubles, it is almost death living under the same roof with her." On top of this, their brother Richard had developed a drinking problem. Catherine found that he had "not returned from the country where he went Wednesday. I guess it will be for the best if he remains there for he had begun to indulge his old habit again."[26] As with so many men their father knew, Richard's drinking had gotten out of control. Their father had been sympathetic to many men who also suffered from alcoholism, but it is hard to imagine how he would have reacted to his oldest children's situations.

William Jr.'s behavior became increasingly erratic. Catherine noticed that he "seldom if ever has any sane moments now and sometimes makes use of very ugly expressions at the table. As he did this morning I wish so much that he could be put under medical treatment." Eventually William's actions became too much for the rest of them to bear. In February 1866, Catherine recounted: "William was in one of his moods this morning, abusing Gramma shamefully and in a very improper manner when Richard spoke to him about it. Nevertheless, his interference only had the effect of turning the tide of abuse on himself. Richard became very angry and went off and had him arrested." A few months later, the family had William confined to a mental institution in New Orleans.[27] Though Catherine had hoped that institutionalization would help her brother, he did not adjust well. William escaped from the asylum three times in the first month and tried to enlist William Hoggatt in his efforts to remain free from the institution, but that did not work. Adam Bingaman wrote to Byron to inform him of William's troubles, and he and his family took it upon themselves to keep an eye on him while he was there.[28] Tene Bingaman visited the Johnsons shortly after the death of Ann Battles Johnson, and Catherine wrote: "I like her better this time then I ever did before. She seemed truer and more attatched to us. And her kindness to poor William wiped out all that was disagreeable in the past."[29] William remained in the asylum for several years. Adam Bingaman continued to write letters to Anna Johnson on his condition, noting in September 1868: "I have not seen William lately. But I know he is well as I required to the Keeper of the Asylum to let me know when he was unwell." A few months later, he wrote: "I saw William the day before yesterday. He looks a little slim, but is in good health. He appeared gladly pleased with your shirts."[30] Once again, their father's relationship with Bingaman continued with the children and provided them comfort and assistance.

Along with her frequent concern over her family's deteriorating circumstances, it is clear from reading her diary that Catherine suffered from depression. William Jr.'s condition manifested itself publicly, but Catherine's was internal, and apparently she felt unable to convey her feelings to others. In one entry, she wrote: "Old friend [the diary], I seldom come to thee except in moments of unhappy thought and feeling when such thoughts as I can not express to a human being like myself. Strange to say I never express a serious thought to anyone." She recognized that instead, people probably thought of her as "light and frivolous," whereas she considered herself "constitutionally defective" and "morally a coward." She diagnosed herself as possessing a "strange affliction" that she wished she could get over.[31] Instead of getting over these feelings, however, they only got worse. Amid the multitude of changes occurring in Natchez in the aftermath of the Civil War, including the loss of financial stability and the ending of slavery, the Johnsons' status as free people of color no longer elevated them over others. As she reflected on these changes, she wrote: "It seems that the times grow harder instead of better and I do so dread poverty. And another thing every body seems so changed and most of all I grieve over the change that has taken place in my self. To the present, the past seems so Bright. So Bright that I dare not call up its memories, for it makes me wretch to think that in reality I can never live them again."[32] Her depression had grown bad enough that she contemplated death as a better option than to continue living with the pain that she felt. When Ann Battles Johnson died in 1866,

Catherine wrote, "Oh if I was only prepared how gladly would i lay dow[n] by her side."[33] The past that she longed for not only was one in which the family was prosperous but no doubt also one in which her father had not been taken from them prematurely.

Catherine never regularly wrote in her diary but took a nearly six-year hiatus between 1866 and 1872, perhaps because her life became far busier and her time more occupied. During this time, Byron, like his father, shifted his interests away from the barbershop and toward farming, but unlike William Sr., Byron was not financially able to purchase land. Instead, like so many southerners after the Civil War, Byron and the family turned to sharecropping. In the late 1860s and early 1870s, Byron leased St. Genevieve and Black Lake Plantations in Concordia Parish, Louisiana, and the Carthage Plantation in Adams County. Byron, Richard, Anna, Juanito, and Carlito Garrus (two free men of color from Cuba who also worked in the barbershop in the 1860s) entered into agreements with freemen to operate these farms.[34]

Byron's murder in 1872 and the conflict that led to it demonstrate that he emulated William Sr.'s sense of masculinity beyond his family role. Byron and Dave Singleton got into an argument on the ferry between Vidalia, Louisiana, and Natchez, resulting in a fight between the two men. The disagreement started over a field hand that Byron had hired away from Singleton. A witness said Singleton called Johnson "A d-d scoundrel and rascal" and said "he could whip him." Byron returned the insult, which led to the fight. The same witness recalled that after the two were separated, Singleton remained "very angry" and "was cursing and saying the thing was not [over]." The witness described Byron as "not much excited," unlike his opponent, and believed he had hurt Singleton and gotten the better of him in the fight.[35] Though Mississippi was not safe for an African American man to get into a public fight in the 1870s, when compared to the same location in the antebellum period, Byron could expect different treatment from locals and the law than his father could have if placed in the same situation. Whereas William Sr. chose to rely on the law to settle his disagreement with Winn, Byron was a free man in an era in which he did not have to worry about being removed from the state for causing a public nuisance. At least in theory, during Reconstruction, he could be considered a full citizen and thus had less at risk in engaging in a fight with Singleton than his father would have.

Like his father, Byron expected adherence to honorable behavior from his opponent and lost his life because of it. After the fight, Singleton joined two other men named Fitzhugh and Coates at Monahan's bar. Several by-standers that evening heard the men say "they were going to kill somebody or be killed." Coates brandished a pistol and told a worker at the bar that "this is fixed for business, this is. It's got seven loads in it." Witnesses re-called that the trio of men went to Johnson's barbershop around 9:00 p.m. looking for Byron. Coates went in the front door and asked if Byron was there while the other two went to the shop's back. Singleton and Fitzhugh knocked on the back door and asked for Byron. When he opened the door, Singleton accused Byron of telling others that he had gotten the better of him during their fight. Byron denied this and offered instead, "I said we had a scrimmage on the ferry and were parted." According to one person present, Singleton seemed satisfied with the denial, but Fitzhugh stated that the two had not settled the matter. As the tension escalated, Byron told the men, "I am not armed," appealing to a sense of fairness from these men who had him at a severe disadvantage. His father might have handled the situation similarly, expecting the men to at least give him a fighting chance in the conflict. Singleton repeated, "I am well armed" several times, and Byron called to Carlito to bring his pistol. Carlito testified that Johnson said he could not "give him satisfaction without arms." Accounts differ on whether Byron got the gun before the shooting started, but all agreed that Singleton shot him in the fight. Juanito and Carlito tried to defend their employer but could not prevent him from being killed.[36]

William T. Martin, the same man who had prosecuted Winn for William Sr.'s murder, was the attorney for the state in the case against Fitzhugh, Coates, and Singleton. The defense offered a different explana-tion of the dispute, but the court rejected their testimony as hearsay, and the three were found guilty of murder. Unlike in William Sr.'s case, Martin (now referred to as "General Martin" after his service in the Confederate army) had a much easier task than he had when trying to prosecute Baylor Winn for William Johnson's murder as no laws could prevent his witnesses from giving their testimony in this case.[37] The account of Byron's murder in the *Natchez Weekly Democrat* resembled many of the stories his father read about during his life or heard about in his barbershop. In those sto-ries, William Sr. always found the men like Byron, who stood up for their reputation in the face of violence, admirable. It is hard to say if this sense of honor led to Byron's death, but he had learned from his father that this was the proper way to behave.

After Byron's murder, Anna took over as head of the household. In 1874, Catherine and Anna, along with their younger sisters Alice and Josephine, purchased Peachland Plantation, located about twelve miles north of Natchez, and entered into a sharecropping agreement with five freedmen to work the land. Anna and Catherine began teaching in 1870, when Natchez approved creating a "colored school." Anna, Catherine, and later Josephine taught at what was known as the Union School, where their students were the children of the formerly enslaved and the first generation of African Americans born after the end of slavery in Mississippi.[38]

Despite the hardships on the family, Johnson's barbershop operated until 1874, when some kind of mismanagement from Carlito Garrus led to its closing, and Catherine wrote, "The Shop we had failed us."[39] William Johnson spent his life crafting relationships to support his business and help keep the community of free people of color in the region thriving. He had many successes as his apprentices established their own shops and families within a slave society, much like he had. His wealth helped sustain his family for a decade after his murder. Byron followed in his footsteps as a barber, farmer, and the center of a large family. Like his father, Byron served as a model of the same kind of responsible masculinity that his father had cultivated his entire life. William Sr.'s other sons, William and Richard, struggled due to psychological disorders and possible alcoholism, respectively, but for his part, Richard overcame his difficulties well enough to operate the leased Black Lake Plantation after Byron died.[40]

William Johnson could never have predicted the changes in Natchez in the 1860s and beyond. By insisting on and providing for his children's educations, he set them all on a path to be, if not as successful as he had been, at least self-sufficient through the tremendous disruptions of the Civil War, Reconstruction, and the beginnings of Jim Crow America. The Johnsons endured many more tragedies, particularly William Jr.'s health and Byron's murder, neither of which could have been anticipated. Still, that three of his daughters went on to teach a generation of African Americans, all of whom were born free, would no doubt please both his sense of extending rights to all regardless of race and his belief in civic duty. Much as he had done in his barbershop with the young free men of color that he took on as apprentices, Anna, Catherine, and Josephine trained the next generation to succeed in a country that remained hostile to African Americans well after the end of slavery.

Notes

INTRODUCTION

1. Phelps, review of *The Barber of Natchez*, 155–56.

2. Davis and Hogan, *The Barber of Natchez* (hereafter cited as *Barber*), 5, 9.

3. The most glaring example of this can be found in Ronald Davis's *The Black Experience in Natchez:* "His diary, to sum it up, is a richly detailed outpouring of gratitude, written as if Johnson were offering testimony to some unknown or perhaps internalized overseer" (64). It is not clear where this outpouring of gratitude takes place, though, and despite these claims, Johnson repeatedly criticized whites and racist policies. Douglas W. Bristol Jr. offers an excellent and nuanced discussion of free Black barbers throughout the United States but still contends that Johnson "cut himself off from the black community," lived in "isolation," and used his diary to express himself because he was "unable to confide in others" despite his constant, daily interaction with a wide variety of people in Natchez, including his friends (white and Black), his family, and other associates in and around town (Bristol, *Knights of the Razor*, 87). T. H. Breen and Steph Innes aptly pointed out in their study of the free Black community of Virginia's eastern shore in the seventeenth century that lived experiences and social realities challenge abstractions and blur boundaries created by race even in obviously racist milieus, (Breen and Innes, *"Myne Owne Ground,"* 22–23). William L. Andrews offers a more careful reading of the diary in "William Johnson's Diary."

4. For example, Doddington, *Contesting Slave Masculinity;* Lussana, *My Brother Slaves;* Plath and Lussana, *Black and White Masculinity in the American South, 1800–2000;* Buckner and Caster, *Fathers, Preachers, Rebels, Men;* and Forret, *Slave against Slave.*

5. Bederman, *Manliness and Civilization*, 7. Works that cover the various ways men publicly displayed and measured their manliness include Franklin, *The Militant South;* Wyatt-Brown, *Southern Honor;* Stowe, *Intimacy and Power in the Old South;* Rotundo, *American Manhood;* Kimmel, *Manhood in America;* Greenberg, *Honor and Slavery;* Friend and Glover, *Southern Manhood;* and Moon, "Southern Baptists and Southern Men."

6. Citizenship within republican philosophy was reserved for white men, and notions of independence and liberty were most often discussed in gendered language or as a contrast to slavery. The Founders of the United States drew their sense of patriarchy from the writings of John Locke, who used the Bible as a justification for male dominance as Adam was created first and was to be dominant and, as such, all men were superior to women (Locke, *Two Treatises of Civil Government*, 9–69). George Washington, often discussed as the "father" of the American republic, most directly put voice to idea that for white men to submit to the authority of the British made them slaves, writing that "the crisis is arrived when we must assert our rights, or submit to every imposition that can be heaped upon us, till custom and

use shall make us as tame and abject slaves, as the blacks we rule over with such arbitrary sway" (quoted in M. Johnson, *Reading the American Past*, 109). See also Jordan, *White over Black;* E. S. Morgan, *American Slavery, American Freedom;* Frey, *Water from the Rock;* K. M. Brown, *Good Wives, Nasty Wenches, and Anxious Patriarchs;* Bloch, "The Construction of Gender in a Republican World"; and Lyons, *Sex among the Rabble.*

7. Hurricane, "The Negro and His Management," 277. The most complete study of African American fathers in this era is Hilde, *Slavery, Fatherhood, and Paternal Duty.*

8. Baptist, *Creating an Old South*, 88–246; Cashin, *A Family Venture*, 99–246.

9. Buckner, "A Crucible of Masculinity," in *Fathers, Preachers, Rebels, Men*, ed. Buckner and Caster, 23–40; Walker, *David Walker's Appeal*, 7–78; Douglass, *Narrative of the Life of Frederick Douglass*, 65–66; Baptist, "The Absent Subject," in *Southern Manhood*, ed. Friend and Glover, 136–73.

10. Walker, *David Walker's Appeal*, 68.

11. Potter, *A Hairdresser's Experience in High Life*, xii.

12. Elkins, *Slavery*, 81–133.

13. Stampp, *The Peculiar Institution*, 3–430; Elkins, *Slavery*, 2–133; Blassingame, *Slave Community*, 3–332; Genovese, *Roll, Jordan, Roll*, 3–665.

14. Forret, *Slave against Slave*, 1–411; Lussana, *My Brother Slaves*, 1–146; Doddington, *Contesting Slave Masculinity*, 1–215.

15. Doddington, *Contesting Slave Masculinity*, 20–48, 171–210; Walter Johnson, "On Agency," 113–24.

16. Doddington, *Contesting Slave Masculinity*, 49–210; Hilde, *Slavery, Fatherhood, and Paternal Duty*, 67–91.

17. Bristol, *Knights of the Razor*, 4–5; Rotundo, *American Manhood*, 18–25.

18. Free people of color took a wide range of positions on slavery. Examples can be found in M. P. Johnson and Roark, *Black Masters*, 23–25; Hanger, *Bounded Lives Bounded Places*, 55–87; Thomas Ingersoll, "Free Blacks in a Slave Society, 1718–1812," 173–200; Berlin, *Slaves without Masters*, 271–83; Sydnor, "The Free Negro in Mississippi before the Civil War," 769–70; Koger, *Black Slaveowners*, 1–200; and Woodson, *Free Negro Owners of Slaves*, v–vii.

19. W. Johnson, *William Johnson's Natchez* (hereafter cited as *Diary*), 259, 282, 357.

20. This type of masculinity is usually associated with frontiersmen who engaged in "rough and tumble fighting" but could also be applied to planters who used their power not just to dominate their households and the people they enslaved, but their political rivals and anyone else who they felt had slighted them. Though this kind of no-holds-barred fighting was brutal, its ultimate result might not be any different from a ritualized duel which left combatants just as maimed or just as dead (Baptist, *Creating an Old South*, 90–103; Gorn, "Gouge and Bite").

21. As Baptist argued in a different context, "the only way to erase a mark of submissiveness was to kill one's opponent" (Baptist, *Creating an Old South*, 109).

22. Forret, "He was no man attall?," in *Fathers, Preachers, Rebels, Men*, ed. Buckner and Caster, 23–40; Greenberg, *Honor & Slavery*, 1–146; Wyatt-Brown, *Southern Honor*, 341–50; Findlay, *People of Chance*, 44–78; Proctor, *Bathed in Blood*, 61–98.

1. TRAINING BARBERS AND MEN

1. Hilde, *Slavery, Fatherhood, and Paternal Duty*, 88; Genovese, *Roll, Jordan, Roll*, 3–158; Walter Johnson, *Soul by Soul*, 19–44; Phillips, *Life and Labor in the Old South*, 3–304. The idea of paternalism originated with the work of U. B. Phillips, a southern apologist for slavery, who argued that slavery actually was a benevolent institution whose image had been warped by abolitionists. Charles Sydnor's *Slavery in Mississippi* applies Phillips notion of slavery as benign and unprofitable to Mississippi. This view remained the standard until Kenneth Stampp's *The Peculiar Institution* reintroduced the ideas that slavery was brutal and that enslavers made decisions to better their own financial positions, not because they felt a bond with the men and women they enslaved. Eugene Genovese fundamentally altered the debate on slavery by not only accepting that enslaved people had agency but also by reinterpreting the meanings of paternalism. *Roll, Jordan, Roll* uses a Marxist framework to argue that the nineteenth-century American South was precapitalist. This does not suggest planters were not acquisitive, but rather that it was not their purpose to acquire capital simply to acquire more capital. Instead, what emerged was a semifeudal South based not on free labor, but on paternalism—a system of mutual obligations between enslaver and slave. Slavery rested on the assumption that these men and women were property but that their humanity was also recognized. This is not to suggest that the relationship between the two was an equal one. Plainly, the enslaver exerted hegemony over the enslaved, but even though this was a relation of dominance, room for resistance existed. Within this room the enslaved were able to make their own "world." To Genovese, and others, slave culture (language, religion, art, families, etc.) represents resistance to this hegemony. This represents a difference from the paternalism of Phillips who argued that it was a necessity for African Americans who did not possess their own culture. Genovese's paternalism does not present slavery as a benevolent institution. The inherent inequality in the master/slave relationship meant that these mutual obligations were not voluntary on the part of the slave, nor were they without cruelty. Since Genovese, countless scholars have challenged and modified the notion of slaveholder paternalism. Walter Johnson makes the point that slaveholders were not "exercising hegemony" but rather waging a war on the everyday resistance engaged in by the enslaved (Walter Johnson, "A Nettlesome Classic Turns Twenty-Five"). Kathleen Hilliard uses the internal economy of enslaved people to demonstrate the push and pull of slaveholders' power in *Masters, Slaves, and Exchange*. Most scholarship of Mississippi and the region has shifted away from the view that slaveholders were paternalists and recognizes the role of capitalism within slavery; this is best exemplified in Baptist, *The Half Has Never Been Told*.

2. Lussana, *My Brother Slaves*, 71–97; Forret, *Slave against Slave*, 43–411; Doddington, *Contesting Slave Masculinity*, 127–210.

3. Bristol, *Knights of the Razor*, 4–5; Welch, *Black Litigants in the Antebellum American South*, 60–81; Welch, "Black Litigiousness and White Accountability."

4. Some of these ideas are explored in Buckner, "A Crucible of Masculinity," in *Fathers, Preachers, Rebels, Men*, ed. Buckner and Caster, 41–59.

5. Breen and Innes, *"Myne Owne Ground,"* 7–114; Berlin, *Slaves without Masters*, 3–5; Hening, *The Statutes at Large; Being a Collection of All the Laws of Virginia*, 267.

6. Berlin, *Slaves without Masters,* 7; Jordan, *White over Black,* 123.

7. Berlin, *Slaves Without Masters,* 8; Jordan, *White over Black,* 125–26.

8. Berlin, *Slaves without Masters,* 15–24; Quarles, Tate, and Nash, *The Negro in the American Revolution,* 19–200.

9. Berlin, *Slaves without Masters,* 25–33; George Washington's Last Will and Testament, in *The Papers of George Washington,* ed. Abbot, 479–511; Frey, *Water from the Rock,* 243–83. More on manumissions can be found in T. D. Morris, *Southern Slavery and the Law,* 371–423; Kennington, *In the Shadow of Dred Scott,* 117–41; and Schweninger, *Appealing for Liberty,* 70–91.

10. Berlin, *Slaves without Masters,* 35–50; Jordan, *White over Black,* 380–86.

11. Berlin, *Slaves without Masters,* 46–47, 136–37; Sydnor, "The Free Negro in Mississippi before the Civil War," 779n45; Ribianszky, *Generations of Freedom,* 26; Libby, *Slavery and Frontier Mississippi,* 33.

12. Sydnor, "The Free Negro in Mississippi before the Civil War," 769, 774; quote from Randall v. the State, 12 Miss. 349. The most complete summary of the Mississippi Supreme Court's thoughts on free people of color and manumission can be found in Mitchell v. Wells, 37 Miss. 235 (1859).

13. Sydnor, "The Free Negro in Mississippi before the Civil War," 769–71; Howard and Hutchinson, *The Statutes of the State of Mississippi,* 165.

14. Sydnor, "The Free Negro in Mississippi before the Civil War," 770; Howard and Hutchinson, *The Statutes of the State of Mississippi,* 168–69; Welch, *Black Litigants in the Antebellum American South,* 18.

15. Ribianszky, *Generations of Freedom,* 9, 20–21; Hanger, *Bounded Lives Bounded Places,* 24–26.

16. Howard and Hutchinson, *The Statutes of the State of Mississippi,* 157–65, 152.

17. Berlin, *Slaves without Masters,* 226.

18. Lightner and Ragan, "Were African American Slaveholders Benevolent or Exploitative?," 540; M. P. Johnson and Roark, *Black Masters,* 13.

19. Lightner and Ragan, "Were African American Slaveholders Benevolent or Exploitative?," 540–41; M. P. Johnson and Roark, *Black Masters,* 143–45.

20. Lebsock, *The Free Women of Petersburg,* 97–98; Ribianszky, *Generations of Freedom,* 10, 39–80; Brent, *Incidents in the Life of a Slave Girl. Written by Herself,* 44–303. in In *The Hemingses of Monticello,* Annette Gordon Reed takes a different position from Ribianszky, contending that enslaved women like Sally Hemings had more agency in their choices.

21. *Diary,* 15; Gould, *Chained to the Rock of Adversity,* xxvi–xxvii.

22. William Johnson's Petition to the Mississippi Legislature, via the Race and Slavery Petitions Project at the University of North Carolina–Greensboro (hereafter cited as RSPP) PAR# 11082002; B. D. Jones, *Fathers of Conscience,* 98–124.

23. Mitchell v. Wells, 37 Miss. 235 (1859).

24. *Barber,* 16; RSPP PAR# 11082002.

25. P. D. Morgan, *Slave Counterpoint,* 244–46; Bristol, *Knights of the Razor,* 8–14.

26. Ribianszky, *Generations of Freedom,* 107; Bristol, *Knights of the Razor,* 41; Mills, *Cutting along the Color Line,* 15–59; Welch, *Black Litigants in the Antebellum American South,* 62.

27. *Barber,* 16–18; *Diary,* 136; Gould, *Chained to the Rock of Adversity,* 4. Gould suggests that it is probable that white William Johnson remained close to both William and Adelia throughout their lives.

28. *Barber,* 19–20; Gould, *Chained to the Rock of Adversity,* xxviii.

29. R. L. F. Davis, *The Black Experience in Natchez,* 57. A less dim view of barbering can be found in Bristol, *Knights of the Razor.*

30. Walker, *David Walker's Appeal,* 29.

31. Delany, *The Condition, Elevation, Emigration, and Destiny of the Colored People of the United States,* 5; Harris, *In the Shadow of Slavery,* 230–33.

32. Potter, *A Hairdresser's Experience in High Life,* xxiv–xxv.

33. Berlin, *Slaves without Masters,* 60; Bristol, *Knights of the* Razor, 10; Thomas, *From Tennessee Slave to St. Louis Entrepreneur,* 89–90.

34. R. L. F. Davis, *The Black Experience in Natchez,* 60; Tubee, *The Life of Okah Tubbee,* xii–xxxviii. Warner was eventually apprenticed to a blacksmith and given permission to stay in Natchez as a free man, though he may never have formally become free. Warner sometimes called himself James Warner, but he left Natchez, took on the name Okah Tubbee, and claimed a Native American heritage. He later became a performer as Okah Tubbee and wrote an autobiography that never mentioned that he was actually Black and born into slavery. On June 9, 1850, Johnson read a book he called "O. Ka. Chublee" that he described as "a tisue of Lies from beginning to Ending" (*Diary,* 727).

35. R. L. F. Davis, *The Black Experience in Natchez,* 62.

36. R. L. F. Davis, *The Black Experience in Natchez,* 62; Walter Johnson, "On Agency," 113–24; Doddington, *Contesting Slave Masculinity,* 49–88. Doddington makes the point that holding a position of authority, even if appointed by whites, marked status and manliness within a slave society.

37. R. L. F. Davis, *The Black Experience in Natchez,* 63; *Natchez Weekly Courier,* November 9, 1859, quoted ibid.; Behrend, *Reconstructing Democracy,* 81–83.

38. R. L. F. Davis, *The Black Experience in Natchez,* 63; *Natchez Weekly Courier,* November 12, 1866; *Christian Recorder,* October 20, 1866; Behrend, *Reconstructing Democracy,* 81–83; Wyatt-Brown, "The Mask of Obedience," 1228–52.

39. *Diary,* 221, 248–49.

40. *Natchez Courier,* July 2, 1858, in R. L. F. Davis, *The Black Experience in Natchez,* 61.

41. *Diary,* 207.

42. *Diary,* 450.

43. *Diary,* 648.

44. Bristol, *Knights of the Razor,* 41.

45. In Mobile, enslaved barbers eventually displaced free Black barbers (Bristol, *Knights of the Razor,* 80–81; Amos, *Cotton City,* 89–91; Berlin and Gutman, "Natives and Immigrants, Free Men and Slaves," 1186).

46. *Diary,* 61–62, 350; Andrews, "William Johnson's Diary," 26.

47. *Diary,* 28–29, 126.

48. Cashin, *A Family Venture,* 100–103.

49. *Diary,* 330-31.

50. It is not clear from the entry which sister, either Misouri or January, would stay in town or where, but Johnson was able to place her as an apprentice with a woman named Ms. Dowell, though he later removed her because the woman was "too foul mouthed" (Ribianszky, *Generations of Freedom,* 109; *Diary* 333, 333n7, and 334n8; Howard, *Reports of Cases Argued and Determined in the High Court of Errors and Appeals,* 12-15).

51. *Diary,* 69; Adelia Miller to William Johnson, January 2, 1844, in *Chained to the Rock of Adversity,* ed. Gould, 3.

52. Johnson usually wrote entries for any confrontations he had with anyone regarding business issues, but there is no mention of this incident in the first week of January, 1844. Nix was back on the river on January 8 (*Diary,* 470-71).

53. Baily, *Journal of a Tour in Unsettled Parts of North America,* 150.

54. Elliot, "City and Empire: The Spanish Origins of Natchez," 275. See also Crouch, Carr, and Mundigo, *Spanish City Planning in North America,* 1-3, 23-26.

55. *Diary,* 67n9, 232, 234.

56. Camp, *Closer to Freedom,* 18.

57. Gould, *Chained to the Rock of Adversity,* xxviii; B. D. Jones, *Fathers of Conscience,* 54-57.

58. By 1860, only 5 percent of free Blacks lived in white households. Davis, *The Black Experience in Natchez,* 51-62; Syndor, "The Free Negro in Mississippi before the Civil War"; Ribianszky, *Generations of Freedom,* 15-38. Ribianszky discusses "waves" of free Blacks entering Natchez from after 1787, but given that the population of free people of color grows from 22 in 1787 to only 283 in 1840 (an increase of 260 in fifty-three years), it is hard to think of this as a real influx, especially since the enslaved population grew by 13,566 in the same span.

59. Wyatt-Brown, *Southern Honor,* 295.

60. *Barber,* 233-40; Gould, *Chained to the Rock of Adversity,* 36n1.

61. *Diary,* 257.

62. *Diary,* 259.

63. Hilde, *Slavery, Fatherhood, and Paternal Duty,* 39-42; H. B. Brown, *Narrative of Henry Box Brown,* 23.

64. Ribianszky, *Generations of Freedom,* 130-31; Lebsock, *The Free Women of Petersburg,* 109.

65. Johnson beat and whipped his workers who went to these parties without permission (*Diary,* 73, 314; *Barber,* 56-57).

66. *Diary,* 485-87.

67. *Diary,* 489-90.

68. *Diary,* 501.

69. *Diary,* 385.

70. *Diary,* 446.

71. *Diary,* 614.

72. Diary, 771.

73. *Diary,* 771, 782.

74. *Diary,* 28-29, 126.

75. *Diary,* 135.

76. *Diary,* 182.

77. *Diary,* 247, 335.

78. *Diary,* 394-95.

79. *Diary,* 527.

80. *Diary,* 28-29.

81. Hiring out enslaved people might have been "a step toward freedom" in some of the Upper South, but for much of the Deep South, especially in cities, hiring out simply demonstrated the flexibility of the peculiar institution (Eaton, "Slave-Hiring in the Upper South"; Wade, *Slavery in the Cities,* 38-54).

82. Doddington, *Contesting Slave Masculinity,* 20-48, 171-210; Walter Johnson, "On Agency," 113-24.

83. Woodson, *Free Owners of Slaves.* Woodson's argument that free Blacks mostly held family members in nominal slavery was upheld by several other classic works on slavery including Stampp, *The Peculiar Institution,* 194; Oakes, *The Ruling Race,* 47-48; and Franklin, *From Slavery to Freedom,* 224. Other studies of free people of color who owned slaves offer different conclusions, such as Berlin, *Slaves without Masters;* M. P. Johnson and Roark, *Black Masters;* Koger, *Black Slaveowners;* and Lightner and Ragan, "Were African American Slaveholders Benevolent or Exploitative?" See also Schweninger, "Prosperous Blacks in the South, 1790-1880," 31-56; and Schermerhorn, *Money over Mastery, Family over Freedom,* 134-63.

84. Potter, *A Hairdresser's Experience in High Life,* xxv-xxvi.

85. Lightner and Ragan, "Were African American Slaveholders Benevolent or Exploitative?"; Schweninger, "John Carruthers Stanly and the Anomaly of Black Slaveholding."

86. Lightner and Ragan, "Were African American Slaveholders Benevolent or Exploitative?," 540. Michael P. Johnson and James L. Roark offer a detailed study of Ellison's life in *Black Masters,* and a collection of the family's letters can be found in Roark and Johnson, *No Chariot Let Down.*

87. Lightner and Ragan, "Were African American Slaveholders Benevolent or Exploitative?, 543-44. For a full account of Durnford's life, see Whitten, *Andrew Durnford: A Black Sugar Planter in the Antebellum South.*

88. For an example, see J. E. K. Walker, *Free Frank.*

89. The most direct challenge to Woodson's thesis of benevolent Black slaveholders is Larry Koger, *Black Slaveowners,* who argues that free Black enslavers were motivated by profit. Lightner and Ragan use the same data as both Woodson and Koger, but come to a middle ground conclusion that it is true that some African Americans held family and friends in nominal slavery, but that it is also the case that the numbers of African American enslavers is understated and not as well understood as other aspects of the peculiar institution.

90. *Diary,* 481.

91. *Diary,* 783.

92. *Diary,* 568-69; *Barber,* 64.

93. *Diary,* 569; Doddington, *Contesting Slave Masculinity,* 127-70. The stereotype that people of African heritage had insatiable sexual appetites dates back to early interactions between Europeans and Africans. Racist fears about African American men as dangerous sexual predators were mostly constructed after slavery ended (see Jordan, *White over Black,* 32-43, 150-63; and Hodes, *White Women, Black Men,* 1-11).

94. *Diary*, 670. Hilde contends that enslaved communities shunned Black women who voluntarily engaged in sexual relationships with white men (*Slavery, Fatherhood, & Paternal Duty*), 217.

95. Diary of Catherine Geraldine Johnson, September 16, 1864, in *Chained to the Rock of Adversity*, ed. Gould, 72. The Union occupied Natchez in July 1863 (Broussard, "Occupied Natchez, Elite Women, and the Feminization of the Civil War").

96. *Diary*, 72n.

97. *Diary*, 97.

98. A. Rothman, *Slave Country*, x–xi.

99. *Diary*, 185, letter to Mrs. James Miller quoted in 185n26.

100. *Barber*, 64.

101. The domestic slave trade is covered in Tadman, *Speculators and Slaves;* Walter Johnson, *Soul by Soul;* Deyle, *Carry Me Back;* Williams, *Help Me to Find My People;* Pargas, *Slavery and Forced Migration in the Antebellum South;* and Baptist, *The Half Has Never Been Told.* Hilde discusses running away as an expression of masculinity in *Slavery, Fatherhood, & Paternal Duty*, 137–48.

102. Welch, *Black Litigants in the Antebellum American South*, 62.

103. Alcoholism is a physiological illness, but the reasons people drink and the behaviors associated with drinking are determined as much or more by cultural and social expectation as chemical reactions within the body. As one scholar of alcohol consumption has noted, ethanol is probably the most popular drug in world history, but "although it has been known and used in most societies throughout the world, there is no universal use, meaning, or function for alcohol" (Heath, "In Other Cultures, They Also Drink," in *Alcohol, Science, and Society Revisited*, ed. Gomberg, White, and Carpenter, 63; Wyatt-Brown, *Southern Honor*, 41, 68, 278–81).

104. *Barber*, 64; *Diary*, 131n46; Wyatt-Brown, *Southern Honor*, 278–80.

105. *Diary*, 90–91, 134.

106. Noonan v. State, 9 Miss. 562, 1844, in *Reports of Cases Argued and Determined in the High Court of Errors and Appeals for the State of Mississippi*, by Smedes and Marshall, 562–74.

107. Noonan v. State, 9 Miss. 562, 1844.

108. Jolly v. State, 16 Miss. 145; Smedes and Marshall, *Reports of Cases Argued and Determined in the High Court of Errors and Appeals for the State of Mississippi*, 562–74.

109. *Natchez Courier*, August 13, 1840, in *Diary*, 309n52.

110. *Diary*, 223–25.

111. *Diary*, 276, 283, 289, 303, 327, 331.

112. *Barber*, 64–66; *Diary*, 469–70.

113. *Diary*, 424.

114. Potter, *A Hairdresser's Experience in High Life*, xviii–xx; Bristol, *Knights of the Razor*, 41–70; Mills, *Cutting across the Color Line*, 17–59.

2. MANLY COMPETITION: GAMBLING, HUNTING, FISHING, AND FIGHTING

1. Stott, *Jolly Fellows*, 56.

2. Stott, *Jolly Fellows*, 56; Lussana, "No Band of Brothers Could Be More Loving," 876; Wyatt-Brown, *Southern Honor*, 327–61; Forret, "He was no man attall?," in *Fathers, Preachers, Rebels, Men*, ed. Buckner and Caster, 23–40; Gorn, "Gouge and Bite," 18–43.

3. Bristol, *Knights of the Razor,* 13–15.

4. Wyatt-Brown, *Southern Honor,* 341–50; Greenberg, *Honor & Slavery,* 135–45. Both deal with gambling essentially as a sport. A card game certainly has specific rules, but winning a card game requires more than just adhering to the rules of that game. In card games where players compete against one another, the player with the most money, or the willingness to lose the most money, has a decisive strategic advantage over others. John M. Findlay argues that gambling was a chance to demonstrate equality among participants in *People of Chance,* 51.

5. James, *Antebellum Natchez,* 88–89; Schultz quoted ibid., 89.

6. Martineau, *Society in America,* 157.

7. John B. Nevitt Diary, April 3, 1828, as quoted in Wyatt-Brown, *Southern Honor,* 340.

8. *Washington Republican and Natchez Intelligencer,* May 29, 1816, quoted in Beard, "Frontier Port," 33.

9. *Mississippi Herald and Natchez Gazette,* May 20, 1806, as quoted in Beard, "Frontier Port," 37.

10. Hall, "Reminiscence of Natchez Under-the-Hill, My Grandmother's Trick," in *Before Mark Twain,* ed. McDermott, 196–98.

11. Hall, "Reminiscence of Natchez Under-the-Hill, My Grandmother's Trick," in *Before Mark Twain,* ed. McDermott, 196–200.

12. Green, "Gamblers and Suckers," in *Before Mark Twain,* ed. McDermott, 200–204.

13. Beard, "Frontier Port," 40–41; Herring, "Natchez 1795–1830," 117–38; Howard and Hutchinson, *The Statutes of the State of Mississippi,* 677–85.

14. Beard, "Frontier Port," 40–41.

15. There is no direct connection between the rumored revolt and the crackdown on Vicksburg's gamblers in except in terms of the heightened levels of anxiety and suspicion of whites on the fringes of the slave society. Several historians have investigated the insurrection plot in Madison (see C. Morris, "An Event in Community Organization"; Shore, "Making Mississippi Safe for Slavery," in *Class, Conflict, and Consensus,* ed. Burton and McMath, 173–206; Libby, *Slavery and Frontier in Mississippi,* 103–18). The most complete primary source on the execution of the gamblers and the conspiracy is Shackelford, *Proceedings of the Citizens of Madison County, Mississippi, at Livingston,* in *The History of Virgil A. Stewart,* by Howard, 223–25; Freehling, *The Road to Disunion,* vol. 1: *Secessionists at Bay,* 110–11; J. D. Rothman, "Hazards of the Flush Times."

16. Shackelford, Livingston pamphlet, in Howard, *The History of Virgil A. Stewart,* 264.

17. Shackelford, Livingston pamphlet, in Howard, *The History of Virgil A. Stewart,* 263.

18. James, *Antebellum Natchez,* 254; de Montulé, *Travels in America,* 96; Breen, "Horses and Gentlemen."

19. James, *Antebellum Natchez,* 255; de Montulé, *Travels in America,* 96.

20. Walter Johnson, *Soul by Soul,* 24–25.

21. *Barber,* 206; *Diary,* 592.

22. *Diary,* 104–5.

23. *Diary,* 84.

24. *Diary,* 111; *Barber,* 206.

25. *Barber,* 206

26. *Barber,* 206; *Diary,* 592.

27. Wyatt-Brown, *Southern Honor,* 345–46; Welch, *Black Litigants in the Antebellum American South,* 115–18; Merritt, *Masterless Men,* 120–13.

28. *Diary,* 170, 686; Boastful traveling men on the Mississippi who frequented gambling establishments in Natchez-Under-the-Hill and elsewhere often used comparisons to animals to demonstrate their own characteristics; for example, one such individual claimed, "I am an alligator; half man, half horse; can whip any on the *Mississippi* by G-d" (A. K. Moore, *The Frontier Mind,* 115; Gorn, "Gouge and Bite," 28).

29. Proctor, *Bathed in Blood,* 61–74.

30. *Diary,* 142.

31. *Diary,* 148–49, 400

32. *Diary,* 317, 397.

33. *Diary,* 237–38; 244, 310, 485.

34. *Barber,* 247–48; *Diary,* 638.

35. *Diary,* 177.

36. Washington Sterns letter fragment, March 6, 1829; *Diary,* 287.

37. *Diary,* 120.

38. *Diary,* 144n, 288.

39. *Diary,* 337, 282.

40. *Diary,* 252.

41. *Diary,* 348.

42. *Diary,* 518.

43. *Diary,* 624.

44. *Diary,* 513.

45. *Diary,* 658, 702.

46. *Diary,* 718.

47. *Diary,* 492.

48. Stott, *Jolly Fellows,* 40–56; "Moral Education," *De Bow's Review* 18 (March 1855): 432.

49. Cashin, *A Family Venture,* 100–103.

50. Stott, *Jolly Fellows,* 40–56; Wyatt-Brown, *Southern Honor,* 327–61; Gorn, "Gouge and Bite," 18–43; Bruce, *Violence and Culture in the Antebellum South,* 21–160; Lussana, *My Brother Slaves,* 1–124; Forret, *Slave against Slave,* 302–346.

51. *Diary,* 149–50; *Mississippi Free Trader and Natchez Gazette,* December 2, 1836, December 9, 1836.

52. *Diary,* 150.

53. Wyatt-Brown, *Southern Honor,* 352–401; Ayers, *Vengeance and Justice,* 9–33; Franklin, *The Militant South,* 1–95.

54. *Mississippi Free Trader,* November 20, 1835.

55. *Diary,* 77–78.

56. Prentiss, *A Memoir of S. S. Prentiss,* 134.

57. Foote, *Casket of Reminiscences,* 181, 200–201. As Foote's memoir makes clear, dueling could be just as violent as fights by lower-class men and the practice might have led to more

conflict. Baptist makes the argument in *Creating an Old South* that duels were simply refined forms of vengeance; since someone had to lose, duels created hierarchies of masculinity, not equality (107-10).

58. *Diary*, 227-28.

59. *Diary*, 228.

60. *Mississippi Free Trader*, April 16, 1838; see also *Diary*, 228-29.

61. *Diary*, 240. Johnson knew Spielman and had loaned him money in 1837 (*Diary*, 169).

62. *Barber*, 144.

63. *Diary*, 352.

64. *Barber*, 144.

65. *Diary*, 329.

66. *Barber*, 144.

67. *Diary*, 336.

68. *Diary*, 336.

69. *Diary*, 456.

70. *Diary*, 167-68.

71. *Diary*, 604.

3. POLITICS, RACE, AND MASCULINITY

1. *Diary*, 98; McDuffie, "The Natural Slavery of the Negro" (1835), in *The American Debate over Slavery*, ed. Hammond, Hardwick, and Lubert, 139-42.

2. "A Declaration of the Immediate Causes Which Induce and Justify the Secession of the State of Mississippi from the Federal Union" (1860), in *Journal of the State Convention and Ordinances and Resolutions Adopted in January, 1861*, 22. A wide range of proslavery thought is available in Faust, *The Ideology of Slavery*.

3. Berlin, *Slaves without Masters*, 90; Painter, *The History of White People*, 106-7; Wilentz, *The Rise of American Democracy*, 17, 27-28, 82-83, 485; Ribianszky, *Generations of Freedom*, 158.

4. Bederman, *Manliness and Civilization*, 20; Halloran, "Shall I Trust These Men?," in *Fathers, Preachers, Rebels, Men*, ed. Buckner and Caster; Shire, "Sentimental Racism and Sympathetic Paternalism"; Field, *The Struggle for Equal Adulthood*, 53-76.

5. Van Gosse, *The First Reconstruction*, 29-56. Examples of enslaved peoples' politics can be found in Camp, *Closer to Freedom*, 35-138; Hahn, *A Nation under Their Feet*, 13-159; and Field, *The Struggle for Equal Adulthood*, 61-76.

6. Welch, "William Johnson's Hypothesis," 1-36.

7. Phillips, *Life and Labor in the Old South*, 3-304; Baptist, *The Half Has Never Been Told*, 1-144; Cashin, *A Family Venture*, 99-118; Tadman, *Speculators and Slaves*, 111-224. Some historians who disagree are C. Morris, *Becoming Southern;* and Libby, *Slavery and Frontier Mississippi.*

8. The white population of Adams County was 4,005 with 7,953 slaves in 1820 ("Adams County," *The Mississippi Encyclopedia*). On the cotton boom, see J. H. Moore, *The Emergence of the Cotton Kingdom in the Old Southwest*, 1-36.

9. Walter Johnson, *Soul by Soul*, 23; Clarke, *Narrative of Sufferings of Lewis Clarke*, 84; Stroyer, *My Life in the South* 40; Henson, *An Autobiography of the Reverend Josiah Henson*, 44.

10. Sydnor, *Slavery in Mississippi*, 3–22; J. H. Moore, *The Emergence of the Cotton Kingdom in the Old Southwest*, 27–92; Libby, *Slavery in Frontier Mississippi*, 42–105. For a discussion of conditions in the South Carolina lowcountry, see Dusinberre, *Them Dark Days;* Joyner, *Down by the Riverside;* and N. Jones, *Born a Child of Freedom Yet a Slave*. For the work environments of sugar plantations, consult Mintz, *Sweetness and Power;* Schwartz, *Sugar Plantations in the Formation of Brazilian Society;* Tadman, "The Demographic Cost of Sugar"; and Follett, "Lives of Living Death."

11. Anderson, *The Life and Narrative of William Anderson*, 14–15.

12. J. Brown, *Biography of an American Bondsman by His Daughter*, 19, 27.

13. Webb, *The History of William Webb*, 8–9.

14. *Frederick Douglass' Paper*, June, 22 1855.

15. *North Star*, December 29, 1848.

16. Weld, *American Slavery as It Is*, 107.

17. *National Era* (Washington, DC), July 1, 1847.

18. Weld, *American Slavery As It Is*, 108–9.

19. Douglass, *Life and Times of Frederick Douglass,*156.

20. Southerners adapted slavery to urban milieus for most of the antebellum era, though Richard Wade points out that by 1860, it was on the decline in most southern cities (Wade, *Slavery in the Cities*, 243–81).

21. *Diary*, 121, 222.

22. *Diary*, 470.

23. *Diary*, 226. Frances Smith Foster compellingly argues that marriages between enslaved couples were far more binding than enslavers and later generations of white policy makers believed in *"Til Death or Distance Do Us Part."*

24. *Diary*, 227.

25. *Barber*, 144; Camp, *Closer to Freedom*, 7.

26. *Mississippi Free Trader*, August 7, 1841.

27. *Diary*, 281–82.

28. *Diary*, 231.

29. *Diary*, 89; *Mississippi Free Trader*, January 8, 1836.

30. *Diary*, 91.

31. *Mississippi Free Trader*, January 8, 1836; *Diary*, 92.

32. *Diary*, 92.

33. *Mississippi Free Trader*, January 15, 1836.

34. *Diary*, 92.

35. *Diary*, 93; Ribianszky, *Generations of Freedom*, 63.

36. *Diary*, 94.

37. Lavinia Miller to Ann Johnson, November 23, 1850, in *Chained to the Rock of Adversity*, ed. Gould, 10.

38. *Barber*, 39–40. For instances of his money lending activity, see *Diary*, especially the year 1836; Welch, "Arteries of Capital"; and Welch, *Black Litigants in the American Antebellum South*, 116–19, 125.

39. *Barber*, 41–42.

40. *Diary*, 162–63.

41. *Diary*, 32, 163; *Barber*, 44; Welch, "Arteries of Capital."

42. Baptist, *The Half Has Never Been Told*, 224–26; Wilentz, *The Rise of American Democracy*, 379; James, *Antebellum Natchez*, 101–35; *Woodville (MS) Republican*, June 27, 1846, quoted in James, *Antebellum Natchez*, 125.

43. *Diary*, 352; *Mississippi Free Trader*, August 27, 1840.

44. *Mississippi Free Trader*, August 31, 1840.

45. *Mississippi Free Trader*, August 31, 1840. George Mason Hooe's letter and information on the court-martial can be found in *House Documents, Otherwise Publ. as Executive Documents*, 59–62.

46. Kendall, "The Case of Lieutenant Hooe," in *The Extra Globe*, ed. Kendall and Blair, 157–59, emphasis in original.

47. *Diary*, 183; Snyder, *Great Crossings*, 60–61.

48. Emmons, *Authentic Biography of Col. Richard M. Johnson of Kentucky*, 30–37.

49. Ramage and Watkins, *Kentucky Rising*, 121; National Parks Service, "Autumn, 1813: Tecumseh's Death Launches Artwork and Political Careers," www.nps.gov/articles/death-of-tecumseh.htm.

50. Snyder, *Great Crossings*, 52–62.

51. *Jinnoowine [genuine] Johnson Ticket*.

52. Robinson, *An Affecting Scene in Kentucky*.

53. Synder, *Great Crossings*, 302.

54. *Diary*, 760.

55. *Diary*, 290.

56. *Diary*, 290.

57. *Diary*, 290.

58. *Diary*, 291.

59. *Diary*, 291–92.

60. *Diary*, 292–93; *Natchez Weekly Courier and Journal*, September 3, 1840.

61. *Diary*, 343.

62. *Diary*, 380.

63. *Diary*, 486, 529.

64. *Diary*, 498. Henry Clay's visit is discussed on page 418.

65. *Diary*, 507.

66. *Diary*, 588. He bet Winston on a city election later and won fifteen dollars (*Diary*, 602).

67. *Diary*, 589.

68. *Diary*, 590–91.

69. *Diary*, 632–33.

70. *Natchez*, March 5, 1831, in James, *Antebellum Natchez*, 175.

71. Sydnor, *Slavery in Mississippi*, 204.

72. Sydnor, *Slavery in Mississippi*, 205–6; American Colonization Society, *The African Repository and Colonial Journal* 5:182; Wilentz, *The Rise of American Democracy*, 210–11.

73. Sydnor, *Slavery in Mississippi*, 207–8; James, *Antebellum Natchez*, 175.

74. Gales, *The Debates and Proceedings in the Congress of the United States*, 1047–51; Ford, *Deliver Us from Evil*, 449–534.

75. The Constitution of Mississippi 1817, via Mississippi History Now, https://mshistorynow.mdah.ms.gov/issue/mississippi-constitution-of-1817; The Constitution of Mississippi 1832, via Mississippi History Now, https://mshistorynow.mdah.ms.gov/issue/mississippi-constitution-of-1832.

76. The 1832 annual report of the Mississippi Colonization Society appears in the *Woodville Republican*, March 31, 1832; and Sydnor, *Slavery in Mississippi*, 210-11.

77. Gloster Simpson and Archy Moore in Knight, *The New Republic*, 116-17.

78. Gloster Simpson appears in the Monrovia Census of 1843 along with Abigail and his daughters Hester Ann and Nancy. See the Roll of Emigrants at https://ccharity.com/contents/roll-emigrants-have-been-sent-colony-liberia-western-africa/emigrants-to-liberia-census-lists/monroviacensus5/. Gloster Simpson was still living in Monrovia and corresponding with Benjamin Drake, a Methodist minister in Natchez at least through 1845 (Benjamin Drake and Family Papers, MDAH). Archy Moore, his brother David, and their families arrived in Monrovia via the same ship, the *Rover*, as the Simpson family in 1835 (*African Repository* 11, no. 4 [April 1835]: 121-26, 153-54).

79. Sydnor, *Slavery in Mississippi*, 211.

80. Walker, *David Walker's Appeal*, 6, 15. Frederick Douglass deals with this version of manliness in his autobiographies when discussing his time with the slave-breaker, Edward Covey. In each instance, Douglass uses his fight with Covey to demonstrate "how a slave became a man" through fighting back against a white man in authority (Douglass, *Narrative of the Life of Frederick Douglass*, 65-66). The language changed somewhat in two subsequent autobiographies, but the sentiment remained the same. See also Doddington, *Contesting Slave Masculinity*, 1-48; Fraser, "Negotiating their Manhood," in *Black and White Masculinity*, ed. Plath and Lussana; and Barber, 3-13. For northern free Blacks who resisted colonization, see Power-Greene, *Against the Wind and Tide;* and Guyatt, *Bind Us Apart*, 197-305. Black barbers in the North actively took on community and political issues and, like most activists of the era, opposed colonization (Bristol, *Knights of the Razor*, 77-79).

81. *Diary*, 226.

82. John Ker's letter, written June 25, 1831, is quoted in Sydnor, "The Free Negro in Mississippi before the Civil War," 785. White supporters of colonization had divergent views about why free Blacks should be removed from the country, and some believed that Blacks were inferior because of conditions in the United States rather than innate biological traits, but all shared the racist notion that they could not remain in the country (Frederickson, *The Black Image in the White Mind*, 6-20).

83. *Diary*, 371-73; *Natchez Weekly Courier*, February 11, 1842.

84. Ross et al. v. Vertner, 6 Miss. 305; James, *Antebellum Natchez*, 176; Sydnor, *Slavery in Mississippi*, 225-26. See also James, *Antebellum Natchez*, 176; and Huffman, *Mississippi in Africa*, 1-144.

85. *Natchez Weekly Courier*, February 11, 1842.

86. Ross et al. v. Vertner, 6 Miss. 305.

87. Ross et al. v. Vertner, 6 Miss. 305; Brazy, *An American Planter*, 66.

88. Sydnor, *Slavery in Mississippi*, 229-230; *African Repository* 26: 59-61, 77, 210-211; 25: 118-21; Wiley, *Slaves No More*, 155-56.

89. Quitman quoted in James, *Antebellum Natchez*, 176. By 1859, the Mississippi High Court of Errors and Appeals ruled it was "the policy of this State, as evinced by its legislation, to *'prevent the increase of free persons of color'*" (Mitchell v. Wells, 37 Miss. 235 [1859]).

90. Chambers, *Trials and Confessions of Madison Henderson, Alias Blanchard, Alfred Amos Warrick and Others;* Berlin, *Slaves without Masters,* 332; "Civis," published in the *Mississippi Free Trader,* May 13, 1841; Sydnor, "The Free Negro in Mississippi before the Civil War," 776.

91. *Natchez Courier,* August 7, 1841, quoted in *Chained to the Rock of Adversity,* ed. Gould, xxxi.

92. Ribianszky, *Generations of Freedom,* 121; B. D. Jones, *Fathers of Conscience,* 54–55, 121–22.

93. Ribianszky, *Generations of Freedom,* 33; Leiper v. Hoffman et al., 26 Miss. 615; Sydnor, "The Free Negro in Mississippi before the Civil War," 776–77; Broussard, *Stepping Lively in Place,* 126–28; B. D. Jones, *Fathers of Conscience,* 121–22.

94. Leiper v. Hoffman et al., 26 Miss. 615; Sydnor, "The Free Negro in Mississippi before the Civil War," 776–77.

95. Ribianszky, *Generations of Freedom,* 15–38; Sydnor, "The Free Negro in Mississippi before the Civil War," 769–70.

96. Sydnor, "The Free Negro in Mississippi before the Civil War," 669–70; B. D. Jones, *Fathers of Conscience,* 105–6.

97. Sydnor, "The Free Negro in Mississippi before the Civil War," 774; B. D. Jones, *Fathers of Conscience,* 105–6; RSPP, PAR# 11082203,

98. Hinds, et al. v. Brazealle, et al., 3 Miss. 837; B. Jones, 55–56.

99. Sydnor, "The Free Negro in Mississippi," 770–75.

100. Sydnor, "The Free Negro in Mississippi before the Civil War," 770–71; Howard and Hutchinson, *The Statutes of the State of Mississippi,* 168–69; Berlin, *Slaves without Masters,* 332; *Diary,* 342.

101. Berlin, *Slaves without Masters,* 332; *Diary,* 341–43.

102. *Diary,* 344.

103. West, *Family or Freedom,* 53–74.

104. *Diary,* 345–46.

105. *Diary,* 348.

106. *Mississippi Free Trader,* September 22, 1841; *Diary,* 348–49.

107. *Mississippi Free Trader,* September 23, 1841.

108. *Diary,* 499–500.

109. *Diary,* 502; Woodson, "Free Negro Owners of Slaves in the United States in 1830," 42. Hogan and Davis found that Samuel Gibson died in 1832, but Carter Woodson lists him as still alive in 1844 and that he freed six slaves in Ohio that year.

110. *Diary,* 502.

111. *Natchez Courier,* November 30, 1849, reprinted in *Diary,* 680n; Hutchinson, *Code of Mississippi,* 948–49.

112. *Diary,* 728.

113. *Diary,* 476.

114. *Diary,* 664–65.

115. *Diary,* 665; Salt, *The Unfinished Revolution,* 113–52.

4. PROTECTING AND PROVIDING FOR A FAMILY

1. Blassingame, *The Slave Community*, 149–322; Genovese, *Roll, Jordan, Roll*, 482–94; Malone, *Sweet Chariot*, 251–72; Hilde, *Slavery, Fatherhood, and Paternal Duty*, 29–66.

2. Hilde, *Slavery, Fatherhood, and Paternal Duty*, 21, 67–91; Ribianszky, *Generations of Freedom*, 136–37.

3. *Barber*, 18.

4. Ribianszky, *Generations of Freedom*, 2–3; M. P. Johnson and Roark, *Black Masters*, 51–52, 210; Hilde, *Slavery, Fatherhood, and Paternal Duty*, 150.

5. *Barber*, 78–84. The National Parks Service operates the William Johnson House Museum.

6. *Barber*, 84–85. William Jr. and Richard were probably trained at least partly by their father as barbers, but Byron must have learned from someone else, most likely Robert Mc-Cray or James Miller, as he was too young at the time of his father's murder.

7. The white William Johnson freed Amy and the children, but his son never recorded any kind of relationship between his mother and father. White men had legal, cultural, and financial incentives to sexually exploit Black women in the Old South, see Clinton, "Southern Dishonor," in *In Joy and Sorrow*, ed. Bleser, 52–68; and Wyatt-Brown, *Southern Honor*, 292–324.

8. *Barber*, 82. A new study contends that Amy Johnson suffered from post-traumatic stress disorder (see Ribianszky, *Generations of Freedom*, 73).

9. *Diary*, 90, 107, 127, 132, 140; Eaton, "Slave-Hiring in the Upper South"; Wade, *Slavery in the Cities*, 38–54. An updated discussion on the flexibility, importance, and exploitation of hiring out can be found in Zaborney, *Slaves for Hire*, 1–166.

10. *Diary*, 94, 119.

11. *Diary*, 179.

12. Forret, *Slave against Slave*, 332–83; King, "'Mad' Enough to Kill,'" 37–56; Ribianszky, *Generations of Freedom*, 73–75.

13. *Diary*, 129.

14. Ribianszky, *Generations of Freedom*, 98–101.

15. *Diary*, 183.

16. *Diary*, 187.

17. *Diary*, 187.

18. *Diary*, 187.

19. *Diary*, 187; William Johnson to Mrs. James Miller, October 4, 1837, quoted in *Diary*, 45.

20. *Diary*, 189.

21. *Diary*, 203.

22. *Diary*, 211.

23. *Diary*, 641.

24. *Diary*, 642.

25. *Diary*, 642–43; *Barber*, 84.

26. In *Black Masters*, M. P. Johnson and Roark argue that this was a type of quiet political statement expressing that they were "human and responsible" (222).

27. *Diary*, 47; *New Orleans Daily Delta*, June 19, 1847.

28. Adelia Miller to William Johnson, January 2, 1844, 3-4, and February 16, 1844, in *Chained to the Rock of Adversity*, ed. Gould, 4-5.

29. Gould, *Chained to the Rock of Adversity*, xxv.

30. *Diary*, 440. Hunting and fishing were behaviors that both Black and white men prized as displays of masculinity and competition between one another, which they viewed as important to pass along to the next generation. (see Fraser, "Negotiating their Manhood," in *Black and White Masculinity*, ed. Plath and Lussana; 76-94; Lussana, *My Brother Slaves*, 71-74; Hilde, *Slavery, Fatherhood, and Paternal Duty*, 94; and Proctor, *Bathed in Blood*, 61-75).

31. *Diary*, 443.

32. *Diary*, 443.

33. *Diary*, 444.

34. *Diary*, 445.

35. *Diary*, 454, 458, 474-75.

36. Meachum, *An Address to all the Colored Citizens of the United States*, 44-45; Bellamy, "Free Blacks in Antebellum Missouri, 1820-1860"; Schweninger, "Prosperous Free Blacks in the South, 1790-1880," 43-45.

37. Lawrence W. Minen to Ann Johnson, March 12, 1853, in *Chained to the Rock of Adversity*, ed. Gould, 13, xlvii.

38. *Diary*, 676-77, 714; R. L. F. Davis, *The Black Experience in Natchez*, 65.

39. Hilde, *Slavery, Fatherhood, and Paternal Duty*, 103.

40. *Diary*, 361.

41. *Diary*, 352, 526, 534.

42. *Diary*, 359-61; *Barber*, 84.

43. Gould, *Chained to the Rock of Adversity*, xxxii-xxxiii; *Diary*, 391. Thomas C. Buchanan offers a detailed discussion of the "pan-Mississippian" life of African Americans who lived along or worked on the river in *Black Life on the Mississippi*.

44. Gould, *Chained to the Rock of Adversity*, xxxiii; Buckingham, *The Slave States of America*, 1:479-88.

45. The baptismal records for Anna, Byron, and Richard are available in Folder 01-13, 1842-1856, Legal and Financial Documents, William T. Johnson and Family Papers; Gould, *Chained to the Rock of Adversity* xxxvi; and Roberts, "Slaves and Slavery in Louisiana." See also letters written to Ann Johnson from New Orleans in Gould, *Chained to the Rock of Adversity*, 11, 13; and Hall, *Africans in Colonial Louisiana*, 156-200.

46. *Diary*, 603.

47. *Diary*, 603-4.

48. *Diary*, 611.

49. *Diary*, 755.

50. Some of Lavinia Miller McCary's letters are available in Gould, *Chained to the Rock of Adversity*, 7, 8, 10, 19.

51. *Diary*, 762.

52. *Diary*, 755-56n28, 769.

53. *Diary,* 389.

54. *Diary,* 462.

55. *Diary,* 575; Berlin, *Slaves without Masters,* 6–7, 57–58.

56. *Diary,* 791.

5. CONTRASTING MASCULINITIES: POOR WHITES, FREE BLACKS, AND SUBVERTING THE RACIAL ORDER

1. Baron de Carondelet to Manuel Gayoso de Lemos, May 12, 1792, in C. D. James, *Antebellum Natchez,* 35; Holmes, "Law and Order in Spanish Natchez," 200–201; *Barber,* 44.

2. *Diary,* 65, 78; Andrews, "William Johnson's Diary," 21.

3. *Barber,* 44–45; *Diary,* 501.

4. *Barber,* 45; *Diary,* 526.

5. *Diary,* 539.

6. *Diary,* 540; *Barber,* 45.

7. Sitterson, "The William J. Minor Plantations," 63; Sydnor, *Slavery in Mississippi,* 69.

8. *Diary,* 36–37, 580.

9. *Diary,* 600.

10. A useful discussion of the malleability of the terms "yeomen," "poor whites," and "plain folk" can be found in Hyde, "Plain Folk Reconsidered," 803–30; and McCurry, *Masters of Small Worlds,* 5–276.

11. Gorn, "Gouge and Bite," 34–38; Janson, *The Stranger in America,* 304; Baptist, *Creating an Old South,* 90–103.

12. Woodward, "The Southern Ethic in a Puritan World," 343–70; David Bertelson, *The Lazy South,* 19–246.

13. Hunting was an important way for southern men to establish friendships and to assert belonging to a community around shared interests and a recognition of skills (Proctor, *Bathed in Blood,* 61–75).

14. Diary, 595–96.

15. *Diary,* 596–97.

16. *Diary,* 598.

17. *Diary,* 599.

18. *Diary,* 599.

19. Merritt, *Masterless Men,* 16.

20. Bolton, *Poor Whites of the Antebellum South,* 42–112; Forret, *Race Relations in the Margins,* 20–73; Merritt, *Masterless Men,* 144–285.

21. *Diary,* 599.

22. *Diary,* 600.

23. *Diary,* 635.

24. *Diary,* 636.

25. Ford told a surveyor that he thought Johnson was wrong to dispute his land boundary with Winn and implied that he was trying to get over on Baylor Winn, but he was friendly toward him when he met Johnson in person in Natchez a few months later (*Diary,* 690).

26. *Diary,* 606.

27. *Diary,* 37.

28. *Diary,* 676–77.

29. Though Woodward does not deal with situations in which white men worked for free men of color, he does make the point that southerners rejected the idea that work was the point of life, at least in contrast to northerners (Woodward, "The Southern Ethic in a Puritan World"; Gorn, "Gouge and Bite," 34–37; Baptist, *Creating an Old South,* 90–106).

30. *Diary,* 647.

31. *Diary,* 655–56.

32. *Diary,* 659.

33. *Diary,* 662.

34. *Diary,* 568.

35. *Diary,* 568.

36. *Diary,* 702.

37. *Diary,* 705.

38. *Diary,* 709.

39. *Diary,* 722.

40. *Diary,* 700.

41. *Diary,* 731.

42. *Diary,* 751.

43. *Diary,* 753.

44. *Barber,* 262; *Diary,* 526.

45. Baptist, *Creating an Old South,* 90; Gorn, "Gouge and Bite."

46. *Diary,* 540, 543, 547, 552, 553, 554.

47. *Diary,* 562–63.

48. *Barber,* 266–67. Baylor Winn married Elizabeth Becktell of Tennessee on December 25, 1846. This was his second marriage. His first wife was named Gregory, whom he married in 1826 before he moved to Mississippi. Her status is also questionable, but since their children are never listed as free people of color, the assumption must be that she was also presumed white (*Mississippi, Compiled Marriage Index, 1776–1935*).

49. *Diary,* 588.

50. *Diary,* 588.

51. *Diary,* 595–96.

52. *Diary,* 531, 533.

53. *Diary,* 568.

54. *Diary,* 613.

55. Hodes, *White Women, Black Men,* 78–86; Gordon-Reed, *The Hemingses of Monticello,* 87; Snyder, *Great Crossings,* 55.

56. *Diary,* 613.

57. *Diary,* 631.

58. *Diary,* 680.

59. *Diary,* 725.

60. *Diary,* 747.

61. Gross, *What Blood Won't Tell*, 16–72; Welch, *Black Litigants in the Antebellum American South,* 27–59.

62. *Barber,* 19.

63. West, *Family or Freedom,* 53–74; Gross, *What Blood Won't Tell,* 31–47; Welch, *Black Litigants in the Antebellum American South,* 3–112.

64. RSPP, PAR# 11000016 and 11000024. The exact years of Hagins's petitions are unknown, but they were filed with the territorial legislature, making this either in or prior to 1817. In *White Women, Black Men,* Martha Hodes argues that relationships between Black men and white women was not as uncommon or controversial in the Old South as the casual observer might believe. Hagins's relationship with his wife offers another piece of anecdotal evidence to her argument.

65. RSPP, PAR# 11000016 and 11000024.

66. *Barber,* 248.

67. *Barber,* 248; B. D. Jones, *Fathers of Conscience,* 110; RSPP, PAR # 11082401. On the performative aspects of racial identity, see Lott, *Love and Theft,* 15–173; Roediger, *The Wages of Whiteness,* 43–156; Gross, *What Blood Won't Tell,* 48–72; Welch, *Black Litigants in the Antebellum American South,* 3–112.

68. *Barber,* 249–50; West, *Family or Freedom,* 53–74; RSPP, PAR # 11082401.

69. *Barber,* 249–50; West, *Family or Freedom,* 53–74; RSPP, PAR # 11082401.

70. Ursin Raby et al. v. Jacob Batiste et ux. 27 Miss. 731 (1854); Gross, *What Blood Won't Tell,* 56.

71. *Diary,* 549–50.

72. *Diary,* 530n1, 550.

73. *Diary,* 713.

74. *Diary,* 751.

75. *Diary,* 752.

76. Baptist, *Creating an Old* South, 130–33; Wyatt-Brown, *Southern Honor,* 353.

77. *Diary,* 637.

78. *Diary,* 643.

79. *Diary,* 651.

80. *Diary,* 660. Johnson copied the letter into his diary ("William Moseby deed of conveyance to William Johnson," November 8, 1845," Folder 01-18, 1843-1849, Legal and Financial Documents, William T. Johnson and Family Papers).

81. *Diary,* 662–63.

82. *Diary,* 672–73. Kimberly Welch describes Winn's legal strategy as a claim of adverse possession but also notes that Winn had begun openly threatening Johnson with physical harm (Welch, "William Johnson's Hypothesis," 33–36).

83. *Diary,* 678, 682

84. William Mosbey to William T. Johnson, November 28, 1849, Folder 01-01, 1829-1853, William T. Johnson and Family Papers.

85. *Diary,* 685.

86. *Diary,* 685.

87. *Diary,* 588.

88. *Diary,* 686–87.

89. *Diary,* 689.

90. *Diary,* 690.

91. *Diary,* 695.

92. *Diary,* 695.

93. *Diary,* 695.

94. *Diary,* 695–96.

95. *Diary,* 697.

96. *Diary,* 699.

97. *Diary,* 739. From the territorial period on, residents in the area were responsible for providing labor on roads that would benefit them. Slaveholders were expected to contribute the labor of the people they enslaved for this purpose "in proportion to the lands he holds in the district." Details of roadwork can be found in Folder 3, 1791–1793, Natchez Trace Collection, Dolph Briscoe Center for American History, University of Texas at Austin, Provincial and Territorial Records.

98. *Diary,* 742–43, 749.

99. *Diary,* 751–53.

100. *Diary,* 757–58.

101. *Diary,* 759.

102. *Diary,* 787.

103. *Barber,* 263–64.

104. *Barber,* 264–65.

105. *Natchez Daily Courier,* June 20, 1851. In some records, Winn is spelled "Wynn."

106. *Natchez Daily Courier,* June 20, 1851.

107. *Mississippi Free Trader,* January 7, 14, 21, 1852.

108. Welch, *Black Litigants in the Antebellum American South,* 27–59; Gross, *What Blood Won't Tell,* 31–47.

109. *Barber,* 266–67. This had been a successful strategy in at least one instance in Natchez: Johnson recorded that one woman had been able to remove the label of "free Negro" by proving that she was of white and Native American ancestry.

110. Adams County Tax Rolls 1834–1852, Mississippi Department of Archives and History.

111. *Mississippi Free Trader,* January 28, 1852.

112. James O. Pollard certification of Washington Winn's status as a free negro, March 24, 1852; Certification of Winn family residence in King William County, Va., March 25, 1852; Thomas Dabney list of free negroes over twelve years old in King Williams County, Va., March 26, 1852; Joseph Johnson certification, March 29, 1852, Folder 01-19, 1850–1854, Legal and Financial Documents, William T. Johnson and Family Papers.

113. Montgomery, *Reminiscences of a Mississippian in Peace and War,* 50–52.

114. *Natchez Daily Courier,* April 27, 1852.

115. *Mississippi Free Trader,* May 12, 1852.

116. *Barber,* 268–70; *Woodville (MS) Republican,* June 21, 1853.

117. *Barber,* 270–72; William Johnson Jr. to Ann Johnson, May 14, 1853, in *Chained to the Rock of Adversity,* ed. Gould, 13–14.

118. *1860 United States Federal Census.* Baylor Winn was listed in the Texas muster roll on May 7, 1861, as "2nd sergt" under the command of Captain Edward Walker. Calvin Winn also enlisted as a private in 1864 (*Texas, Muster Roll Index Cards, 1838-1900;* Last Will and Testament of Baylor Winn).

119. Baptist, *Creating an Old South,* 109.

120. *Barber,* 266.

EPILOGUE

1. Newspaper quote in *Barber,* 265.

2. Gould, *Chained to the Rock of Adversity,* xxiii-xxiv.

3. Tax valuations from Gould, *Chained to the Rock of Adversity,* xli.

4. Gould, *Chained to the Rock of Adversity,* xli-xlii.

5. *Diary,* 676-77, 714; Lawrence W. Minen to Ann Johnson, March 12, 1853, in *Chained to the Rock of Adversity,* ed. Gould, 13, xlvii.

6. Byron Johnson to Ann Battles Johnson, November 26, 1850, in *Chained to the Rock of Adversity,* ed. Gould, 11; *Diary,* 603.

7. James Miller to Ann Battles Johnson, June 4, 1853, *Chained to the Rock of Adversity,* ed. Gould, 14.

8. Emma Hoggatt to Ann Battles Johnson, April 10, 1858, in *Chained to the Rock of Adversity,* ed. Gould, 30.

9. Victoire Brustie to Ann Battles Jonson, June 19, 1858, in *Chained to the Rock of Adversity,* ed. Gould, 31.

10. RSPP, PAR # 11085903; RSPP, PAR# 11085911; RSPP, PAR# 11085912. Some South Carolina legislators actually attempted to push through a law that would have enslaved all free people of color who did not leave in 1859 (see M. P. Johnson and Roark, *Black Masters,* 166).

11. RSPP, PAR #11085911; West, *Family or Freedom,* 57, 53-92.

12. Levine, *Searching for Black Confederates,* 1-184. For more on the role of race in the memory of the Civil War, consult Blight, *Race and Reunion;* and G. M. Foster, *Ghosts of the Confederacy.*

13. William Hoggatt to Catherine Johnson, September 7, 1862, Folder 01-03, 1860-1874, Louisiana Digital Library, Correspondence and Manuscript Materials, William T. Johnson and Family Papers.

14. Ann Battles Johnson quoted in *Chained to the Rock of Adversity,* ed. Gould, xlv.

15. The Diary of Catherine Johnson, in *Chained to the Rock of Adversity,* ed. Gould, 72, xlv; Broussard, "Occupied Natchez, Elite Women, and the Feminization of the Civil War." The most complete discussion of Black Natchezians' experience during the Civil War and afterward can be found in Behrend, *Reconstructing Democracy,* 16-116.

16. Catherine Johnson's Diary, in *Chained to the Rock of Adversity,* ed. Gould, 82n4.

17. Glymph, *Out of the House of Bondage,* 137-66.

18. Catherine Johnson's Diary, in *Chained to the Rock of Adversity,* ed. Gould, 69.

19. Catherine Johnson's Diary, in *Chained to the Rock of Adversity,* ed. Gould, 70.

20. Catherine Johnson's Diary, in *Chained to the Rock of Adversity*, ed. Gould, 77.

21. Catherine Johnson's Diary, in *Chained to the Rock of Adversity*, ed. Gould, 77–78.

22. Catherine Johnson's Diary, in *Chained to the Rock of Adversity*, ed. Gould, 79.

23. Catherine Johnson's Diary, in *Chained to the Rock of Adversity*, ed. Gould, 79.

24. Catherine Johnson's Diary, in *Chained to the Rock of Adversity*, ed. Gould, 80.

25. Catherine Johnson's Diary, in *Chained to the Rock of Adversity*, ed. Gould, 80–81.

26. Catherine Johnson's Diary, in *Chained to the Rock of Adversity*, ed. Gould, 81.

27. Catherine Johnson's Diary, in *Chained to the Rock of Adversity*, ed. Gould, 83, 85.

28. A. L. Bingaman to Byron Johnson, May 12, 1866, Folder 01-01, 1860–1874, Correspondence and Manuscript Materials, William T. Johnson and Family Papers.

29. Catherine Johnson's Diary, in *Chained to the Rock of Adversity*, ed. Gould, 86.

30. A. L. Bingaman to Anna Johnson, September 18, 1868, Folder 01-01, 1860–1874, Correspondence and Manuscript Materials, William T. Johnson and Family Papers; A. L. Bingaman to Anna Johnson, December 16, 1868, Folder 01-01, 1860–1874, Correspondence and Manuscript Materials, William T. Johnson and Family Papers.

31. Catherine Johnson's Diary, in *Chained to the Rock of Adversity*, ed. Gould, 71.

32. Catherine Johnson's Diary, in *Chained to the Rock of Adversity*, ed. Gould, 85.

33. Catherine Johnson's Diary, *Chained to the Rock of Adversity*, ed. Gould, 86.

34. Byron Johnson to Anna Johnson, September 21, 1868, in *Chained to the Rock of Adversity*, ed. Gould, 43. Juanito was Eugenia Johnson's husband.

35. *Natchez Weekly Democrat*, January 24, 1872.

36. *Natchez Weekly Democrat*, January 24, 1872.

37. *Natchez Weekly Democrat*, January 24, 1872.

38. Gould, *Chained to the Rock of Adversity*, xlviii; indenture conveying land from Duncan G. Minor to Anna Johnson and family, January 28, 1885, Folder OS 01-03, 1846–1885, Legal and Financial Documents, William T. Johnson and Family Papers.

39. Catherine Johnson's Diary, in *Chained to the Rock of Adversity*, ed. Gould, 89. It is not clear what exactly happened here. Carlito was married to Eugenia Johnson and sharecropped with the family. His brother Juanito was still employed as a barber in Natchez in 1898, which suggests that the shop was still operating (*Natchez Democrat*, June 19, 1898).

40. Gould, *Chained to the Rock of Adversity*, 47–48; Richard M. Johnson to Anna Johnson, May 31, 1872, Folder 01-03, 1860–1874, Correspondence and Manuscript Materials, William T. Johnson and Family Papers.

Bibliography

ARCHIVAL SOURCES

Adams County Tax Rolls 1834–1852. Mississippi Department of Archives and History.
Benjamin Drake and Family Papers. Mississippi Department of Archives and History.
William J. Minor Papers. LSU Libraries and Special Collections.
Natchez Trace Collection. Dolph Briscoe Center for American History. University of Texas at Austin.

Online Archival Sources

William T. Johnson and Family Papers. Louisiana Digital Library. www.https://louisianadigitallibrary.org/.
Mississippi, Compiled Marriage Index, 1776–1935. www.ancestry.com.
Race and Slavery Petitions Project. Digital Library on American Slavery. http://library.uncg.edu/slavery_petitions/.
Texas, Muster Roll Index Cards, 1838–1900. www.ancestry.com.
United States Federal Census 1860. www.ancestry.com.
Baylor Winn. Last Will and Testament. www.ancestry.com

Newspapers and Periodicals

African Repository and Colonial Journal
Daily Delta (New Orleans)
De Bow's Review
Frederick Douglass' Paper
Mississippi Free Trader
Mississippi Free Trader and Natchez Gazette
Natchez Courier
Natchez Daily Courier
Natchez Weekly Courier
Natchez Weekly Courier and Journal
Natchez Weekly Democrat
North Star
Woodville (MS) Republican

Published Primary Sources

Anderson, William. *The Life and Narrative of William Anderson, Twenty- Four Years a Slave [. . .]*. Chicago: Daily Tribune and Job Printing Office, 1857.

Baily, Francis. *Journal of a Tour in Unsettled Parts of North America, in 1796–1797*. London: Baily Brothers, 1856.

Brent, Linda (Harriet Ann Jacobs). *Incidents in the Life of a Slave Girl. Written by Herself*. Boston: Published for the Author, 1861.

Brown, Henry Box. *Narrative of Henry Box Brown: Who Escaped from Slavery Enclosed in a Box Three Feet Long and Two Wide and Two and a Half High*. Boston: Brown and Stearns, 1849.

Brown, Josephine. *Biography of an American Bondsman by His Daughter*. Boston: R. F. Wallcut, 1856.

Buckingham, James Silk. *The Slave States of America*. 2 vols. London: Fisher, Son, and Company, 1842.

Chambers, A. B. *Trials and Confessions of Madison Henderson, Alias Blanchard, Alfred Amos Warrick and Others, Murderers of Jesse Baker and Jacob Weaver, as Given by Themselves*. St. Louis: Chambers and Knapp, 1841.

Clarke, Lewis. *Narrative of Sufferings of Lewis Clarke during a Captivity of More Than Twenty-Five Years amongst the Algerines of Kentucky*. Boston, 1845.

de Montulé, Edouard. *Travels in America, 1816–1817*. Bloomington: Indiana University Press, 1951.

"A Declaration of the Immediate Causes Which Induce and Justify the Secession of the State of Mississippi from the Federal Union" (1860). In *Journal of the State Convention and Ordinances and Resolutions Adopted in January, 1861*. Jackson, MS: E. Barksdale, 1861.

Delany, Martin Robinson. *The Condition, Elevation, Emigration, and Destiny of the Colored People of the United States, Politically Considered*. Philadelphia: The Author, 1852.

Douglass, Frederick. *Life and Times of Frederick Douglass, His Early Life as a Slave, His Escape from Bondage, and His Complete History to This Time*. Boston: De Wolfe and Fiske: 1892.

———. *Narrative of the Life of Frederick Douglass: An American Slave, Written by Himself*. Boston: Anti-Slavery Office, 1845.

Faust, Drew Gilpin. *The Ideology of Slavery: Proslavery Thought in the Antebellum South, 1830–1860*. Baton Rouge: Louisiana State University Press, 1981.

Foote, Henry S. *Casket of Reminiscences*. Washington, DC: Chronicle, 1874.

Gales, Joseph. *The Debates and Proceedings in the Congress of the United States*. Vol 1. Washington, DC: Gales and Seaton, 1855.

Gould, Virginia Meacham, ed. *Chained to the Rock of Adversity: To Be Free, Black and Female in the Old South*. Athens: University of Georgia Press, 1998.

Hammond, Scott J., Kevin R. Hardwick, and Howard Lubert. *The American Debate over Slavery, 1760–1865: An Anthology of Sources.* Indianapolis, IN: Hackett, 2016.

Hening, William W. *The Statutes at Large; Being a Collection of All the Laws of Virginia, from the First Session of the Legislature, in the Year 1619.* 13 vols. New York: R. & W. & G. Bartow, 1823.

Henson, Josiah. *An Autobiography of the Reverend Josiah Henson An Autobiography of the Rev. Josiah Henson ("Uncle Tom"). From 1789 to 1881. With a Preface by Mrs. Harriet Beecher Stowe, and Introductory Notes by George Sturge, S. Morley, Esq., M. P., Wendell Phillips, and John G. Whittier.* London, Ontario: Schulyer, Smith, 1881.

House Documents, Otherwise Publ. as Executive Documents. Vol. 7: *13th Congress, 2d Session–49th Congress, 1st Session.*

Howard, H. R. *The History of Virgil A. Stewart and His Adventure in Capturing and Exposing the Great "Western Land Pirate" and His Gang, in Connection with the Evidence; Also of the Trials, Confessions, and Executions of Murrell's Associates in the State of Mississippi during the Summer of 1835, and the Execution of Five Professional Gamblers by the Citizens of Vicksburg, on the 6th of July, 1835.* New York: Harper and Brothers, 1836.

Howard, Volney E. *Reports of Cases Argued and Determined in the High Court of Errors and Appeals of the State of Mississippi.* Vol. 4. St. Paul, MN: West, 1910.

Howard, V. E., and A. Hutchinson. *The Statutes of the State of Mississippi of a Public and General Nature, with the Constitutions of the United States and of This State: and an Appendix Containing Acts of Congress Affecting Land Titles, Naturalization, &c. and a Manual for Clerks, Sheriffs and Justices of the Peace.* New Orleans: E. Johns, 1840.

Hurricane. "The Negro and his Management." *Southern Cultivator* 18 (September 1860).

Hutchinson, A. *Code of Mississippi: Being and Analytical Compilation of the Public and General Statutes of the Territory and State, with Tabular References to the Local and Private Acts, from 1708 to 1848.* Jackson: Price and Fall, 1848.

Janson, Charles William. *The Stranger in America.* London: James Cundee Albion Press, 1807.

Jinnoowine Johnson Ticket. Political cartoon. Cincinnati, 1836. www.loc.gov/resource/cph.3a38727/.

Johnson, William. *William Johnson's Natchez: The Ante-Bellum Diary of a Free Negro.* Edited by William Ransom Hogan and Edwin Adams Davis. Baton Rouge: Louisiana State University Press, 1951.

Kendall, Amos. *The Extra Globe: Containing Political Discussions, Documentary Proofs, &c.* Washington, DC: Globe Office, 1838.

Knight, Helen C. *The New Republic.* Boston: Sabbath School Society, 1850.

Locke, John. *Two Treatises of Civil Government.* Edited by Thomas Hollis. London: A. Millar, et al., 1794.

Martineau, Harriet. *Society in America*. London: Saunders and Otley, 1837.

McDermott, John Frances, ed. *Before Mark Twain, a Sampler of Old, Old, Times on the Mississippi*. Carbondale: University of Southern Illinois Press, 1968.

Meachum, John B. *An Address to All the Colored Citizens of the United States*. Philadelphia: King and Baird, 1846.

Montgomery, Frank A. *Reminiscences of a Mississippian in Peace and War*. Cincinnati, OH: Robert Clarke, 1901.

Prentiss, S. S. *A Memoir of S. S. Prentiss*. Edited by George Lewis Prentiss. New York: Scribner, 1886.

Report of the Proceedings of the Colored National Convention, Held at Cleveland, Ohio, On Wednesday, September 6, 1848. Rochester, NY: John Dick, at the North Star Office, 1848.

Robinson, Henry R. *An Affecting Scene in Kentucky*. Political cartoon. New York: Henry R. Robinson, 1836. www.loc.gov/pictures/item/2008661287/.

Smedes, W. C., and T. A. Marshall. *Reports of Cases Argued and Determined in the High Court of Errors and Appeals for the State of Mississippi*. Vol. 9. Boston: Charles C. Little and James Brown, 1844.

Stroyer, Jacob. *My Life in the South*. Salem: Salem Observer, 1889.

Washington, George. *The Papers of George Washington*. Edited by W. W. Abbot. Retirement Series, vol. 4: *20 April 1799–13 December 1799*. Charlottesville: University Press of Virginia, 1999.

Webb, William. *The History of William Webb, Composed by Himself*. Detroit, MI: Egbert Hoekstra, 1873.

Weld, Theodore Dwight. *American Slavery as It Is: The Testimony of a Thousand Witnesses*. New York: American Anti-Slavery Society, 1838.

Walker, David. *David Walker's Appeal, in Four Articles; Together with a Preamble, to the Coloured Citizens of the World, but in Particular, and Very Expressly, to Those of the United States of America, Written in Boston, State of Massachusetts, September 28, 1829*. Edited by Sean Wilentz. New York: Hill and Wang, 1965.

SECONDARY SOURCES

"Adams County." In *The Mississippi Encyclopedia*. https://mississippiencyclopedia.org/

Amos, Harriet E. *Cotton City: Urban Development in Antebellum Mobile*. Tuscaloosa: University of Alabama Press, 1985.

Andrews, William L. "William Johnson's Diary: The Text and the Man behind It." *Southern Quarterly* 43, no. 2 (Winter 2006): 18–33.

Ayers, Edward. *Vengeance and Justice: Crime and Punishment in the 19th-Century American South*. New York: Oxford University Press, 1984.

Baptist, Edward E. *Creating an Old South: Middle Florida's Planation Frontier before the Civil War.* Chapel Hill: University of North Carolina Press, 2002.

———. *The Half Has Never Been Told: Slavery and the Making of American Capitalism.* New York: Basic, 2014.

Beard, Michael. "Frontier Port on the Mississippi: A History of the Legend of Natchez-Under-the-Hill, 1800-1900." Master's thesis, Louisiana State University, 1981.

———. "Natchez-Under-the-Hill: Reform and Retribution in Early Natchez." *Gulf Coast Historical Review* 4 (1988): 29-48.

Bederman, Gail. *Manliness and Civilization: A Cultural History of Gender and Race in the United States, 1880-1917.* Chicago: University of Chicago Press, 1995.

Behrend, Justin. *Reconstructing Democracy: Grassroots Black Politics in the Deep South after the Civil War.* Athens: University of Georgia Press, 2015.

Bellamy, Donnie D. "Free Blacks in Antebellum Missouri, 1820-1860." *Missouri Historical Review* 67, no. 2 (January 1973): 198-226.

Berlin, Ira. *Slaves without Masters: The Free Negro in the Antebellum South.* New York: New Press, 1974.

Berlin, Ira, and Herbert G. Gutman. "Natives and Immigrants, Free Men and Slaves: Urban Workingmen in the Antebellum American South." *American Historical Review* 88, no. 5 (December 1983): 1175-200.

Bertelson, David. *The Lazy South.* New York: Oxford University Press, 1967.

Blassingame, John W. *The Slave Community: Plantation Life in the Antebellum South.* New York: Oxford University Press, 1979.

Bleser, Carole, ed. *In Joy and Sorrow: Women, Family, and Marriage in the Victorian South, 1830-1900.* New York: Oxford University Press, 1991.

Blight, David W. *Race and Reunion: The Civil War in American Memory.* Cambridge, MA: Harvard University Press, 2001.

Bloch, Ruth. "The Construction of Gender in a Republican World." In *A Companion to the American Revolution,* edited by Jack P. Greene and Jack Richon Pole, 605-9. Hoboken, NJ: Wiley and Blackwell, 2000.

Bolton, Charles. *Poor Whites of the Antebellum South: Tenants and Laborers in Central North Carolina and Northeast Mississippi.* Durham, NC: Duke University Press, 1993.

Brazy, Martha Jane. *An American Planter: Stephen Duncan of Antebellum Natchez and New York.* Baton Rouge: Louisiana State University Press, 2006.

Breen, T. H. "Horses and Gentlemen: The Cultural Significance of Gambling among the Gentry of Virginia." *William and Mary Quarterly* 34, no. 2 (April 1977): 239-57.

Breen, T. H., and Stephen Innes. *"Myne Owne Ground": Race and Freedom on Virginia's Eastern Shore, 1640-1676.* New York: Oxford University Press, 2004.

Bristol, Douglas Walter. *Knights of the Razor: Black Barbers in Slavery and Freedom.* Baltimore, MD: Johns Hopkins University Press. 2015.

Broussard, Joyce Linda. "Occupied Natchez, Elite Women, and the Feminization of the Civil War." *Journal of Mississippi History* 70 (Summer 2008): 179–207.

———. *Stepping Lively in Place: The Not-Married, Free Women of Civil War Era Natchez, Mississippi.* Athens: University of Georgia Press, 2016.

Brown, Kathleen M. *Good Wives, Nasty Wenches, and Anxious Patriarchs: Gender, Race, and Power in Colonial Virginia.* Williamsburg, VA: Published for the Omohundro Institute of Early American History and Culture by the University of North Carolina Press, 1996.

Bruce, Dickenson D. *Violence and Culture in the Antebellum South.* Austin: University of Texas Press, 1979.

Buchanan, Thomas C. *Black Life on the Mississippi: Slaves, Free Blacks, and the Western Steamboat World.* Chapel Hill: University of North Carolina Press, 2004.

Buckner, Timothy R., and Peter Caster, eds. *Fathers, Preachers, Rebels, Men: Black Masculinity in U.S. History and Literature, 1820–1945.* Columbus: Ohio State University Press, 2011.

Burton, Orville, and Robert McMath Jr. *Class, Conflict and Consensus: Antebellum Southern Community Studies.* Westport, CT: Greenwood, 1982.

Camp, Stephanie M. H. *Closer to Freedom: Enslaved Women and Everyday Resistance in the Plantation South.* Chapel Hill: University of North Carolina Press, 2004.

Cashin, Joan E. *A Family Venture: Men and Women on the Southern Frontier.* Baltimore: Johns Hopkins University Press, 1991.

Crouch, Dora P., Daniel J. Carr, and Axel I. Mundigo. *Spanish City Planning in North America.* Cambridge, MA: MIT Press, 1982.

Davis, Edwin Adams, and William Ransom Hogan. *The Barber of Natchez.* Baton Rouge: Louisiana State University Press, 1959.

Davis, Ronald L. F. *The Black Experience in Natchez 1720–1880.* Natchez: National Historic Park, 1993.

Deyle, Steven. *Carry Me Back: The Domestic Slave Trade in American Life.* New York: Oxford University Press, 2005.

Doddington, David Stefan. *Contesting Slave Masculinity in the American South.* Cambridge, UK: Cambridge University Press, 2018.

Dusinberre, William. *Them Dark Days: Slavery in the American Rice Swamps.* New York: Oxford University Press, 1996.

Eaton, Clement. "Slave-Hiring in the Upper South: A Step toward Freedom." *Mississippi Valley Historical Review* 46, no. 4 (March 1960): 663–78.

Elkins, Stanley. *Slavery: A Problem in American Institutional and Intellectual Life.* Chicago: University of Chicago Press, 1959.

Elliot, Jack D. "City and Empire: The Spanish Origins of Natchez." *Journal of Mississippi History* 59 (1997): 270-321.

Emmons, William. *Authentic Biography of Col. Richard M. Johnson of Kentucky.* Boston: For the Proprietor, 1834.

Field, Corinne T. *The Struggle for Equal Adulthood: Gender, Race, Age, and the Fight for Citizenship in Antebellum America.* Chapel Hill: University of North Carolina Press, 2014.

Findlay, John M. *People of Chance: Gambling in American Society from Jamestown to Las Vegas.* New York: Oxford University Press, 1986.

Follett, Richard. "'Lives of Living Death': The Reproductive Lives of Slave Women in the Cane World of Louisiana." *Slavery & Abolition* 26, no. 2 (August 2005): 289-304.

Forret, Jeff. *Race Relations in the Margins: Slaves and Poor Whites in the Antebellum Southern Countryside.* Baton Rouge: Louisiana State University Press, 2006.

———. *Slave against Slave: Plantation Violence in the Old South.* Baton Rouge: Louisiana University Press, 2015.

Foster, Frances Smith. *"Til Death or Distance Do Us Part:" Love and Marriage in African America.* New York: Oxford University Press, 2010.

Foster, Gaines M. *Ghosts of the Confederacy: Defeat, the Lost Cause, and the Emergence of the New South, 1865-1913.* New York: Oxford University Press, 1987.

Franklin, John Hope. *From Slavery to Freedom: A History of Negro Americans.* New York: Knopf, 1967.

———. *The Militant South, 1800-1861.* Cambridge, MA: Harvard University Press, 1956.

Frederickson, George M. *The Black Image in the White Mind: The Debate on Afro-American Character and Destiny, 1817-1914.* Middletown, CT: Wesleyan University Press, 1987.

Freehling, William W. *The Road to Disunion.* Vol. 1: *Secessionists at Bay, 1776-1854.* New York: Oxford University Press, 1990.

Frey, Sylvia R. *Water from the Rock: Black Resistance in a Revolutionary Age.* Princeton, NJ: Princeton University Press, 1991.

Friend, Craig Thompson, and Lori Glover, eds. *Southern Manhood: Perspectives on Masculinity in the Old South.* Athens: University of Georgia Press, 2004.

Genovese, Eugene D. *Roll, Jordan, Roll: The World the Slaves Made.* New York: Vintage, 1974.

Glymph, Thavolia. *Out of the House of Bondage: The Transformation of the Plantation Household.* New York: Cambridge University Press, 2008.

Gomberg, Edith, Helene White, and John Carpenter, eds. *Alcohol, Science, and Society Revisited.* Ann Arbor: University of Michigan Press, 1982.

Gordon-Reed, Annette. *The Hemingses of Monticello: An American Family*. New York: Norton, 2008.

Gorn, Elliott J. "'Gouge and Bite, Pull Hair and Scratch': The Social Significance of Fighting in the Southern Backcountry." *American Historical Review* 90 no. 1 (February 1985): 18–43.

Gosse, Van. *The First Reconstruction: Black Politics in America from the Revolution to the Civil War*. Chapel Hill: University of North Carolina, 2021.

Greenberg, Kenneth S. *Honor and Slavery: Lies, Duels, Noses, Masks, Dressing as a Woman, Gifts, Strangers, Humanitarianism, Death, Slave Rebellions, the Proslavery Argument, Baseball, Hunting, and Gambling in the Old South*. Princeton, NJ: Princeton University Press, 1996.

Gross, Ariela J. *What Blood Won't Tell: A History of Race on Trial in America*. Cambridge, MA: Harvard University Press, 2008.

Guyatt, Nicholas. *Bind Us Apart: How Enlightened Americans Invented Racial Segregation*. New York: Basic, 2016.

Hahn, Steven. *A Nation under Their Feet: Black Political Struggles in the Rural South from Slavery to the Great Migration*. Cambridge, MA: Harvard University Press, 2004.

Hall, Gwendolyn Midlo. *Africans in Colonial Louisiana: The Development of Afro-Creole Culture in the Eighteenth Century*. Baton Rouge: Louisiana State University Press, 1992.

Hanger, Kimberly. *Bounded Lives, Bounded Places: Free Black Society in Colonial New Orleans, 1769-1803*. Durham, NC: Duke University Press, 1997.

Harris, Leslie M. *In the Shadow of Slavery: Africa Americans in New York City, 1626-1863*. Chicago: University of Chicago Press, 2003.

Herring, Todd Ashley. "Natchez 1795-1830: Life and Death on the Slavery Frontier." PhD diss., Mississippi State University, 2000.

Hilde, Libra R. *Slavery, Fatherhood, and Paternal Duty in African American Communities of the Long Nineteenth Century*. Chapel Hill: University of North Carolina Press, 2020.

Hilliard, Kathleen M. *Masters, Slaves, and Exchange: Power's Purchase in the Old South*. New York: Cambridge University Press, 2014.

Hodes, Martha. *White Women, Black Men: Illicit Sex in the 19th Century South*. New Haven, CT: Yale University Press, 1997.

Holmes, Jack D. L. *Gayoso: The Life of a Spanish Governor in the Mississippi Valley*. Baton Rouge: Louisiana State University Press, 1965.

———. "Law and Order in Spanish Natchez, 1871-1798." *Journal of Mississippi History* 25 (1963).

Huffman, Alan. *Mississippi in Africa: The Saga of the Slaves of Prospect Hill Plantation and their Legacy in Liberia Today*. Jackson: University Press of Mississippi, 2010.

Hyde, Samuel, Jr. "Plain Folk Reconsidered: Historiographical Ambiguity in Search of Definition." *Journal of Southern History* 71, no. 4 (November 2005): 803-30.

Ingersoll, Thomas. "Free Blacks in a Slave Society, 1718-1812." *William and Mary Quarterly*, 3rd ser., 48 (1991): 173-200.

James, Clayton D. *Antebellum Natchez*. Baton Rouge: Louisiana State University Press, 1968.

Johnson, Michael P., ed. *Reading the American Past: Selected Historical Documents*. 2 vols. Boston: Bedford/St. Martin's, 2005.

Johnson, Michael P., and James L. Roark. *Black Masters: A Free Family of Color in the Old South*. New York: Norton, 1984.

Johnson, Walter. "A Nettlesome Classic Turns Twenty-Five." *Common-Place* 1, no. 4 (July 2001).

———. "On Agency." *Journal of Social History* 37, no. 1 (Autumn 2003): 113-24.

———. *Soul by Soul: Life Inside the Antebellum Slave Market*. Cambridge, MA: Harvard University Press, 1999.

Jones, Bernie D. *Fathers of Conscience: Mixed-Race Inheritance in the Antebellum South*. Athens: University of Georgia Press, 2009.

Jones, Norrece. *Born a Child of Freedom Yet a Slave: Mechanisms of Control and Strategies of Resistance in Antebellum South Carolina*. Middletown, CT: Wesleyan University Press, 1990.

Jordan, Winthrop. *White over Black: American Attitudes toward the Negro, 1550-1812*. New York: Norton, 1968.

Joyner, Charles. *Down by the Riverside: A South Carolina Slave Community*. Urbana: University of Illinois Press, 1984.

Kennington, Kelly M. *In the Shadow of Dred Scott: St Louis Freedom Suits and the Legal Culture of Slavery in Antebellum America*. Athens: University of Georgia Press, 2017.

Kimmel, Michael. *Manhood in America: A Cultural History*. New York: Free Press, 1996.

King, Wilma. "'Mad' Enough to Kill: Enslaved Women, Murder, and Southern Courts." *Journal of African American History* 92, no. 1 (Winter 2007): 37-56.

Koger, Larry. *Black Slaveowners: Free Black Slave Masters in South Carolina, 1790-1860*. Columbia: University of South Carolina Press, 1985.

Lebsock, Suzanne. *The Free Women of Petersburg: Status and Culture in a Southern Town, 1784-1860*. New York: Norton, 1984.

Levine, Kevin M. *Searching for Black Confederates: The Civil War's Most Persistent Myth*. Chapel Hill: University of North Carolina Press, 2019.

Libby, David. *Slavery and Frontier Mississippi, 1720-1835*. Jackson: University of Mississippi Press, 2004.

Lightner, David L., and Alexander M. Ragan, "Were African American Slaveholders Benevolent or Exploitative? A Quantitative Approach." *Journal of Southern History* 71, no. 3 (August 2005): 535–58.

Lott, Eric. *Love and Theft: Blackface Minstrelsy and the American Working Class.* New York: Oxford University Press, 1993.

Lussana, Sergio. *My Brother Slaves: Friendship, Masculinity, and Resistance in the Antebellum South.* Lexington: University Press of Kentucky, 2016.

———. "'No Band of Brothers Could Be More Loving': Enslaved Male Homosociality, Friendship, and Resistance in the Antebellum South." *Journal of Social History* 46, no. 4 (2013): 872–95.

Lyons, Clare. *Sex among the Rabble: An Intimate History of Gender and Power in the Age of Revolution, Philadelphia 1730–1830.* Chapel Hill: University of North Carolina Press, 2006.

Malone, Ann Patton. *Sweet Chariot: Slave Family and Household Structure in Nineteenth-Century Louisiana.* Chapel Hill: University of North Carolina Press, 1992.

McCurry, Stephanie. *Masters of Small Worlds: Yeomen, Households, Gender Relations, and the Political Culture of the Antebellum South Carolina Lowcountry.* New York: Oxford University Press, 1997.

Merritt, Kerri Leigh. *Masterless Men: Poor Whites and Slavery in the Antebellum South.* Cambridge: Cambridge University Press, 2017.

Mills, Quincy T. *Cutting along the Color Line: Black Barbers and Barbershops in America.* Philadelphia: University of Pennsylvania Press, 2013.

Mintz, Sidney W. *Sweetness and Power: The Place of Sugar in Modern History.* New York: Viking, 1985.

Moon, David T., Jr. "Southern Baptists and Southern Men: Evangelical Perceptions of Manhood in Nineteenth-Century Georgia." *Journal of Southern History* 81, no. 3 (August 2015): 563–606.

Moore, Arthur K. *The Frontier Mind.* Lexington: University Press of Kentucky, 2015.

Moore, John Hebron. *Agriculture in Ante-bellum Mississippi.* New York: Bookman Associates, 1958.

———. *The Emergence of the Cotton Kingdom in the Old Southwest, Mississippi, 1770–1860.* Baton Rouge: Louisiana State University Press, 1988.

Morgan, Edmund S. *American Slavery, American Freedom: The Ordeal of Colonial Virginia.* New York: Norton, 1975.

Morgan, Phillip D. *Slave Counterpoint: Black Culture in the Eighteenth-Century Chesapeake and Lowcountry.* Chapel Hill: University of North Carolina Press, 1998.

Morris, Christopher. *Becoming Southern: The Evolution of a Way of Life, Warren County and Vicksburg Mississippi, 1770–1860.* New York: Oxford University Press, 1995.

———. "An Event in Community Organization: The Mississippi Slave Insurrection Scare of 1835." *Journal of Social History* 22 (1988): 93-111.

Morris, Thomas D. *Southern Slavery and the Law, 1619-1860.* Chapel Hill: University of North Carolina Press, 1996.

Oakes, James. *The Ruling Race A History of American Slaveholders.* New York: Knopf, 1982.

Painter, Nell Irving. *A History of White People.* New York: Norton, 2010.

Pargas, Damian Alan. *Slavery and Forced Migration in the Antebellum South.* New York: Cambridge University Press, 2015.

Phelps, Dawson A. Review of *The Barber of Natchez,* by Edwin Adams Davis and William Ransom Hogan. *Alabama Review* 8, no. 2 (April 1955): 155-56.

Phillips, Ulrich Bonnell. *Life and Labor in the Old South.* Boston: Little, Brown, 1929.

Plath, Lydia, and Sergio Lussana, eds. *Black and White Masculinity in the American South, 1800-2000.* Newcastle upon Tyne, UK: Cambridge Scholars Publishing, 2005.

Potter, Eliza. *A Hairdresser's Experience in High Life.* Edited by Xiomara Santamarina. Chapel Hill: University of North Carolina Press, 2009.

Power-Greene, Ousmane. *Against the Wind and Tide: The African American Struggle against Colonization.* New York: New York University Press, 2014.

Proctor, Nicolas W. *Bathed in Blood: Hunting and Mastery in the Old South.* Charlottesville: University of Virginia Press, 2002.

Quarles, Benjamin, Thad W. Tate, and Gary Nash. *The Negro in the American Revolution.* Chapel Hill: University of North Carolina Press, 1996.

Ramage, James A., and Andrea S. Watkins, *Kentucky Rising: Democracy, Slavery, and Culture from the Early Republic to the Civil War.* Lexington: University Press of Kentucky, 2011.

Ribianszky, Nik. *Generations of Freedom: Gender, Movement, and Violence in Natchez, 1779-1865.* Athens: University of Georgia Press, 2021.

Roark, James L., and Michael P. Johnson. *No Chariot Let Down: Charleston's Free People of Color on the Eve of the Civil War.* Chapel Hill: University of North Carolina Press, 1984.

Roberts, Kevin D. "Slaves and Slavery in Louisiana: The Evolution of Atlantic World Identities, 1791-1831." PhD diss., University of Texas at Austin, 2003.

Roediger, David. *The Wages of Whiteness: Race and the Making of the American Working Class.* London: Verso, 1991.

Rothman, Adam. *Slave Country: American Expansion and the Origins of the Deep South.* Cambridge, MA: Harvard University Press, 2007.

Rothman, Joshua D. "The Hazards of the Flush Times: Gambling, Mob Violence, and the Anxieties of America's Market Revolution." *Journal of American History* 95, no. 3 (December 2008): 651-77.

Rotundo, Anthony. *American Manhood: Transformations in Masculinity from the Revolution to the Modern Era.* New York: Basic, 1993.

Salt, Karen. *The Unfinished Revolution: Haiti, Black Sovereignty and Power in the Nineteenth-Century Atlantic World.* Liverpool, UK: Liverpool University Press, 2019.

Schermerhorn, Calvin. *Money over Mastery, Family over Freedom: Slavery in the Antebellum Upper South.* Baltimore, MD: Johns Hopkins University Press, 2011.

Schwartz, Stuart. *Sugar Plantations in the Formation of Brazilian Society: Bahia, 1550–1835.* Cambridge: Cambridge University Press, 1985.

Schweninger, Loren. *Appealing for Liberty: Freedom Suits in the South.* New York: Oxford University Press, 2018.

———. "John Carruthers Stanly and the Anomaly of Black Slaveholding." *North Carolina Historical Review* 67, no. 2 (April 1990): 159-92.

———. "Prosperous Free Blacks in the South, 1790-1880." *American Historical Review* 95, no. 1 (February 1990): 31-56.

Shire, Laurel Clark. "Sentimental Racism and Sympathetic Paternalism: Feeling Like a Jacksonian." *Journal of the Early Republic* 39, no.1 (Spring 2019): 111-22.

Sitterson, J. Carlyle. "The William J. Minor Plantations: A Study in Ante-Bellum Absentee Ownership." *Journal of Southern History* 9 (February 1943): 59-74.

Snyder, Christina. *Great Crossings: Indians, Settlers, and Slaves in the Age of Jackson.* New York: Oxford University Press, 2017.

Stampp, Kenneth. *The Peculiar Institution: Negro Slavery in the Antebellum South.* New York: Knopf, 1956.

Stott, Richard. *Jolly Fellows: Male Milieus in Nineteenth-Century America.* Baltimore, MD: Johns Hopkins University Press, 2009.

Stowe, Steven M. *Intimacy and Power in the Old South: Ritual in the Lives of the Planters.* Baltimore, MD: Johns Hopkins University Press, 1987.

Sydnor, Charles. "The Free Negro in Mississippi before the Civil War." *American Historical Review* 32 (1929): 769-88.

———. *Slavery in Mississippi.* Baton Rouge: Louisiana State University Press, 1933.

Tadman, Michael. "The Demographic Cost of Sugar: Debates on Slave Societies and Natural Increase in the Americas." *American Historical Review* 105, no. 4 (December 2000): 1534-75.

———. *Speculators and Slaves: Masters, Traders, and Slaves in the Old South.* Madison: University of Wisconsin Press, 1989.

Thomas, James. *From Tennessee Slave to St. Louis Entrepreneur: The Autobiography of James Thomas.* Edited by Loren Schweninger. Columbia: University of South Carolina Press, 1984.

Tubbe, Okah. *The Life of Okah Tubbe.* Edited by Daniel F. Littlefield. Lincoln: University of Nebraska Press, 1988.

Tyrrell, Ian R. "Drink and Temperance in the Antebellum South: An Overview and Interpretation." *Journal of Southern History* 48, no. 4 (November 1982): 485-510.

Wade, Richard C. *Slavery in the Cities: The South, 1820-1860.* New York: Oxford University Press, 1964.

Walker, Juliet E. K. *Free Frank: A Black Pioneer on the Antebellum Frontier.* Lexington: University Press of Kentucky, 1995.

Welch, Kimberly. "Arteries of Capital: William Johnson and the Practice of Black Moneylending in the Antebellum US South." *Slavery & Abolition* 41 no. 2 (2020): 304-26.

———. *Black Litigants in the Antebellum American South.* Chapel Hill: University of North Carolina Press, 2018.

———. "Black Litigiousness and White Accountability: Free Blacks and the Rhetoric of Reputation in the Antebellum Natchez District." *Journal of the Civil War Era* 5, no. 3 (September 2015): 372-98.

———. "William Johnson's Hypothesis: A Free Black Man and the Problem of Legal Knowledge in the Antebellum United States South." *Law & History Review* 37, no. 1 (2019): 1-36.

West, Emily. *Family or Freedom: People of Color in the Antebellum South.* Lexington: University Press of Kentucky, 2012.

Whitten, David O. *Andrew Durnford: A Black Sugar Planter in the Antebellum South.* New Brunswick, NJ: Transaction, 1995.

Wilentz, Sean. *The Rise of American Democracy: Jefferson to Lincoln.* New York: Norton, 2005.

Wiley, Bell I., ed. *Slaves No More: Letters from Liberia, 1833-1869.* Lexington: University Press of Kentucky, 1980.

Williams, Heather A. *Help Me to Find My People: The African American Search for Family Lost in Slavery.* Chapel Hill: University of North Carolina Press, 2012.

Woodson, Carter G. "Free Negro Owners of Slaves in the United States in 1830." *Journal of Negro History* 9 (1924): 4-85.

———. *Free Negro Owners of Slaves in the United States in 1830 Together with Absentee Ownership of Slaves in the United States in 1830.* Washington DC: Association for the Study of Negro Life and History, 1924.

Woodward, C. Vann. "The Southern Ethic in a Puritan World." *William and Mary Quarterly* 25 no. 3 (July 1968): 343-70.

Wyatt-Brown, Bertram. "The Mask of Obedience: Male Slave Psychology in the Old South." *American Historical Review* 93 (1988): 1228-52.

———. *Southern Honor: Ethics and Behavior in the Old South.* New York: Oxford University Press, 1982.

Zaborney, John J. *Slaves for Hire: Renting Enslaved Laborers in Antebellum Virginia.* Baton Rouge: Louisiana State University Press, 2012.

Index

www.ingramcontent.com/pod-product-compliance
Lightning Source LLC
Chambersburg PA
CBHW020444100426
42812CB00036B/3440/J